The Pocket Guide to Building Your Own Home

The Pocket Guide to Building Your Own Home

David Snell

EBURY
PRESS

1 3 5 7 9 10 8 6 4 2

Published in 2008 by Ebury Press, an imprint of Ebury Publishing

A Random House Group Company

Text © David Snell 2008
Photographs © David Snell 2008

The Random House Group Limited Reg. No. 954009

Addresses for companies within the Random House Group can be found
at www.randomhouse.co.uk

A CIP catalogue record for this book is available from the British Library

The Random House Group Limited supports The Forest Stewardship
Council (FSC), the leading international forest certification organisation.
All our titles that are printed on Greenpeace approved FSC certified paper
carry the FSC logo. Our paper procurement policy can be found at
www.rbooks.co.uk/environment

To buy books by your favourite authors and register for offers visit
www.rbooks.co.uk

Printed and bound in Singapore by Tien Wah Press

ISBN 9780091926601

Contents

Introduction

Building Your Own Home (Ebury Press), first published in the mid-1970s, was the first of the modern self-build books. Over time it has got bigger and bigger, but in truth so have all the other self-build books on the market. Perhaps it's because the subject is becoming ever more complicated with constant changes in legislation. Perhaps it's because we authors are learning new things as we go along and feel that we have to include them. In any case, when it comes out, the nineteenth edition of *Building Your Own Home* will really be a weighty tome.

For some time I have felt that a concise guide, containing all of the essential information but fewer of the anecdotal stories and still fewer of the personal opinions, was necessary. I was minded of this by the reality of my hobby and passion in life, birds, where the huge books that make a nasty dent in your thighs whenever you read them are balanced by the lightweight pocket guides that can be used in the field.

I had to look no further than the notes that I had prepared for the various lectures that I give around the country plus assorted articles that I had written for *Homebuilding & Renovating* magazine. This book, written in the third person (not my usual style), is therefore a compilation and distillation of those notes and articles. Essentially, it is portable: I do hope that you will be able to keep it in the car or take it on site or, perhaps, read it on the train on the way to work.

chapter one

Sorting Out the Money

I f you don't get the finances right for your new home, if you don't budget properly, you will get into trouble. While many coming new to the self-build table might think that finding the plot is the only important criterion, it is in fact the finance that is essential to get right, because, unless you do, you will miss out on that plot or end up with a project you can't afford to take forward. Get the boring bits about money sorted out first so that you can charge into the market, knowing exactly what you can afford to buy and to build, with the backing that sound finances can give. And don't forget to think about the extraneous money issues such as tax; you may think they don't matter but if you don't do things right you could find yourselves in trouble.

Setting the budget

Before you buy the plot for your self-build and before the design is even formulated it is next-to-nigh impossible to predict the costs of building your

The self-build budget

The self-builder's budget is made up from the following elements:

- Equity in an existing home
- Whatever is available to borrow as a mortgage
- Any cash or other equity that can be raised

That total budget will then have to be apportioned between:

- The land itself
- Construction – labour and materials

PLUS

- Any bridging/finance
- Any warranties
- Any insurances
- Architects'/surveyors'/engineers' fees
- Payments to local authorities for planning and building Regulations approvals
- Payments to service suppliers for things such as gas, water, electricity and sewage connections
- VAT paid out during the construction – this has to be financed even though it may be recoverable (see p. 7)
- The contingency fund

own house to pinpoint accuracy. But you have to start somewhere, and the only way of doing this is to make some broad assumptions, at the very beginning, regarding the costs of both the land and the type and size of the new home you are hoping to build.

Land cost

The land cost is probably the one factor with which you are more or less stuck. Although there are loose formulae (see Chapter 3, p. 29) to determine the true value of a plot, the brutal fact is that, with plots in such scarcity, it is a seller's market. Basically, anyone with any land to sell is going to charge as much as they can get for it. To find out what you are going to have to pay for what you are looking for, study the back pages of the self-build magazines for plots advertised by the land-finding agencies. Be aware, though, that if you are seeing plots in the magazine, they go to print some three months before they hit the shelves and many of the plots may have already been sold. If you want a more up-to-date picture of land costs you will have to register with one or both of them.

Construction costs

Once you have found your plot and know almost exactly how much it is going to cost, it will be possible to work out what you have got left and to determine your building budget and how big your new home can be. But, once again, it is a bit like 'putting the cart before the horse' because without a final design and plans you have got to make yet more assumptions and the only way of determining the possible or probable costs is via the £s per sq. metre method. If you look in the back pages of *Homebuilding & Renovating* magazine you will see a constantly updated table of average building costs that will provide a useful and surprisingly accurate guide. Those of you who already have *Building Your Own Home* by David Snell (Ebury Press) or *The Housebuilder's Bible* by Mark Brinkley (Ovolo Publishing) will also be able to access the more detailed information contained within them.

When you look at these building-cost tables you will see that the method of building – either using a builder, building with direct labour (subcontractors) or a combination of the two – is a factor in the cost variation. You will also discover that the area in which you are building introduces a further cost variation. But the biggest, single, determining factor of building costs is the level of the specification. At the time of writing (2007) the average building costs indicated within the building-cost tables are as follows.

Average building costs, per sq. metre

- Managing subcontractors with a fair amount of DIY – £794
- Managing subcontract labour – £840
- Using a builder to weather-tight shell plus subcontractors for second fix – £887
- Using a builder for the whole job – £933

But costs can be much higher: in London and the inner cities they may even reach £1500 per sq. metre. On the other hand, in outlying rural areas they may be much lower, perhaps down to £533 per sq. metre. However, another factor creeps in here, in that in many outlying areas materials have to be of better quality, and therefore higher cost, to fit in with the local vernacular.

In order to understand the principle of £s per sq. metre, it is necessary to know just how big most types of home are. The measurements, given in the table below, refer to the net floor area, meaning the area by reference to the measurements inside the outside walls for each usable floor.

Typical areas of houses and bungalows

- *Up to 65 sq. metres*
  Holiday chalets, tiny one- or two-bedroom bungalows.
  Granny annexes.

- *65–75 sq. metres*
  Very small two- or three-bedroom semi-detached houses.
  Small two-bedroom bungalows.

- *75–85 sq. metres*
  Small three-bedroom bungalows and semi-detached houses
  with integral lounge/dining room.

- *90–100 sq. metres*
  Large, older, semi-detached houses. Pokey four-bedroom
  modern-estate houses. Four-bedroom bungalows with very
  small bedrooms. Three-bedroom bungalows with separate
  dining room. Luxury two-bedroom bungalows.

- *Around 120 sq. metres*
  Many modern four-bedroom estate houses. Detached houses
  and bungalows with the possibility of a small study, a utility
  room and/or a second bathroom.

- *Around 150 sq. metres*
  Comfortable four-bedroom family houses or bungalows,
  often with en-suite facilities to master bedrooms, studies or
  family rooms and a utility room.

- *Around 185 sq. metres*
  Large four- and perhaps five-bedroom houses and bungalows
  with the possibility of en-suite facilities to more than one
  bedroom and with a separate family room.

All of these sizes exclude garaging accommodation, which can
have the effect of adding 30–40 sq. metres.

Don't expect a site to look pretty.

Labour costs

Materials account for some £400 per sq. metre for average-specification houses and bungalows, so it is the labour factor that creates the cost differentials. In areas where labour is expensive, such as in London and the other major conurbations, the materials might cost no more than in some of the cheaper areas. And of course it goes without saying that if you dispensed with labour altogether, and there are a few hardy souls who do so from time to time, the only building costs would be the material costs.

The contingency fund

When first formulating your budget, never forget the final item in the list of costs: the contingency fund. Contrary to popular opinion, the contingency fund is not usually used up in one or even a number of disastrous occurrences. Instead it is gradually absorbed in the creep of costs throughout the build process; sometimes as a result of little errors but mainly because of the reality and uncertainty of actual building as opposed to the strict measurement of plans beforehand. On a normal site with few problems a contingency fund of 10 per cent would suffice. On more complicated sites or where the design is a complex one, this could rise incrementally to 20 per cent.

A word of warning

Pounds per sq. metre is a very good way of assessing costs, especially if used, as *Homebuilding & Renovating* magazine suggests, in conjunction with the limiting and varying factors. They can, in fact, be remarkably accurate and it is not at all unusual for self-builders to find that their original cost assumptions are pretty much on the ball. But they are, in large part, a fairly rough-and-ready way of calculating costs, and they cannot be used in the minutiae. Don't expect that just because you lop off or increase the size by a few sq. metres and then use the multiplier, it will necessarily translate to an accurate saving or increase. A 24 sq. metre room might have the same number of doors, windows, radiators and electrical outlets as a 30 sq.

metre room. The only saving will be in space with perhaps slightly fewer bricks and blocks that may, in any event, already be accounted for by having to go to full loads for deliveries or by adding in the wastage factor.

Mortgages

Most self-builders need a mortgage, and they are pretty well served within the financial market. Nevertheless, it is perhaps best to deal with either one of the specialist companies, such as BuildStore, or a building society that specifically trumpets its knowledge and understanding of the self-build market. The fact is that it is not a self-build mortgage unless there are stage payments. Usually these are given in arrears at stages that vary according to method of construction (see table below). Other forms of construction, discussed in Chapter 6, are treated individually with stage payments subject to negotiation.

Construction methods

Traditional (brick and block)
- Purchase of land
- Foundation level
- Wall plate level
- Wind and watertight
- First fix and external render (if appropriate)
- Final completion

Timber-frame
- Purchase of land
- Foundation level
- Kit erection
- Wind and watertight
- First fix and external rendering (if appropriate)
- Final completion

The biggest single advance in self-build mortgages over the past years has been the introduction of the BuildStore Accelerator mortgage, where the stage payments are given in advance of the stages rather than in arrears. This allows the self-builder to have a positive cashflow throughout the build and has largely prevented the stop–start syndrome that previously afflicted so many self-build projects.

Many of the building societies working within the self-build industry will now advance up to 95 per cent on the land plus 95 per cent of the build costs up to a maximum of 95 per cent of the final value of the property. Once again, a quick look in the back pages of *Homebuilding & Renovating* magazine will indicate a table or tables listing those companies active within the market, their rates, the percentages they will lend and the likely cost of borrowing.

Tax

In all of the excitement at the prospect of building your own home, tax, a subject many habitually ignore, is an important consideration, not least because, for the self-builder, there are numerous distinct advantages to be had from the system.

Stamp Duty

The first tax that the self-builder will come across is Stamp Duty, payable on the purchase of land or on the granting of a lease of more than seven years. It is paid by the purchaser and is usually added to the solicitor's bill and passed over to Revenue and Customs by them. There is Stamp Duty relief in certain deprived urban areas. Stamp Duty is paid only on the cost of the land. It is not payable on the building costs.

Stamp Duty: rates and cut-off points

Up to £125,000	nil
£125,001–£250,000	1%
£250,001–£500,000	3%
Over £500,001	4%

Therefore those building a house where the land and building costs add up to £250,000 will, if the land costs less that £125,000, be paying no Stamp Duty. Whereas anyone going out and buying a house for £250,000 will have a bill for £2500.

VAT

The VAT Notice No. 719 allows self-builders to reclaim VAT paid out during construction. New build is zero rated; that is, if you are building a new dwelling from scratch you pay no VAT on the labour – you do, however, have to pay 17.5 per cent on purchase of materials, which you recover at the end of the project.

Conversions (the changing of a non-residential building into a dwelling) are also zero rated, but you do have to pay 5 per cent VAT on the labour as well as 17.5 per cent on the materials, which you then recover at the end.

Renovations and extensions are fully VAT-able at the standard rate. But a renovation is counted as a conversion if it has been unoccupied for at least ten years.

In addition, although not strictly applicable to self-building:

- The rate on all conversions carried out by developers (even those not covered by the self-build scheme) is dropped to 5 per cent.
- There is also a special rate of 5 per cent for:
  - Renovation of dwellings unoccupied for two years
  - Conversion of an existing dwelling into multiple dwellings (flats)
  - Conversion of a dwelling into a care home
  - Conversion of a dwelling into bed-sit accommodation

If your project is eligible for a VAT reclaim then you can recover VAT paid in the UK, including VAT paid at the port of entry for goods imported from outside the EU. You can also recover VAT paid in the EU for goods used in the construction of your new home. This is recovered at the rate paid and at the exchange rate on the date of purchase.

Be careful not to pay VAT incorrectly. If you do, inadvertently, pay the builder at the wrong rate for a conversion or VAT for labour on a new build, the Excise will not entertain your claim and your only resort would be to ask the builders to give it back to you.

Listed buildings are not covered by the 719 scheme, but it is possible to avoid paying VAT on certain approved extensions and alterations. This does not apply to repairs. The relief is given by allowing a builder to zero rate the work. There is no personal relief and no refund system.

Inheritance (gift) tax (IHT)
Most people think that IHT will never affect them, but with recent rises in property values many more of us are being drawn into its net. The tax is on gifts made in a lifetime and is payable upon the death of the donor. However, there are certain thresholds and exemptions that are important and mean that if careful plans are made, the tax can often be avoided.

When a gift is made it becomes what is known as a Potentially Exempt Transfer (PET). If the person making the gift lives for seven years after the donation, then the gift falls out of any calculation for IHT purposes. Taper relief is available for gifts made between three and seven years prior to death.

The current threshold for IHT is £300,000 per person, rising in April 2008 to £325,000 and then to £350,000 by 2010. Most importantly, transfers between couples within either a marriage or a civil partnership are exempt, and new rules allow the unused portion of one partner's threshold to be passed to the other on their death. This can effectively double up the 'tax free' inheritance that a couple may pass to their beneficiaries.

Unmarried couples and civil partnerships This exemption does not apply to long-term relationships outside marriage or a civil partnership. To avoid this, it is sometimes better for couples in this situation to decide, while both are still alive, to change their ownership so that they hold the property as 'tenants in common' rather than as 'joint tenants'. This allows each partner to will their portion to another party.

Additional IHT exemptions There are additional gifts, however, that are exempt, specifically:

- A person may give away £3000 in any one year and, if no gift has been made in the previous year, may backdate an additional £3000.
- On a marriage, each parent can give a further £5000, grandparents £2500 and others £1000.

Capital Gains Tax (CGT)
Gains made from the sale of your Principal Private Residence (PPR), or part of it, are exempt, so long as it has been your main home throughout your ownership, no part of it has been let for business (that doesn't mean working from home) and the disposal does not exceed half a hectare. There are various exemptions and reliefs available including:

- An annual personal exemption, currently £9200 per person.
- Roll-over relief allows for gains to be deferred if replacement assets are required.
- Indexation Allowance adjusts gains for the effects of inflation up to April 1998.
- Taper relief reduces chargeable gain by a sliding scale according to the number of years you have owned the asset. The government indicated in 2007 that they might be reviewing this relief.

Quick Q&A tax checklist

If I make a big profit when I sell my home, do I have to pay any Capital Gains Tax?

Any profit or gain in equity that you make when you sell your main home, or Principal Private Residence, is normally exempt from Capital Gains Tax. It must have been your main residence throughout the period you have owned it, ignoring the last thee years of ownership, and the total area of land that you are disposing of must not exceed half a hectare.

How do I nominate my home as being my Principal Private Residence?

You don't need to do anything. The only time this should crop up is when filling in your Tax Return Form. In that there is a question, 'If you have disposed of your only or main residence, do you need the Capital Gains pages?' If the home you have sold is or was your Principal Private Residence, you would obviously answer 'No' to that question.

Are there any circumstances where I could be liable for Capital Gains Tax on the sale of my home or part of my home?

Yes. If part or all of the home has been let out or used as a business, or if the area of the disposal is greater than half a hectare. If you are seen to be buying and selling homes on a regular basis and the Revenue deem that you are trading, you could be liable for Income Tax.

How long do I have to live in a new house in order for it to qualify as my main home?

Strangely enough there is no set time limit. The figure of 12 months is often bandied about, probably because it is a figure that appears in the legislation in various concessions. The simple answer is that, in normal circumstances, 12 months would be deemed to be safe. But if the taxman saw that you were moving every 12 months, they could deem that you were trading, unless there was a reasonable explanation, and you could demonstrate another viable source of income. On the other hand, if you could cite circumstances to prove that you needed to move on in less than 12 months, the Revenue would probably let it go, unless, once again, you started making a habit of it.

If I get planning permission for part of my garden, will I have to pay Capital Gains Tax when I sell it?

In normal circumstances, there is no tax liability, so long as the sale of the land is a bona fide one 'at arm's length' and the total area of the land of which you are disposing does not exceed half a hectare.

If I get planning permission on part of my garden and I build myself a new house on it, will I get stung for Capital Gains Tax when I sell my existing house?

Not at all, so long as you were simply moving from one main home to another and so long as the area of the disposal was not greater than the half hectare allowed within the exemption ruling. However, if you did this sort of thing rather too often and could not demonstrate an alternative viable income, then you could be deemed to be trading and taxed accordingly.

If I build myself a new home and then have difficulty selling my old house, will I have to pay Capital Gains Tax?

There is a concession that allows for this situation to go on for 12 months with a further 12 months' extension for factors outside the taxpayer's control. This extension is at the taxman's discretion and good reason must be demonstrated. There is no facility to extend the period beyond the two years. If this situation is likely to occur, then it is perhaps better to retain the old house as your Principal Private Residence until such time as it is sold and then, once it is gone, the exemption will move on to the new home. Be aware, however, that any gain made on the new house, for the period beyond the concession period and the time of it becoming your PPR, could be taxable, when and if you sell on.

If I decide to build on part of my garden and then sell off the new house, will I be liable for tax?

Yes, you will. The Revenue will decide that you are trading or making a business, and you will be liable for Income Tax, rather than Capital Gains Tax. Furthermore, you will be deemed to have commenced trading at the time of your application for planning permission. The pre-planning value of the land will be counted as your capital input to the new business and therefore the profit you make when you sell the house will include the uplift in the value of the land. With the tax liability being Income Tax rather than Capital Gains Tax, you will not be able to use up your annual exemptions and, if you have another source of income, you will probably have used up all your other allowances.

What happens if I buy a plot for two houses, build them and then live in one of them, selling off the other one?

The Revenue will again deem that you have been trading and you will have to pay Income Tax on any profit that you make on the house you sell.

Day 1 on site, clearing an almost impenetrable jungle.

What if I sell off my home and retain part of its land in the hope that I can get planning permission on it at a later date in order to sell it separately?

Even if the holding, before you split it off, were your Principal Private Residence, the land has to be so occupied at the time of disposal. You would therefore have to pay CGT on any gain made on the land that you sell at a later date.

There is an old house with a large garden that's got planning permission on it. If I buy this, build myself a new home on the plot and sell off the old house, what tax liability will I incur?

It all depends on whether you move into the old house. If you sell your existing home, move into the old house while you're building and then move again into the new house when it's ready, then all you will have done is move from one main home to another. If you stay in your current home while you're building and sell off the old house, you could be liable for CGT on any profit that you make on it. However, you would be entitled to set any costs of refurbishment and the costs of separation against any possible profit. If you let out the old house, you would be liable for Income Tax on any rental monies received and then when you eventually sell it the CGT liability would still be there.

What happens if I buy a plot and take a long time to build my new house?

If you buy a plot in order to build a house on it that will become your main home, or if you buy property that you intend to renovate and convert as your new main home, you are allowed 12 months to carry out the works and sell off your existing Principal Private Residence. This is extendable for another 12 months for events that are outside your control, such as the need to go to Appeal. There is no facility to extend this period beyond the two years.

What happens if I own a parcel of land, not part of my main home, for which, eventually, I obtain planning permission and build myself a new home – am I liable for Capital Gains Tax?

Yes, you are. Where you do not use the property as your only or main residence within the period allowed (one year, extendable in certain circumstances to a maximum of two years), no relief will be given for the period before it is so used. For example, let's say you own a paddock in a nearby village with which you do nothing for several years and then you decide to try for planning permission. You're successful, so you build yourself a new house and move into it. From that moment forward it becomes your Principal Private Residence. But, when you sell it, you are liable for CGT on any gain made before the property became your main home, including the uplift in value due to the granting of planning permission.

If an elderly relative gives me a plot of land, are there any tax liabilities?

A gift of land or property could fall foul of both Inheritance Tax and Capital Gains Tax. Inheritance Tax first. Gifts of money or property given during a person's lifetime are known as Potentially Exempt Transfers and if the donor lives for seven years following the gift, there is no IHT liability. However, if a donor dies within the seven-year period, tax will become payable on the total value of the estate on death, including gifts made within the seven-year period prior to death, for any amounts that exceed their unused thresholds and exemptions. If a person gives you property or land that does not qualify or fall within the rules for Private Residence Relief, there can also be a Capital Gains Tax liability. If the donor pays the CGT on a gift, the payment is ignored for IHT valuation purposes. If the recipient pays the tax, it is deducted from the value transferred.

What reliefs or exemptions are there for Capital Gains Tax?

There are annual exemptions, which currently amount to £9200 per person. There are a number of other reliefs, including Roll-over, which allow for gains to be deferred if replacement assets are required. Indexation Allowance adjusts gains for the effects of inflation up to April 1998 by means of tables setting out multipliers that can be applied to the original acquisition costs to reduce the tax liability. Taper relief applies to gains made after 5 April 1998. This reduces the amount of gain chargeable to tax by a sliding scale of percentage points, according to the whole number of years the asset has been in your ownership. None of these reliefs is exclusive, and one or more can apply to any gain.

What thresholds, reliefs or exemptions exist for Inheritance Tax (IHT)?

If the value of an estate on death, including the value of gifts given within seven years of death, exceeds the unused thresholds of the donor(s), there is an IHT liability. If tax is payable on gifts made within the seven-year period, they may be subject to Taper relief. This has the effect of reducing the tax payable on a sliding scale for gifts made between three and seven years prior to the donor's death. Gifts made by an individual, so long as they do not exceed £3000 in any one year, are exempt although if nothing were given in the year before, this can be doubled. Outright gifts that can be classed as normal expenditure 'out of income' are allowable, as are gifts made on the occasion of a marriage. Here, parents can each give £5000, grandparents £2500 and anybody else can give £1000.

When is any Inheritance Tax payable?

Inheritance Tax liability usually comes into effect and is payable only upon the death of the donor, although with certain Discretionary Trusts the liability can be immediate.

Do I need to worry about this tax? Surely this is only for the very rich?

Creeping inflation has meant that many more of us are at risk from our estates being drawn into the IHT net. Many couples living in London and the inner cities are now in possession of houses that breach the individual threshold and in many cases both parties' combined individual thresholds. Many more of us stand to inherit money or property that, taken into account and added to the value of our existing homes and estates, will push them above the thresholds.

What if I die and leave my half of the house to my partner – will they be liable for tax?

Transfers between those in a marriage or civil partnership are exempt for Inheritance Tax purposes. However, long-term partnerships do not enjoy this exemption. Therefore a couple living and owning a home together as joint tenants, or indeed as tenants in common, where they leave their share of the home to their partner, could be faced with an IHT liability if on the death of one of them the value of their share of the property exceeds the current personal threshold.

If either my wife or I die, leaving our share of the estate or property to the other, does the threshold for the surviving spouse double up?

Yes. For those within marriage or a civil partnership (including surviving partners of those who died before 2007), the unused portion of their exemption threshold can now be passed to the surviving partner. This may not always be a doubling up as the deceased partner's threshold may have already been used up in part or in whole.

What Stamp Duty will I have to pay?

Stamp Duty is applied to the purchase of all land and property that exceeds £125,000. If you buy a plot of land for less than this amount, no Stamp Duty is payable. If you buy land or property that exceeds £125,000, even by £1, then the duty is levied at the rate of 1 per cent. Above £250,001 the rate rises to 3 per cent and at £500,001 it goes up to 4 per cent. Stamp Duty is only payable on the purchase of land or property – it is not payable on the building or construction costs of a new self-built home, a renovation or a conversion.

Warranties

A warranty covers for structural defects caused by faulty design, workmanship or materials. They are available for cover periods between 10 and 15 years. Anyone contemplating building a new home should seriously consider having a warranty, which, in all probability, will be a requirement of any lender. Even if you don't need a mortgage, think what might happen if you needed to sell within the first ten years and the probability that any purchaser might want a mortgage.

Principal warranty providers

- NHBC – Buildmark/Solo for Self Build
- Zurich – Building Guarantee Self Build 10
- Premier Guarantee (administered by BuildStore and Project Builder)
- LABC (Local Authority Building Control) – New Home Warranty

Architects' certificates, where an architect inspects the building work at various stages, are not strictly speaking a warranty, although many building societies will accept them in lieu. They are not transferable. Any liability the architect may have is not passed on to any subsequent owner or even to the building society unless a collateral contract is entered into. To have any worth, the architect must have relevant and current Professional Indemnity.

Insurance

A self-build insurance policy offers cover for three main risks:

- Contractors' All Risk
- Employers' Liability
- Public Liability

Insurance vs warranty

To understand the practical implications of the difference between insurance and warranty it helps to consider the example of the construction of a wall in a new home.

If the wall falls down *during* construction:

- It will be put back up under the contractors-all-risk section of the self-build insurance policy.
- Any damage to a neighbour's property or person will be covered by the public-liability section of that same policy.
- Any injury to subcontractors will be covered by the Employers' Liability within the self-build insurance policy.

If the wall falls down *after* construction:

- It will be put back up by the householder insurance policy.
- Any injury will be covered by public-liability/personal-accident section of the householder policy.
- Damage caused will be covered by public-liability/personal-accident section of the householder policy.

However, if a wall falls down *within* the warranty period, during or after construction, because it has been badly built or wrongly designed, then cover to put it back up is provided for within the warranty.

But, there is no Public or Employers' Liability within the warranty and therefore:

- If the wall falls down during construction, cover for injury and damage to other property is given by self-build insurance.
- If the wall falls down after construction, then injury and damage to others' property is covered by a householder insurance policy.

chapter two

Finding that Elusive Plot

John Lennon sang that life is what happens to you when you're busy making other plans and for those seeking a plot, there are no truer words. No matter how long you have been looking, no matter how diligently you apply yourself to the task, in the end most successful self-builders just seem to stumble on to their plot. But you have to be ready for it. You have to be able to recognise it when you see it, and you have to be in a position to secure it.

Unfortunately, there is a large group of people who go for years without finding anything, many of whom give up in the end and even start to doubt what they have been reading in the books and magazines. What are they doing wrong? Sometimes their complaints strike a chord with similarly unsuccessful readers. Sometimes their insistence that 'there aren't any plots in my area' simply doesn't ring true, especially when it is directed at those who have got first-hand knowledge of plots that they have obviously missed.

There are plots around. Even the briefest of look at the web pages of the land-finding agencies proves that point and a more sustained study will confirm that these are not just the 'throwaway' plots that the general

A digger makes short work of even the densest growth.

market does not want and that there is quite a considerable turnover. True, some estate agents would prefer not to sell to a self-builder, preferring instead to sell to their builder/developer chums who will then retain them to sell the house that they build. But many more, and particularly those represented on the land-agencies' lists, are aware of the existence of the self-build market and know that within and from it, they can perhaps get a better price for their clients. They know too that a large proportion of self-builders go on to do it again and again, becoming serial self-builders, and that they can, therefore, look upon them as repeat business.

Talk to any self-builder who has finished their project and they will tell you of land. Maybe that is because the agents, having dealt with them, let them know about potential plots. Maybe it is because they have learnt how to evaluate plots and recognise worthwhile opportunities. So the essential task for the first-time would-be self-builder is to elevate yourself to that level of knowledge; to try, as far as possible, to leapfrog those barren early-learning stages. If you find that you are always missing out then you need to take a long, hard look at things and ask yourself 'Ten key questions about plot-finding'.

Ten key questions about plot-finding

Are you looking at things in the right way? You need to learn to look at things as they will be, as you are going to make them and not as they might at first appear. Look beyond all those old sheds, tangled undergrowth or rusting cars. When people sell houses they do all they can to make them attractive. When people sell plots they do nothing of the sort; in fact they may even bung all their rubbish on them, thinking that the builders will get rid of it. What you have got to do is to close your eyes and imagine the finished home.

Have you got your finances arranged? Plots don't hang about on the market and you have got to be able to 'put your money where your mouth is'. Make sure that if you find that ideal plot you have the facilities and the ability to beat others to the punch and be able to offer vendors a quick Completion.

Are you being too bashful? It is no good being shy when you are looking for plots. When you go and see one that somebody else has told you about you will need to be able to talk to the neighbours and ask around to find out as much as you can about it. If you identify the plot yourself then you will have to have the courage to ask about it and maybe even walk up somebody's driveway to ask if they are willing to sell.

Are you in the right place at the right time? Finding a plot is a mixture of perseverance and luck. Just putting your name down at the estate agent's office as 'looking for land' won't produce much, if anything, at all. You need to do the rounds. Get to know names and build up a relationship so that when a plot does come on to their books you are either there in their office or top of their list of people to contact.

Is the area in which you are looking too restricted? Confining yourself to one village, a very small radius or maybe a particular bus route or school catchment area, is always going to lessen your chances of success. Widen your horizons and look at plots in other areas and maybe, just maybe, you will find what you want in the end anyway.

Are you being proactive? Just concentrating on one way of finding land is never going to work and you will need to get out there and talk to people about what you are hoping to achieve. Let everybody know what you are hoping to do and explore every avenue. Read the local papers, especially the property sections, from cover to cover.

Are you too hung up on the idea of a greenfield site? While such a site may be superficially attractive and seem to present fewer problems, the reverse is actually true. Many self-builds are as the result of a 'one-for-one' replacement. And there are wonderful benefits. Such a site may well have the garden done, the drains and services connected, the fencing in and the drive-way established – all things that will save you money.

Have you got the money right? Are the plots of your dreams all above your budget? Being prepared to pay that little bit more for the land might well mean that you have to restrict what you have available to spend on the build. But there is no build without the plot and once you have got the land you could either design something that is that little bit cheaper to build or build it in such a way that it could be improved upon at a later date, when money is not so tight.

Are you being too fussy? You might not get everything you want. The views might not be the same as in your dream. The size of the plot might not be as great as you would prefer. It might not be in the exact village that you had hoped for. But self-building is about making the best of things and, very often, it is about jumping several rungs up the property ladder. So could this be a step on the way to your ultimate house?

Have you 'boned up' on all of the pitfalls of buying land? Many people get put off plots needlessly when, with a little bit of knowledge and foresight, they could have held on to it. Above all, look at everything. Estate agents are not always good at preparing details for plots, and the most attractive can be lost in simple one-line descriptions with no photographs and little or no background information. Equally, elaborate details can mask unattractive features. So make a point of viewing all plots in your area, which, if nothing else, will help you build up a dossier of availability and increase your knowledge of how to look at land and relative values. Your constant taking of details and willing-ness to get out there and look will also stand you in good stead with agents by keeping your name and requirements to the fore. And that, more than anything, is what is likely to lead to success.

Land for sale: the agencies

Estate agents

The estate-agency profession comes in for a pretty bad press, sometimes deservedly. But the fact is that an estate agent is there not just for the short time frame in which you are trying to self-build but also the duration. Theirs is an ongoing business, and like all businesses they rely on sewing the seeds for future ventures in the course of their normal trading activities. Small wonder then that their first thought is for a plot to be sold to a builder or developer who will, in return, engage them for the sale of whatever gets built on the land.

Selling a plot to a self-builder is just a bit too long term for most agents. The consensus of opinion is that somebody taking the time and trouble to build their own home is going to build exactly what they want and then live in it happily ever after. It is not true of course. Most self-builders do it again at some stage, and some move and build homes more often than most people buy and sell their houses. Sometimes they are driven by finance and the need to reduce or wipe out a mortgage. Or they have simply got the building bug or want to improve upon what they have already achieved.

Estate agents do, of course, have a duty to their clients – the vendors of the land. Many are now realising that the self-builder can perhaps give that little bit more for the plot than the builder or developer. More importantly, many vendors are also cognisant of this fact. The days of self-building existing in a parallel universe, undiscovered and misunderstood, are long gone. Most estate agents will know of the land-finding agencies and the market they serve, as some clients are only too well aware, to the point where they are beginning to cut out agents and advertise their land directly.

Getting around the agents

An estate agent selling a piece of land gets a relatively small fee for so doing. What interests them of course is the much higher fee for the sale of the resulting house – that and the thought that their advertising board will be on a prestigious site for months to come. Try representing yourself as a 'private house builder'. Give the impression that you are going to sell the house when it is finished. Talk about values and the best way of selling. After all, as already identified, the likelihood is that you will be selling and moving on again in any event. When you do find your plot, start talking immediately about your next plot. The probable truth is that you are repeat business, so make sure that the agents understand that fact.

Visit the offices at the weekend. Some firms have weekend staff whose only job is to 'mind the shop'. Tell them that you are looking for land and on the land list. Check your details with them and ask them to check their files to see if any land has come in during the intervening time. You might see files or details of land that the principal staff have neglected to tell you about and, on the Monday morning, when proper business resumes, you might be able to get further information. In turn they might wonder how you heard of the land and they might well have something to say to their weekend staff.

Does any of this seem underhand? Well, it shouldn't. You want a plot. The vendor wants to sell the plot to the highest bidder and it's the agents' job to do just that. All you've done is assist them in that task.

Getting in before the agents

The maxim, which needs repeating, is that as self-builders rather than property speculators, you should not buy land without planning permission or at least the certainty of it. But that doesn't mean that you have to wait for all that to happen before you register your interest or come to an agreement with a landowner.

You don't have to own land in order to make a planning application. All that is required is that you serve notice on the owners. But to go around making planning applications on land that you don't own might be extremely costly unless you have made some prior agreement with the owners. You do need to tie up some sort of legal agreement, either in the form of an 'exchange of contracts', 'subject to receipt of satisfactory planning consent', or in the form of a legally binding option to purchase. Otherwise there would be nothing to stop a vendor simply saying, 'Thank you very much for all of the work you've done in getting planning on my land, but I'm selling it to somebody else.'

The Ordnance Survey is Britain's national mapping agency – contactable for all general public general enquiries via the Helpline (Tel: 08456 050505) or website (www.ordnancesurvey.co.uk). Study the Ordnance Survey maps of your local or chosen area. Look out for obvious plots. Look out for streets where infill has already taken place but where certain properties have not taken advantage of this opportunity. Look out for signs of previous backland development, where properties have been built in the rear gardens of houses with either shared access or a new access down the side. Watch out for houses with long back gardens that front on to a side road or where one house has a road frontage that could lead to a number of back gardens forming a viable plot.

When you have identified possible sites, get out there and check them on site. Sometimes the maps might be out of date. Sometimes there are physical reasons why plots can't be developed. In England, Wales or Northern Ireland, if you do identify a plot and have difficulty in finding out who owns it then it might be registered with HM Land Registry (www.landregistry.gov.uk Tel: 0207 917 8888). In Scotland the registry of land and property is held by Registers of Scotland (www.ros.gov.uk Tel: 0131 659 6111). A registered title includes details of the address and location with details of the owners and any charges, covenants and Easements affecting the land. For a small fee you can send off for or inspect the indexed maps held by the Registry and if the plot you're interested in appears on them, you should be able to find the owners. You can also access the maps on line, downloading copies of title information for a small fee payable by credit or debit card via their website.

Next, visit the planning office and ascertain what chances there are of these 'plots' obtaining consent. Maybe they'll be negative. If so perhaps it is best to move on to another possibility. Maybe they'll be non-committal, but maybe, especially in the light of recent government directives to utilise land more intensively, they'll accept the fact that this is a potential building plot. If so, ask them if they would prefer a 'Full' application, rolling the outline and detailed stages into one. That can save time and money and, while not a certainty, means that the project stands a pretty good chance of success.

The hardest part of course is to convince the landowner that they should sell to you. They can only say yes or no. They may welcome your approach, especially if you represent yourself to them as private individuals looking to build your new home. They may well tell you to get lost – but nothing ventured, nothing gained.

Getting in behind the agents

While you are in talking to the planners, ask to see the Planning Register. This is not a secret document. It is open for public inspection, as indeed are all of the files on applications. Study this register and you will see that it is a list of all of the planning applications that are currently under consideration. Some of them will be for things like extensions. Ignore those. Some will be for Approval of Reserved Matters pursuant to an original Outline consent. Maybe they are not worth that much attention as they probably indicate that whoever owns the land has already decided what to do with it. But don't discount them if they're exactly what you're looking for.

Pay the most attention to the Outline applications. Make a note of the applicant's name and address, especially if it's clear that they live next door. You will also notice that there is often an applicant's agent. And guess what? That will probably be one of those estate agents who has already told you that they don't have any land for sale and that they don't know of any that is coming up! So it is no good writing to them. They have already decided that they don't want to deal with you on this project. Write instead to the owners. Tell them that you are potential self-builders hoping to build your own home and that if they ever want to talk to you about you buying their land, you would be delighted to hear from them. Maybe you will hear nothing. But on the other hand, you might one day get a call from them.

When people get planning for part of their garden they are delighted at the cash windfall that this usually represents. The agent will, in all probability to gain the business in the first place, have told them top-dollar price. Then when they have had time to think about things they start to

Beginning to look the part.

worry. What will it be like? What effect will it have on their enjoyment of their home? What effect will it have on the value?

If the agent has 'sold' the land to local developers, what sort of house will they be building? Will they be building the biggest house they can and to hell with the consequences or the effect on their existing home? Are they paying the right price?

Many a time the offer that comes in, as a result of the cosy relationship between agent and builder, is a lot less than the figure that was first quoted. Not only that but the sale can drag on with the builders not wanting to commit financially until they have either sold the previous house they have built or actually got planning permission for what they want to build. And it is then that the owner may well go to the file, turn up your letter and contact you – for you are offering not only to buy the land but also to be their neighbour. And you can sit down and talk to them as potential neighbours about all of their fears and empathise with the mutual need to preserve values and enjoyment. And most importantly you can offer them the right price.

Land-finding agencies

The first port of call for many would-be self-builders are the land-finding agencies. Plotsearch at BuildStore (www.buildstore.co.uk/plotsearch Tel: 0870 870 9004) has lists containing upwards of 6000 plots or renovation opportunities at any one time. Plotfinder.Net (www.plotfinder.net Tel: 0906 557 5400) has around 4000 plots or development opportunities on its books, and it would be wrong to assume that because a plot is on one register, it will automatically be on the other. Rightmove (www.rightmove.co.uk) is also a very good source.

It is obviously a mammoth task to keep this data up to date but the agencies have been getting better and better at it. Perhaps the most important information to be gleaned from the lists is which estate agents or others specifically and consistently deal in land. You can also deduce from them the going rates for plots in any area and the general availability and distribution. A day spent on the telephone going through the lists can often lead to far more opportunities than are listed – stay on the line if the plot you are telephoning about has gone and ask about up-and-coming opportunities.

Land for sale: other sources

Local authorities and English Partnerships (formerly CNT)

Some local authorities are well known for selling plots marketed specifically at the self-builder, often taking precautions to make sure that builders or developers do not purchase them. It is worth phoning your local authority to ask what plots they might have in this category and if there is none available, whether they have plans to identify and release any. Those that do so are quite proficient at it and the plots they sell are often highly desirable with all roads, sewers and services taken care of. It is worth contacting the Estates Department of authorities with no policy of identifying and releasing land for this purpose, as they sometimes have spare plots left to them by circumstance or history, suitable for a single dwelling.

The national regeneration agency, English Partnerships, sells fully serviced plots in the new towns up and down the land. They are contactable via their website (www.englishpartnerships.co.uk) or central switchboard (Tel: 01908 692692), and they will put you through to the relevant area office closest to where you are looking. There is no doubt, however, that this is a diminishing resource, with the notable exception of Milton Keynes, where there is still a ready supply of really good plots at sensible prices, many of which are heavily oversubscribed upon release.

The media
National newspapers and self-build magazines are a source of land but local newspapers and classified papers are a far better one. Subscribe to the local papers in your chosen area and don't forget that there is quite a bit of over-lap, so subscribe to those in the adjoining areas. If you see a plot advertised then get on to it immediately and don't wait for the weekend. If it's a private advertiser then be aware that they will be bombarded with offers from estate agents and others and that you, as a private individual, might well have to fight hard for their attention. Play up the fact that you are looking to self-build as an individual or a family. Vendors, especially those who will continue to live next door, are often apprehensive about any loss of control over what happens on the plot, and you might well be able to put their mind at ease by addressing any fears within your proposed design. Newspapers work both ways in that you can advertise for plots yourself. Be prepared for some time wasters, as not all of the replies will have planning permission or even the hope of it. Be prepared also to hear from vendors who have instructed the same estate agents who have told you they don't have any land for sale!

Self-build clubs & associations/Internet & discussion forums
Some builders' merchants run self-build clubs where you can go along to meet other self-builders and attend meetings and seminars to discuss self-building in general as well as trade topics and products. These clubs often run a land list in their regular newsletters and by the nature of the merchant's position in the market, they often have insight into availability that's denied to others. The Association of SelfBuilders (Tel: 01604 493757) tries to keep its members advised of available land for sale that comes to its attention and keeps a note of local-authority plots.

The Internet is not yet a powerful force for land sales but many estate agents are getting on line, and it's worth keeping a check on their various websites, where plots often form a distinct category. Of course the Internet is really a bridge between many of the recognised ways of finding land, and it can contain elements of all the other categories. Discussion forums, while not designed to sell land, do nonetheless throw up plots from time to time, particularly where someone wants to sell off a plot or plots on a multiple site that they are buying or wants someone to join them in buying a larger site.

The self-build industry
While they cannot always seek to provide a comprehensive and up-to-date list of plots, many of the package-deal companies and their local representatives might know of available land. Quite often prospective vendors contact well-known companies asking if they have clients looking for land. Do not expect the companies to tell you about plots that other clients are contemplating buying or building upon because that would be anarchic.

However, clients do sometimes have to drop out or are unable to proceed for reasons that have little or nothing to do with the suitability of the plot. In those cases, if you're in touch with the staff it might well be possible to 'take over' the contract and plot. Architects and surveyors, being more local, often have a far greater knowledge of plot availability in their area and, just like the package-deal companies, there may also be a 'wastage factor' in that, from time to time, clients might drop out of a project. If you as a prospective customer can impress them with your keenness, then at a point where they are fearful that a lot of work could have been wasted, you might well be the answer to their problem.

Land for sale: lateral thinking

Piecing together a plot

This involves looking out for something slightly different. When studying the Ordnance Survey maps you would normally look out for the obvious plot that exists either in its own right or is able to be subdivided from a larger property. However, it is possible to make a plot by stitching together smaller areas of land. The drawback is that in doing so you end up with several vendors, but the trick is to devise the scheme and tie it all up with legally binding options from each of the owners, allowing you to purchase in the event of satisfactory planning permission. Beware trying to go too far without such an option as, once you've got planning consent, a single owner, maybe with landlocked land that has no intrinsic value other than as part of your plot, could hold you to ransom. Look out for a row of houses where the back gardens are quite long and where at least one of them fronts a viable access. Remember that once again, it's important to demonstrate that you are a private self-builder, that the scheme can be realised with little or no detriment to their continued occupation and that it is unlikely adversely to affect their values.

Utilising part of your own land/garden

Before going out bothering prospective plot owners with offers to convert their garden into your dream plot, take a close look at your own home. Is your house in a street where the density of dwellings is rising due to large gardens being divided off as plots? If not, is it possible that you could start the trend? Maybe your garden backs on to or is side on to a road where a new access could be formed. Maybe the rear garden is so long that it might be possible to create a new driveway down the side of your house and build at the bottom with very little detriment to your existing home in either amenity or financial terms? A visit to your local planning department will either confirm or deny your hopes and cost nothing to investigate unless you decide to go for an application. Prepare the ground first, though, and look out for precedents that you can quote if necessary. And if you live in a semi-detached or end-of-terrace house on a corner or between blocks in a high-density location, consider whether there's room to extend the terrace with a similar house attached to yours.

Local builders and developers

When the housing market is buoyant, developers buy up land and form their own land bank. When the market is sluggish and sales of their houses are down they might be persuaded to off-load surplus plots just to keep some sort of cashflow going. However, it is always worth contacting them as they might have plots with which they are willing to enter into a 'turnkey' arrangement whereby they will build the house to your design. It is not strictly self-building and there is unlikely to be a significant saving over buying a house 'off the peg' but it can get you what you want. Occasionally developers have plots to sell on partially finished estates. Large estates of houses need areas set aside for site huts and compounds that are required almost up to the end of a project. At times, a new and more attractive proposition can come up and the smaller developer might well be persuaded to cut his losses on the old site in order to make a clean start on to the new one. The beauty of these plots is that they are serviced but the drawback is that you might be limited in design expression.

Be proactive
Get in the car and drive around looking for plots. In all of the dire warn-ings about not buying land that doesn't have planning permission, there are obvious circumstances where a piece of land can be considered as a plot and where you can either take out an option or agree to buy subject to receipt of satisfactory planning. Look out for areas where infilling has occurred and carefully seek out the undeveloped plot. While the owners might have originally resisted selling, time can change things. Look for unexplained gaps in the street scene. They could have been the village pond or be the route of a drain or service but they could just as easily be an access to land at the rear that is no longer required. Ask around. Try to find the oldest person or the village busybody to identify vacant land that might lie behind hedges or walls. Get some flyers printed and deliver them door to door in chosen villages or streets, making it clear that you are private individuals seeking to self-build and not developers. Put notice cards in shop windows, again making it clear that the land is for your own use rather than pure profit.

Public utilities (telephone and gas companies, electricity and water boards, Railtrack, etc.)
Telephone relay stations, gas regulators, pumping stations and electricity transformers used to take up large areas of land in the middle of residen-tial areas. In some cases the buildings that used to house these things were the size of small bungalows. Nowadays what went on in there can be accommodated in a box the size of chest of drawers, and the land and buildings have become redundant, with planners often more than happy to see the street scene tidied up by replacement of these anachronisms. The drawback with these plots is that the land might well be contaminated in some way or that there might be a considerable amount of equipment and pipework to remove. Additionally, provision for access to any replace-ment equipment might be needed and there may well be sterile zones. Try writing to the various companies, explaining what you want to do and asking if they have any surplus and suitable land for sale. Better still, get out there and identify these things yourself and then write or call in to ask directly about a specific property.

Railtrack owns many parcels of land, not all of which are close to railway lines. It has an Estates Department that actively seeks to develop and dispose of surplus land.

Multiple plots

Sometimes self-builders have double plots or obtain planning for more than one dwelling and want to sell off the spare plots. The chances are that when they do they'll try to sell to another self-builder through the self-build media or discussion forums rather than through estate agents. Sometimes prospective self-builders will want to bid for a multiple site and will advertise for other self-builders to join in with them. In such cases vendors are often reluctant to sell to multiple buyers so it might be necessary for one party to purchase with collateral agreements to sell on the remaining plots to the others.

Plotsearch has Plotshare, whereby it will put you in touch with like-minded people who only want one plot on a multiple-plot site. It is also moving towards creating plots for self-builders by buying up suitable development land and putting in the services.

If there are to be four or more homes requiring a new access, it is likely that the authorities will require the road and the drains under it to be constructed to Highway standards, with a bond to lead to formal adoption. This costs a great deal of money and is complicated, as either a single person or some formal body has to take legal responsibility for the bond.

Change of use/conversions

The UK is dotted with countless redundant and unoccupied buildings from old barns to shops, factories, water towers and churches, many of which, with flair and imagination could be converted to residential use if only the planners would allow it. The situation varies from area to area with some local authorities enthusiastically welcoming the renewal and regeneration of these buildings while others actually state that they'd prefer to see them fall down rather than contemplate them becoming homes. Check out your local authority's standpoint on this one but even so it's often worth making a case for a change of use or conversion. Take out an option before taking things too far so as not to see your efforts, if successful, enjoyed by others. Remember that planners and conservation officers are often afraid of buildings being developed in an unsympathetic way; if you can demonstrate that you really want to preserve the essential aspects and historical relevance of the building, your case will be considerably strengthened.

Renovations or extensions

The land-agency lists are full of renovation opportunities that vary from almost complete re-builds to properties that just need a makeover such as a new kitchen or bathroom. However, unless the change envisaged is fundamental there is unlikely to be the equity gain that is available with new build. Look for the house that is really the missed opportunity; for example the 1960s house that is too small or of a design out of character with the local vernacular, yet enjoys an enviable plot. Rendering or cladding, new windows, modern heating systems, thermal insulation and even, at times, new roofing material more in keeping with the area can make a huge difference to enjoyment and value. Investigate Permitted Development Rights (see Chapter 5, The Planning Maze, p. 85) and whether they apply; if so, utilise them to the full before making any planning application, where an extension's acceptability might well be related the size of the dwelling.

Farming and rural enterprise plots

Development of agricultural land is usually only allowed if it can be proven that it is necessary for the proper maintenance and running of a viable agricultural enterprise or an approved rural industry. That doesn't mean that if you've got couple of horses in the field you can build to be near them; on the other hand, if you run a successful livery or riding stables with a proven track record of economic viability, you might just get consent. It's often easier to demonstrate necessity on larger farms but it is also possible to prove a need for a dwelling on smaller enterprises such as nurseries, intensive units and specialist growers. The important thing to realise is that the land and its use, rather than the house, is paramount. As such many new enterprises are required to demonstrate that they have been successfully up and running for some time before a dwelling is finally approved and that it's really necessary for someone actually to live on site. This means that the applicants might have to contemplate living in a mobile home for some time and any planning consent that is granted might limit the occupation of the dwelling to those engaged in running the enterprise.

Replacement dwellings

A large proportion of self-build projects are not greenfield plots but one-for-one replacements. Large numbers of houses built since the war, even as late as the 1970s, have run their course. They are structurally unsound, incapable of being brought up to modern requirements for thermal insulation and energy efficiency, and fall short of the sort of accommodation that we all now expect. Estate agents don't always recognise this fact. Sometimes they take a property at face value and try for ages to sell a substandard bungalow or house, with a string of disappointed mortgage applications, little realising that this should more properly be a plot. When you are putting your name down for plots, consider also asking for details of properties in need of refurbishment. If you're at a distance, you might want to separate the two issues and register this other interest under a different name or address.

Replacement dwellings have huge advantages over plots. While there may be demolition costs, in most cases these are insignificant or unlikely to detract from the value of the plot. Furthermore, many of the infrastructure costs associated with a greenfield plot are taken care of. Almost certainly all or most of the services are already in. The sewers might well be connected, the driveway and entrance may already have been formed and the garden and fencing are likely to be capable of re-use.

Many local authorities restrict the size of any replacement dwelling to a certain percentage increase over the original building. You may be able to 'beat' this restriction by your knowledge and use of Permitted Development Rights as outlined in Chapter 5 on planning.

Imagination is what brings most people to the self-build table. A desire to achieve what they want for want they've got. Finding the plot is the first hurdle at which most would-be self-builders fall. But with dedication and a little knowledge, the odds are definitely shortened.

chapter three
Checking Out & Buying the Plot

Finding plots is never easy, and it sometimes seems that all the really good plots get snapped up so quickly by builders and developers that the poor old self-builder hardly gets a look in. But there are plots that hang around and appear never to sell. These are the difficult plots: the ones with unusual ground conditions, the ones without mains services and the ones where the topography, shape or orientation of the site mean that standard design formats simply won't fit. For the self-builder these plots can represent a golden opportunity just so long as you have the perseverance and determination properly to assess the problems, research the solutions and calculate the costs of putting things right. Builders and developers simply don't have the time to do all of this. They are after the quick-and-easy return, and plots like this can stay on the market for ages. This is often reflected in the price, and if the costs of the building, including the additional costs necessary plus the cost of the land, still leave a margin, then these plots are well worthy of consideration.

If a plot is absolutely no good then the self-builder should know enough to be the first to walk away. But, if there is any real potential, you should be the last to do so. The secret is not to give up. Not every problem is capable of being solved. Some sites can simply never be an economic prospect but, for far more, a slightly different mindset or willingness to look at things from another perspective can certainly bring rewards.

Most people's ideal of a building plot is a lovely rectangle of closely cropped lawn with a neat hedge or fence, along a quiet road with superb views in all directions. They are of course out there, but they are few and far between, and the potential self-builder has to get used to seeing a succession of pieces of land that seem to bear no real relationship to the dream. When people sell a house they go to extraordinary lengths to make it attractive even to the point of putting on a fresh pot of coffee or baking bread in the oven for the aroma. However, when people sell building plots they leave them covered in rubbish, derelict buildings, rusty cars and tangled undergrowth. Why this should be is a mystery. But the first lesson that any potential self-builder needs to learn is to look at a plot as it is going to be, as you are going to develop it and not as it is. But in order to evaluate a plot fully there are some pretty major considerations.

The context: surrounding sites and land value

Don't look at the plot in isolation
In any assessment of a potential plot it is important to look beyond the immediate boundaries of the property you have come to see. Don't start looking at things as you arrive at the site. Start miles away. When you have located the plot, drive on past and approach it from the other direction. As

you get near it from either direction, watch out for changes in the social profile of the area. If you are thinking of building an upmarket house, then an approach through a local-authority housing estate, even if quite removed from the actual site, might detract. Look out for the For Sale signs and phone the agents to check on local property values. If there are loads of properties up for sale, ask yourself why. Worry about the general tidiness of the area. The value of our homes depends to a large degree on those around and about us sharing those values.

Ask yourself why nobody's built on it already

Decent plots have been hard to come by almost everywhere for a long time now. Start any assessment of the plot by asking yourself why nobody has built there already. There may be a simple answer. The plot may have been part of somebody's garden. Their lifestyle and aspirations may have changed, or they may have simply got too old to manage the larger plot and finally given in to the need to realise cash. The planners, spurred on by government directives, might only recently have agreed to this intensification of use. The plot may have served some other purpose, such as providing access to fields at the rear, which is no longer required. But just as possibly, the site might be wholly or partly sterilised by the presence of a high-pressure main or be the subject of some 'live' restrictive covenant. Maybe those obstacles are negotiable? Maybe problems such as bad ground, which made the plot uneconomical in the past, can now be resolved by newly invented solutions and mitigated by rising property values? Maybe it is just because nobody ever thought of it?

Starting the foundations.

Consider what you should pay for the land

A plot derives its worth from the value of the eventual house or bungalow that is or should be built upon it. Establishing that value is important but there is no mystery to this. There are no complicated formulae. One home is simply assessed in direct comparison to similar homes and the values they have achieved on the market. We all do this. Our worth is quantified by our property value and that is a calculation we all make on a continuous basis. The only difference between the lay person and the estate agent is that the latter may have a larger mental database upon which to draw. But a look through the lists of property for sale or advertised in estate-agents' windows can quickly bring you up to date.

All property has a ceiling value, a price beyond which it is no longer economically viable. If a plot is in an area where it would best be developed as a four-bedroom house and somebody decides, for reasons of their own, that they would like to build a six-bedroom house instead, they might find that, despite spending a great deal more money on building costs, the eventual house is not worth much more than the smaller homes. They would have overdeveloped and exceeded the carrying capacity of the plot. On the other hand, if somebody decides that they only want to build a two-bedroom bungalow on this same plot of land, then they will never realise the full potential of the plot. They would have underdeveloped the plot.

In the past, the 'third, third, third' rule was often quoted, where the land cost would form one-third of the eventual house value, the building costs would form another third and the balance would be the profit or equity increase. It was an ideal, and in some regions it still holds good. Elsewhere, the availability of land and/or high or low property values have distorted it. In the final analysis the most you could pay for the land would be the market value of the house less the building costs. But that would leave no margin and, if that were the norm, most developers and many self-builders simply wouldn't bother. So in fact the average margin is around 33 per cent on equity rather than final value. Thus somebody buying a plot in Gloucestershire for £100,000 and spending £200,000 on the build could expect to finish up with a home worth around £400,000. The land would be around a quarter of the finished value and the profit would be one-third of the amount spent. But, in Surrey, they might have to pay £500,000 for a similar plot and £220,000 to get the same type of house built. On the other hand, with the new home being worth in the region of £960,000, while the land accounts for over half the final value, the yield on equity remains the same, at one-third.

Think about what you can build

When you go out to view a plot, don't just arrive at the site and start look-ing around. On your way in make a note of the local architectural styles. Take particular note of new houses that have been built – they give the clue as to just what sort of design the local planning authority is prepared to accept. They also give the clue as to those properties that find favour in the market. If you decide that you want to buck that trend then be aware that you might be limiting your resale value or market acceptability.

While some areas can carry an eclectic mixture of styles and house sizes, others are of a more consistent nature. Make sure that what you propose to build is going to fit in. If you think that a four-bedroom house is going to look incongruous set in a street of two-bedroom bungalows then you are probably right. The planners won't like it and even if they did, when it comes to sell it you will have trouble. What fits into the street scene will, in most cases, represent the best property to build and the best return on your investment.

Any potential problem with pollution from noise, smell or vibration

Even the most ideal-looking site can suffer from noise pollution. In some cases fairly dramatic solutions may be necessary but, often, simple re-orientation or careful thought within the design may be all that is needed to alleviate the problem. If there is an identifiable noise source, such as a factory or a busy road, any design should attempt either to put a blank wall on the problem side or, at the very least, only site utility or non-habitable rooms there. The shape of a building can be crucial. A horseshoe- or courtyard-shape opening on to the noise source will trap and magnify any sound. Turn the same design the other way round and introduce a baffle in the form of outbuildings or garaging and noise pollution is mitigated.

Most sites send away vast quantities of spoil, and this costs money. An earth bank or bund built between a busy road and the house, possibly planted with evergreen trees, can literally absorb or throw off noise; insulation of the walls and ceilings can be achieved through the use of plasterboard bonded to an acoustic foam or by the use of acoustic mineral board bonded to impregnated rubbers in a multi-layered sandwich. These systems can significantly reduce sound levels from airborne, flanking and impact noise, almost to the point of eradication. It is, however, important that all gaps between walls and ceilings and, in particular, at floor zones are sealed. If the outside noise is such that opening windows is undesirable, whole-house ventilation may be the solution, with or without heat-recovery options. This can also help solve the problem of smell within the house, although in the garden there is little or nothing that can be done. Vibration can occur through busy roads, local industrial premises or from trains or underground railways. A normal floating floor, particularly where there is a thicker-than-average foam underlay, preferably in multiple layers, can go a long way to solving this. Alternatively, there are specific bonded or underlay products on the market that reduce airborne or acoustic sound between floors.

Planning considerations

Planning permission

What makes the corner of a field or part of somebody's garden into a building plot? The answer is planning permission; either the actuality or the certainty of it. Most self-builders would be well advised not to buy property without it having express planning permission. That does not mean that you cannot *agree* to buy land before it has planning consent. What it does mean, though, is that if you do, you should do so only subject to receipt of satisfactory planning permission, and you should only pay for the land once, and if, it gets it.

Most land that is sold by agents will have details of the planning permission or a note of the consent number, appended to the brochure. Sometimes all that is shown is the front page. This is not enough. Always read the whole of the planning consent and check the timing and duration of the consent. Chapter 5, The Planning Maze, will explain the various types of planning permission and why it is so important to understand the differences.

Sometimes land comes on to the market with an expired planning permission. Now, in many and most cases a pragmatic local authority will accept that the principle of development has been established and they will entertain and grant a Full application. But in some cases, particularly where there has been a change of policy, they might be reluctant to do so, making it of utmost importance that if such a situation arises the self-builder is only committed to purchase only in the event of planning being granted.

Always read all of the conditions on a planning consent and make sure that they are capable of being satisfied. If you are buying land where work has already been started and the planning has apparently therefore been perpetuated, make sure that all of the conditions in the original consent have been satisfied or enacted. If not, then it is possible for the consent to be invalidated or counted out of time.

An example of this is where there is a condition on a consent requiring the approval of external materials by the local authority, in writing, before commencement of work. If this is overlooked then any work carried out under the consent could be deemed to be unlawful or in breach of the conditions. In most cases the local authority will grant approval for the materials and validate the consent retrospectively. However, in certain cases, where the policy of the authority is or has turned against development in that situation or where the consent was granted on Appeal in defiance of the planning authority's wishes or in green belt, it might not be so accommodating.

Permitted Development Rights (PDR)

Before walking away from a plot where the planning authorities have imposed a condition limiting the development to a single storey or stipulating a maximum size for the dwelling, check the position regarding Permitted Development Rights or PDR (see Chapter 5, p. 85). If you want to build rooms in the roof or a bigger house, then you might still get what you want. If the rights are not impaired they give implied consent for a wide range of developments, among which are construction of garages or outbuildings, occupation of the roof void and extension of up to 15 per cent of the original house volume or 70 cu. metres, whichever is the greater, up to a maximum of 115 cu. metres.

Strictly speaking PDR apply to the dwelling only once it is occupied. Some local authorities accept an intention to use them for future development in the basement or the loft, so long as it has no effect on the overall size and height of the dwelling. Others maintain that if such development breaches the required size of the dwelling, it should not be allowed. It may be better, therefore, to neglect to show the basement or loft as occupied space on the planning drawings. You will need to show them on the Building Regulations application but even here, it might be best to start off by referring to them as 'storage' or 'void'.

If PDR have been removed, consider whether, if it is a replacement dwelling, you could utilise the rights accruing to the existing property and then incorporate them within your overall scheme. Be careful, however, if there is clause in the consent requiring demolition of all existing buildings prior to occupation of the new dwelling.

Very rarely, a consent requires a minimum size. To get around this, design your new home so that it can be built in phases and then build only what you can afford in the first instance.

Archaeological interest

Sometimes planning permission is granted where reference is made to an archaeological interest in the site. There may be a requirement for an archaeological survey to be carried out and while, at first, this might seem innocuous it can have serious cost implications, not only in the initial expense but also as a result of the findings. There might be at times an almost indefinite delay on the development of the site or a requirement, if development goes ahead, for special foundations to be laid to allow for future access to the site.

In most cases the interests of the various societies and bodies can be satisfied by agreeing to a watching brief. With this, you undertake to allow the authorities and interested parties to come out and inspect your foundations as they proceed.

Access considerations

In order to qualify as a plot, a piece of land must have a legal right of access that is physically achievable. Most plots have access to a main or adopted road. Check to see that there is no 'ransom strip' between your plot and the adopted Highway. This is a small strip of land, maybe even as narrow as 150 mm, in the ownership of another party. In many cases this has been put there deliberately by a previous vendor in order to cash in on any uplift in value should the land gain planning permission.

Strictly speaking, any ransom amounting to around one-third of the land value should be paid by the vendor. But not all vendors are as honest as one would hope. Some may deliberately try to cover up the existence of the ransom. Others might either not be aware of its existence or fail to understand the significance. Check all dimensions and study the plans from the Land Registry or those contained in the title deeds for any discrepancy that might indicate the existence of a ransom strip. If it does appear that one exists and you are unable to find the beneficiary then it is possible to obtain an indemnity policy, and it is normal for the premium to be paid for by the vendor.

Some plots have rights of way over other land or existing driveways. In many cases these rights of way are detailed in the legal documentation for both parcels of land. In other cases, the rights are lost in the mists of time or have never been fully documented. In most cases such an established right of way can be formalised but in others an indemnity policy can be employed to guard against someone challenging the right of way.

The 20-year rule that is generally accepted means that if you can prove that a property has enjoyed unencumbered and uninterrupted access over land for a period of 20 years or more, a legal right of way is capable of being established. These are known as Prescriptive Easements. They allow the acquisition of a right through long usage or enjoyment, provided that the right was lawfully granted or obtained at common law, by lost modern grant or under an 1832 Act of Parliament.

As you would expect, there are a number of caveats. Firstly, the right must have been obtained without force, secrecy or permission. Secondly, it must attach to a freeholder, although, if the right were established by a tenant it may still stand but would attach to the land it benefits rather than the tenant. Thirdly, the use must be continuous, although The Prescription Act of 1832 allows a break of up to one year. Most importantly, the access must not be illegal and, since the passing of the British Transport Commission Act 1949, it has not been possible to acquire rights over railway land or land owned by the British Waterways Board. Crown land is naturally exempt. Highways land is also exempt but as it is expressly there for the purpose of public access, there is therefore no need to acquire additional rights.

As vehicular passage over common land without the owner's permission is illegal, until The Countryside & Rights of Way Act 2002 came into force you could not acquire rights over common land. All that has now changed and an owner of property who can prove that they have driven over common land for a period of 20 years or more can now apply to the owners for an Easement or legal right of vehicular access. This has to be accompanied by a valuation of the house, which the Easement is proposed to serve, and compensation or payment has to be made at the rate of 2 per cent of the house value. This is reduced to 0.5 per cent for houses built before 31 December 1930 and 0.25 per cent for houses built before 31 December 1905.

A subsequent House of Lords' decision holds that it is possible to acquire Prescriptive Rights over common land. This turns much of the above on its head. Quite what it will mean is not yet clear, apart from the fact that many people who have paid substantial amounts of money to acquire rights may now feel extremely aggrieved.

Visibility splays

One condition that is quite common in planning permissions is that the entrance shall be formed to the requirements of the Highways or local authority. That is fine, just so long as you know what they are in your particular case and that they can be satisfied.

If your plot is on a busy road there may be a requirement for sight lines and visibility splays. That means that at a certain point measured back from the carriageway edge in the centre of your proposed driveway a line may have to be drawn to a point in each direction, back to the carriageway edge. The distance that this line has to be taken will vary in each case but the requirement will be that all parts of the resulting triangles of land should be kept free of any obstruction. If the sight lines remain within your ownership then there is no problem. But if they cross adjoining property then, in order to satisfy the planning condition, you will need to enter into a legal agreement with the neighbours to keep this land free from obstruction in perpetuity.

If they are ambivalent about the development of the land, at worst they might refuse and at best they might demand payment. Make sure that you identify this potential problem before buying the land and that if any payment is made it is made by the vendors and not by you.

Ground conditions/subsoil considerations

Most of what the groundwork trade does is covered up afterwards and never seen again. That doesn't mean it isn't important. In fact, it is the most important trade of them all with the whole structural stability and integrity of your new home depending on whether it was done properly. No wonder that those contemplating building worry more about this aspect of the build than any other. It is the one part of the building process where the self-builder can feel out of control, where costs can spiral and where dramatic changes of direction or even design can be forced upon you.

And yet it is undoubtedly the most exciting part. For a start, it is the first of the trades, and their commencement means that a long cherished dream is now coming true. Huge changes can be wreaked in minutes. Diggers tear into the ground, chainsaws hum and trees come crashing down. Mechanical arms swing and old buildings are reduced to rubble. It all looks chaotic, and you can be left wondering if any order will ever be restored. But it always is and the site that is a churned mess of ruts, heaps and trenches will one day bear your new home and be transformed into an ordered garden.

Clues to potential problems

In most cases problems within the ground and the requirement for extra or different foundations are things that can and should be flagged up at an early stage. The first and most common mistake people make when visiting a site for the first time is to start looking at things only when they get there. As you approach any site, look at the other houses. As you get to within a mile study them carefully for various pointers. Look for signs of cracks in the walling that may have been crudely repointed. One house, and it may be a problem that is peculiar to that building; several houses, and it may be an indication of a general ground problem in the area.

Pay particular attention to new buildings or those under construction. Study the disturbed ground to see what type the subsoil is, whether it is clay, loam, gravel or chalk. Look in trenches to see not only the strata they display but also whether the sides hold up. If there is a lot of rock around, find out what type it is, whether it was consistent or loose shale. Find out what type of foundations they have employed, as the chances are that you will have to use the same. When on site you will obviously redouble your efforts to discover these things but vendors might not take too kindly to you digging holes. Instead, look into flowerbeds and especially around recently planted trees or hedges for signs of filled ground such as broken glass, bricks or tiles.

Nature also offers some significant clues. Discarding obvious exotic planting, look for what is there naturally. Oak trees do well in heavy clay soils. Native conifers prefer damp, acidic upland peat. Willow and alder like wet loam close to watercourses. Beech thrive in light clay soils overlying chalk, whitebeam in chalk downs and lime trees in limestone. It is not an exact science and complicated by transplanting, but it can give clues. So too with grasses, particularly soft rushes or sedges, which only thrive in conditions of poor drainage. A high water-table may not, of itself, mean that the ground is poor for building purposes. But it will mean that you may have to think carefully about which foundation system you use.

Soil survey

Despite all of this, do you need a soil survey? The short answer has always got to be 'Yes'. If there is any suspicion or your own investigations reveal any possible problem then it doesn't make sense to go any further without one. But before you do, drop into the local authority and have a chat with the Building Inspector. They have seen everything from a whole house to a new porch, and they will be well aware of ground conditions throughout their area. If they think there is a likely problem then they will say so and, equally, if they think it unlikely, they may tell you to save your money.

A clean foundation trench waiting for concrete.

If you do have a soil survey then the surveyors will normally want to open between three and four trial holes. These will be dug around the site, normally outside the eventual excavation, to a depth of between 1 and 3 metres. If they need to go deeper then it will have to be a specialist borehole. The important thing to remember is that these trial holes are telling the surveyor what is found within them, and they will extrapolate that information to produce their report and recommendations. Normally that is sufficient and their findings can be translated to the whole site and your eventual foundations. Occasionally what is found when the real foundation holes are dug is different and the surveyors might have to come back and re-design to accommodate the reality. A soil investigation will cost between £300 and £1000 for most sites and in most cases is a worthwhile expenditure.

What are they looking for? The surveyors are looking for the type of subsoil and may well relate that to the presence of trees. What they find will determine the type of foundation you will have to use, and it is important to know this before you start, as it is not always easy to change once building has commenced.

Trees Particularly important when combined with heavy clay, trees take enormous quantities of water from the subsoil. Even beneath small trees, the ground is always dry and friable. In most soil conditions this presents no problem, but in clay with a high plasticity it can cause what is known 'heave'. Dry clay, when wet, will expand in volume. If a tree is removed or killed by buildings works, the subsoil will expand and rise, or heave, with a pressure that, while hardly visible, is inexorable and strong enough to crack ordinary foundations.

Rock The presence of rock might at first seem beneficial. Rock is of course nature's concrete. But you can't just go building straight on to it and that might mean having to employ some pretty powerful machinery to cut into it, only to replace it with man-made concrete. Loose rock or shale can be a problem. It might have good bearing but it is difficult to get the trench sides to remain constant and in certain situations the shale is so loose that it can slide over itself, losing all compressive strength.

Chalk This is about the best medium in which you can build. Chalk drains well, it bears well, and it can be cut to quite precise trench widths. The problem is that it often occurs in concert with other soil types and in that case, unless you are able to follow the chalk, you may be faced with having to design a foundation that can deal with differential settlement.

Sand has good bearing strength but when it is waterlogged it can develop a treacle-like consistency and is then known as running sand. It is almost impossible to dig into, and it may mean reverting to a specialised foundation type or system. Dry sand is normally good but the trench sides can be very unstable.

Mining activity In current or recent mining areas a mining survey is necessary, because mining activity can cause problems, and it is usual to build with a raft foundation. This is basically a reinforced concrete platform upon which the house is built, that is designed to 'float' over any changes in the supporting ground. A big problem is where outcrops of coal appear within the foundations. Usually these seams are relatively thin and can be dug out. They cannot, however, be left in.

A bigger problem, prevalent in places like Cornwall, is bell mining where a relatively narrow surface entrance balloons out below, leaving an empty chasm. These are often unmapped and occasionally they open up unexpectedly, making the news headlines. The solution, which is expensive, is almost invariably to fill them up with large amounts of concrete.

Most sites will have a normal vegetable loam or topsoil overlying an inert subsoil comprised of a mixture of clays, sand and stones. Any foundation must be created below the vegetable layer and only inert material can be left beneath them or the oversite. Organic material such as coal or asphalt must be removed, and the presence of a seam of coal can be bad news, although, happily, most are fairly shallow.

Contamination Another thing the surveyor will be looking for is contamination. In most cases the possibility of contamination will be obvious, as when purchasing an old filling-station or industrial premises. Owners of land and vendors must notify the local authority if any contamination is likely to affect an underground watercourse, humans, livestock or the natural environment. Unfortunately, not all vendors are as scrupulous as they should be and not all local authorities are up to speed on compiling lists of contaminated sites. Flagging up the existence of contamination, most of which can be cured, means that any costs will be borne by the vendors and not the self-builder.

Foundation solutions

If conditions on site mean that you do have to employ a special foundation it may seem like the end of the world. But the truth is that in most cases the costs are easily absorbed or covered by the contingency fund and, even in the very worst cases, the extra costs are unlikely to exceed 10 per cent of the original budget. The principal types of foundation and their relative costs are standard strip, trenchfill, deep trenchfill, piled and ringbeam, and reinforced concrete raft.

Standard strip For most soil conditions this is the best and cheapest way of constructing your foundations. A trench 450–600 mm wide is dug 1–1.2 metres deep beneath all external and loadbearing walls. In the bottom of this a layer of concrete, at least 225 mm thick, is placed, and upon this the foundation walls are built in blockwork with two skins to external walls and a single skin to internal loadbearing walls. The costs for a building roughly 10 ˉ 7 metres with one cross wall would be around £8000, and it would take the average team of groundworkers a maximum of two weeks or ten working days to get to oversite level.

Trenchfill Where the water-table is high or the trench sides are unstable it is often better to revert to this type of foundation. The trenches are essentially the same except that, instead of just putting concrete in the bottom, you fill them almost to the top. This means that you are out of the ground in one day and it also means that the amount of below damp proof course blockwork is reduced. The costs, for the same size building, rise to around £9000 but the time taken for the job should be no longer and perhaps even shorter.

Deep trenchfill Where heavy clay is in the presence of trees it is necessary to take the foundation below the level at which the tree's thirst for water is active. This can mean digging to a depth of 3 metres and filling the trenches with massive amounts of concrete. At these levels special care needs to be taken and shoring might be required. Additionally it is usually necessary to insulate the foundation from any ground movement by lining one or both sides of the trench with a compressible material plus a slip membrane. The costs can rise to as high as £14,000, and it will take an extra week. At some stage it is no longer economically or physically possible to dig any deeper by conventional means. Additionally the cost of sending spoil away becomes prohibitive and it is at this point that it becomes economically viable to switch to a piled foundation.

Piled and ringbeam   Piled and ringbeam foundations are also used in situations where the top layers of ground have poor bearing capacity and good bearing can only be found at deeper levels. The piles are driven or bored into the ground to support a reinforced concrete ringbeam (groundbeam) spanning from cap to cap to support the house walls. This ringbeam can be cast in situ or delivered as a prefabricated unit. Systems are also available, which combine the ringbeam with the floor as a stable platform upon which the house can be built. A piled system for a 10 ˜ 7 metre home will cost £12,000–£18,000 depending on the depth at which bearing strata is found and the number of piles required. The time taken for an in situ cast groundbeam type will be around three weeks and for the prefabricated systems no longer than ten working days, if everything is properly co-ordinated.

Reinforced concrete raft   This system is used where the ground has good bearing but is inherently unstable due to geological or mining conditions far below the surface. A large hole is dug and filled with consolidated layers of hardcore. Upon this a specially designed reinforced-concrete raft is cast, and it is this raft or slab that supports the whole house. It uses a lot of concrete, and it needs to be carefully designed, but in areas where it is common, most groundworkers see it as 'standard'. The time taken is 10–15 working days at a cost of £12,000–£15,000.

In most cases homes built with either timber frame or masonry will share precisely the same foundations, and no distinction will be made between the two. In a few cases, where loads are critical, the lightweight timber frame or other prefabricated-type structures may be able to have lesser foundations. This is particularly applicable with a piled and ringbeam foundation, where it might sometimes be possible to reduce the number of piles. All foundations should be accurate to the plan, but in the heat of battle that is not always possible. However, if you are building in timber, frame foundations should be level to within 20 mm and square to within 12 mm.

Flooding
The government has set its face against the granting or renewal of planning permissions on floodplains. Nevertheless there are still a considerable number of viable plots that can be affected by flooding. Building beside a river is many people's dream, but it can have its disadvantages. One solution is to raise the floor level above the known maximum flood level with all underbuilding designed to allow the free passage of water. Essentially, this means that the house is built up on brick piers. The area beneath the floor can be used for storage or parking but at no time should it be enclosed. The problem comes when this solution is linked to roof height restrictions, effectively limiting development to a raised bungalow.

Properties that are liable to intermittent flash flooding can be protected, to a degree, by earth bunds or barriers plus a sump-and-pump disposal system. This works by having a series of perforated pipes set in the ground leading to a sump with a dual pump to send any water back outside the barrier. The pumps are designed to cope with up to 75 mm of rainfall per hour, but they have to have somewhere to dump the water, and if the flood gets above the barrier it will cease to have any effect. The biggest single problem with flooding is either the mixing of sewage with the floodwater or the backing up of the drains into the house.

The first of these problems can be mitigated by siting any private sewage systems outside the bund. The second can be solved, except in the case of a flood breaching the bund, by the installation of non-return valves in the foul drains. Insurance is the biggest problem. Most insurers have announced that they will continue to hold cover for existing customers in areas liable to flooding, but the premiums could still rise. They and others don't want to be in the position of 'drawing red lines around areas', but the fact remains that for some properties the premiums may make development uneconomic and a smaller number may even be uninsurable.

Radon gas

In certain parts of the UK, particularly in those areas where the underlying rock is granite, there is a naturally occurring radioactive gas called radon that seeps up from the ground. This gas is present everywhere in the atmosphere, and accounts for 50 per cent of natural background radiation. Normally it is quite harmless, but in modern houses with good draught-proofing concentrations can build up, and in some areas this health hazard is now recognised as making a significant contribution to the statistics for deaths from lung cancer.

As a result there are now special design requirements for houses built in areas where there is a high level of radon seepage, and Building Inspectors will advise on this as a matter of course. The precautions involve making foundation slabs gas tight, and in some areas of high risk providing ways for the radon to be discharged into the atmosphere. This is not complex, difficult or expensive but it has to be done. The Health Protection Agency (www.hpa.org.uk) has a range of free leaflets about this and even offers test kits to indicate radon levels.

Contaminated ground

As mentioned already, local authorities have a statutory duty to register and inspect land in their area that is subject to contamination and likely to affect adversely an underground watercourse, humans, livestock or the natural environment. The problem is that these registers are still in the process of being compiled, and landowners are not always as scrupulous as they should be in advising interested parties of the possibility of contamination. Where contamination is identified, the authorities can require the problem to be cleaned up by serving a Remediation Notice, which, if it is ignored, allows them to do the necessary work and charge the cost to the landowner. If vendors wilfully fail to disclose known contamination then they can lay themselves open to a civil action from a purchaser.

It is quite likely that your solicitor will carry out an environmental search on the land. This isn't automatic, and they may ask if you want to bother. If there is any doubt at all then it is a wise precaution. One of the most common problems is a site that used to be an old filling-station. Local village filling-stations are no longer economically viable, and it is these older premises that are the most likely to have leaking concrete or brick tanks. That should not mean, just so long as the price being asked for the land reflects the fact, that such a site cannot be adequately cleaned up. Sometimes this means digging out the contaminated soil, carting it to an approved dumping site and replacing it with fresh. This is the expensive option in cash and environmental terms with costs in the £20,000–£30,000 range. Another way of doing things is to cap the site with an impermeable layer or to treat the soil in situ with processes referred to as 'bio-remediation', where microbes are cultured or encouraged to proliferate on site to break down the long hydrocarbon chains and neutralise the problem.

Human Health Risk Assessment has become an issue, whereby, if it can be proved that a hazard, though present, is manageable, the authorities can be persuaded that no intrusive action is necessary. Such is often the case where sometimes quite high levels of arsenic, used in earlier times for pest eradication, are found but where it can be proven that the amounts that anyone would need to ingest to cause them harm would make a problem unlikely.

Always be ready to shore up and support trenches, where necessary.

Service considerations

Getting the services connected to a site can be very expensive. Even in a suburban street the cost of supply and connection to electricity can be around £700 with about £300 required by the gas suppliers. Sewage and water connections will add at least £1200.

Rural or isolated sites are at a premium, and any property that gets built on them will have a correspondingly high market value. Nevertheless, many people are put off either by the fact that there is often no mains electricity or by the prohibitive cost of getting it laid on. There are alternatives. Solar panels can supply up to 40 per cent of the hot-water needs of a house, even in inclement weather. However, they are not that good at providing hot water for space heating. Photovoltaic (PV) panels, many of which actually work better in diffused light than full sunshine, convert sunlight into DC electricity, which can then be converted to AC current. It is unlikely that they can supply 100 per cent of a normal household's needs, but if they are coupled with other alternatives, such as wind turbines, and backed up by a generator then most if not all electricity requirements can be met.

Quite a lot has been written about wind turbines. The cost is around £1500 for a 1kW machine, but an average-size house would need at least 6kW, and that cost would rise to around £16,000 after grants, which is about a 15-year payback. The trouble is that in many areas of the UK there simply isn't enough wind, and on the coldest days, when it's frosty or foggy and the air is still, there is no wind at all. The other problem that rarely gets mentioned is the noise and vibration, which can resonate through the structure and cause considerable annoyance.

For those aiming at a low or nil carbon-emission rate, if used in conjunction with a mains supply, these on-site generation systems can mean that excess current can be put back into the grid. When used in isolated situations, electricity can be stored in batteries for use at night. A full array of photovoltaic panels will typically cost anywhere between £12,000 and £25,000. However, the government, through the Energy Saving Trust, is giving grants towards their installation.

The type of site that is divorced from mains-water supply is likely to be isolated and, in many people's eyes therefore, desirable. The principal alternative to mains-water supply is to employ a borehole. The *Yellow Pages* lists the drilling companies under 'Water Engineers', and there are likely to be quite a few in each area. The cost will vary between £5000 and £20,000 depending on the depth and the ground conditions but, in general, a borehole will work in most areas of the United Kingdom, with the water from them being 99 per cent likely to be potable or capable of being made so. It is, however, necessary to satisfy the Environmental Health Department of your local authority that the water you will be drinking is safe. In the *Yellow Pages* the companies that test and analyse water are listed under 'Water Treatment'. The same companies usually supply and install treatment systems using either chemical or mechanical filtration, or ultraviolet treatment designed to screen out or remove most pollutants. They will also provide the householder with a home test kit to make sure that the water remains safe.

Drains and sewers

If mains foul drains are available then the authorities will usually require that you connect to them, even if there are cheaper options. Connection might mean having to cross land in the ownership of others, in which case a legal right will have to be established, for which you might have to pay. Such payments often fall to the purchaser simply because the need is not established until after the sale has completed. Check all sewage routes. Check not only on the legal front but also the physical characteristics. Most situations can be resolved. If the levels are not right, it might be necessary to utilise a pump. There is a cost involved but there may also be a saving. A gravity drain has to be laid to precise falls, the drains must be surrounded in pea shingle and if it changes direction there is a requirement for manholes. The 50-mm flexible pipe from a pump can be laid in a simple, narrow trench at imprecise levels without having to go in straight lines.

Just because a plot doesn't have access to mains sewers does not mean that it should be discounted. Most sites are capable of being developed using alternative on-site systems and these are discussed in greater detail in Chapter 6, Building.

Sterile zones

One of the reasons a site hasn't been built on before may be because there are services running over or above the land. The Easement that the relevant Statutory Undertaker has taken out over the land may prohibit any building over or under the service or within a certain distance of it. This is known as a sterile zone. Sometimes, particularly with high-pressure gas, sewage or water mains, there is simply no way around the problem and if the site is not capable of being developed without interfering with the sterile zone, it is perhaps best to move on. If you feel that the service is capable of being moved you will need the utmost patience to deal with the monolithic company that really doesn't share your enthusiasm for tampering with something that is quite all right as it is. If you can get a quotation then, whatever the cost, it is an admission that the service is capable of being moved. If the price paid for the plot reflects this cost then what you have is a viable plot.

Having received a quotation for the service provider to move the pipes or cables you can sometimes negotiate the price down by offering to do some of the work, such as the excavation, yourself. If a private sewer crosses your land, this may not be the problem that it first appears. In fact, it could be of benefit. It costs money to open up a road and connect to drains. If the sewers are already on your land then you can usually connect up to them and even if that means that you have to divert them around your house, this is likely to prove considerably cheaper than having to connect in the Highway.

If you build near power lines or electricity supply lines and your works, including the scaffolding, come within 3 metres then you will have to arrange for an electricity board to sleeve them and, in certain cases, erect safety nets or screens. In most domestic cases there is no charge for this.

Legal considerations

Incomplete or defective titles

Whenever land is sold, it has to be registered with HM Land Registry. This first became compulsory in parts of London in 1899 but did not extend to the whole country until December 1990. By its very nature, vacant land will often, therefore, fall into the category of unregistered land. The most common problem that can occur is where the deeds have been lost and, while it can be quite obvious just who owns what, the proof is not there. On the face of it this might seem an impossible situation. However, one of the principles behind much property law is that land should always serve a useful function, and that is only served if there are mechanisms in place to establish ownership or lawful possession. The solution to this particular problem, and to related problems, is to obtain Statutory Declarations from the would-be vendors and other associated parties and neighbours. With these it is then possible to obtain a Defective Title indemnity policy, which is effectively a single-premium insurance policy, that usually costs no more than £200.

Unknown owners and Adverse Possession

Sometimes you will come across a dream site, but nobody knows who owns the land. Now, you could try the Land Registry but not all land is registered; the details and title deeds may be lying, gathering dust, in some solicitor's basement. Sometimes the landowner may live close by but just doesn't want anyone to know that they own the land or perhaps they went abroad or were killed in war. Occasionally, an elderly person may simply have forgotten about their ownership of the land. What can you do about it? Well, very little except ask around, take out adverts and possibly put a notice on the site, all of which may alert all the other prospective self-builders in the area to the existence of the plot; meaning that, when an owner does surface, you could find yourself in a long queue.

But there is one other way of gaining title to land. And this is often referred to and is best known as Squatter's Rights. It dates back to the very earliest of times when all land was vested in the Crown and the kings and queens saw land as always having to serve a useful purpose, the primary purpose being to benefit them. The thought of land just lying vacant and unused was therefore a complete anathema. In England and Wales, where land is occupied 'without let or hindrance' for a period of at least 12 years, the occupier can register what is known as a Possessory Title and, with the passage of a further 12 years, an Absolute Title. If anyone comes along within the first 12 years and either allows you to continue your occupation upon payment of rent (a let) or tells you to get off their land (a hindrance), then the clock stops and the Adverse Possession has failed. If someone comes along during the period of the Possessory Title then the matter may well have to go to court. Providing the squatter has done things properly, they, or their successors in title, may well be granted the absolute title. But there may also be some element of recompense for the original owner.

All land has to be registered with the Land Registry whenever it is sold or mortgaged or if a lease of more than seven years is granted. However, there is no requirement for land to be registered unless one of these transactions takes place, and it is this unregistered land, with untraceable owners, that is most likely to be the subject of a claim for Squatter's Rights. An Adverse Possession is most unlikely to succeed if the land is registered and the registration has been kept up to date, with the owner's current address listed. Under the Land Registration Act 2002, anyone contemplating an Adverse Possession must give the Registry two years' clear notice of their intention to register a Possessory or Interim Title. The Registry will then make their own efforts to contact or establish an owner and give them due warning.

The most common occurrence of a Possessory Title being offered is where a vendor has moved the fence over to take in some overgrown or unused land at the side. The main plot will then be offered with an absolute title and the acquired bit with a Possessory Title. If you are offered land with a Possessory or Incomplete Title you should make certain that there is a single premium indemnity policy in place to cover the eventuality of an absent owner turning up to dispute your occupation. The premium for this policy is, by the way, usually the responsibility of the vendor.

Boundary disputes fall into a similar category. Your solicitor will be able to tell you any dimensions of the land from the deed plans but it is really up to you to make sure that these dimensions are available on the ground. If you do notice signs of encroachment or opportunistic and acquisitive behaviour from neighbours, you do need to seize the initiative. Get some stakes and wire, and clearly mark your boundaries, sending a letter by recorded delivery to the neighbour stating that you have established your boundaries and fenced your property accordingly. 'Possession being nine tenths of the law', it is then your neighbour who has the uphill struggle to establish his claim, unless, of course, he has already done so by means of an Adverse Possession. In which case, you will need to renegotiate your contract with the vendor.

Footpaths and rights of way

It is possible to have a footpath or public right of way moved. However, the realignment must be to the benefit of those using the footpath rather than just for the convenience of your property. Footpaths are not only protected by law but also jealously guarded by local authorities and various other bodies such as the Ramblers' Association.

If there is a footpath crossing your land then it is safe to assume that, in most cases, its existence and route must remain unaltered and, unless you have a lot of time and resources, you should plan any development accordingly.

Compulsory purchase

The most usual occurrence that affects a plot is where land is taken for road widening or the creation of a footpath. In most cases this transaction is noted on the deeds and registered with the Land Registry, but there are times when this doesn't happen. It is possible for the land to be taken and for the Highways authority not to realise or remember that it has actually taken up their acquisition. If you do become aware of such a compulsory purchase, take careful measurements from fixed points such as other buildings, to establish the extent of the loss. Do not fall into the trap of measuring from the road edge as this can only serve to exacerbate any discrepancy. If it is obvious that the land has not been taken, it is open for you to try to negotiate to buy it back. Sometimes road-widening schemes are abandoned. Sometimes changes in planning policy and the planner's recognition of the variant nature of building lines in villages render a previous acquisition obsolete.

Whatever you do, do not assume that by keeping quiet, you can re-establish ownership of the land. Highways land cannot be the subject of an Adverse Possession.

Agricultural ties and Section 106 Agreements

If a consent is granted in the countryside where there would normally be a presumption against the granting of planning permission, it is quite likely that it is what is known as an 'agricultural consent'. In all likelihood this is established by means of a condition within the consent that a person shall only occupy the property if they are wholly or mainly engaged in agriculture, last engaged in agriculture or the widow or widower thereof. It means what it says. Only a person fulfilling those criteria can legally live in the property. The encumbrance has the effect of devaluing the property and of limiting or precluding the involvement of many of the lending institutions.

Agricultural ties are often reinforced by a Section 106 Agreement, a legal agreement that is part of the Town & Country Planning Act 1990, which is entered into by the local authority and the owners, and binds their successors in title. These agreements can also be used to enshrine various other commitments and to ensure that planning requirements are upheld in perpetuity. It is possible to have an agricultural tie or Section 106 Agreement overturned. Application has to be made for its removal. It is necessary to prove that the need for the tie has lapsed. It might also be a requirement that one proves that the property is not capable of being sold in its encumbered form.

If persons who do not qualify occupy an agriculturally encumbered property it is possible to ask for and get a Certificate of Lawful Use, which effectively overturns the requirement. This is mandatory so long as there has been no overt attempt at concealment and the occupation has gone unchallenged by the authorities. The qualifying period for unchallenged occupation prior to the issuing of a Certificate of Lawful Use was ten years, until a ruling by the House of Lords in August 2006 indicated that the qualifying period should only be four years.

Covenants and Easements

Covenants are clauses in an earlier contract for the sale or purchase of land that are binding on all future owners. They normally require that something shall not be done on the land or that the land either remains undeveloped or is developed in a particular way. Restrictive covenants can fall into disuse. They may well have originally been imposed to protect the view of or from a large property, which has subsequently been demolished. Although the original beneficiary property has gone, the covenant remains. In such circumstances it is possible to get the covenant removed by the Lands Tribunal, but this is a very expensive and time-consuming exercise, and the best way of covering for this situation is, once again, to employ a single-premium indemnity policy.

The most usual covenant that can affect land is one that requires the developer of land to seek the approval of the vendors for their proposals. Even if they not used, the words 'such consent not be unreasonably withheld' are implied. It is therefore possible to argue, in certain situations, that the granting of planning consent, where all of the needs and interests of adjoining owners and properties are taken into account, means that to oppose the proposals would be unreasonable.

Easements are similar to covenants, although they tend to grant specific rights of passage or use over land rather than modify how land is used. Statutory undertakers take out Easements or Wayleaves to enable them to cross land with electricity cables, gas pipelines and sewers. In many cases these Easements include a sterile zone on either side of the line of the service, where no building can take place. It is sometimes possible to have these services diverted. It is nearly always prohibitively expensive so to do, although if you can arrange to do all or part of the work yourselves, you might be able to mitigate the costs. As with covenants, there is a right of application to the Lands Tribunal, but once again this is a time-consuming and expensive process. In many cases Easements run to the benefit of the land, granting rights of access or the right to connect to drains or services and their existence can be mutually beneficial.

Wildlife

The existence of native fauna or flora on a site can have severe implications for the use and enjoyment of land. It is, for example, illegal to disturb a badger's set or to dig up certain rare plants or do anything that would endanger them. Newts, birds and bats are also recipients of considerable protection. Government and local authorities have an imperative to identify and maintain Sites of Special Scientific Interest (SSSIs or Triple-SIs).

Pouring foundation concrete.

In addition there are international conventions, such as the Convention on Wetlands (or Ramsar Convention), which effectively prohibit development and severely curtail activities on adjoining land.

Where endangered or protected wildlife is identified on a site it might be necessary to provide a survey, which will require specialists to maintain a watch on activities and may subsequently require long-term remedial measures. These can involve fencing in the site for a season to prevent newcomers and then removal of the 'captive' fauna to a suitable and agreed alternative site.

Neighbours

Proximity to boundaries

Most people will want to have a pathway down at least one side of the house although this is not always possible. Strangely enough there are no hard and fast planning rules on building close to boundaries. While some local authorities may have minimum requirements, most will consider each application on its own merits with the deciding factors being the appearance of the building and its impact on neighbours.

The Building Regulations are equally vague. Quite obviously there has to be access for drains and services, but if these can be accommodated at the front or if they can safely run under the oversite, then this is perfectly acceptable. Some authorities will not allow buildings to have guttering or downpipes overhanging a neighbour's land but as walls must be built centrally on a footing, this effectively means that the closest one can actually build a detached house to a boundary is 150 mm. Suitable space for refuse bins must also be demonstrated.

Fire regulations within the Building Regulations also come into play. These preclude an opening of glass or timber of greater than 1 sq. metre adjoining the boundary and limit openings 1 metre away to 5.6 sq. metres.

The Access to Neighbouring Land Act 1992 gives access, upon due serving of notice, for the purposes of maintenance only. It does not confer any right to enter upon land to build and those building close to a boundary may have to consider building overhand from scaffolding that is set up inside the building.

The Party Wall etc. Act 1996 seeks to provide a framework for the prevention and resolution of disputes in relation to party walls, boundary walls and excavations that are close to neighbouring buildings. It requires that, whenever such work is proposed, those intending to carry out the work must give the adjoining owners notice in writing. There is no penalty within the Act for non-compliance, but it recognises that if the proper notices and procedures are not followed, then legal redress or an injunction might be sought in the courts. The implication is that non-compliance would count against any offending party.

Work on existing party walls The Act lists works that may be done to existing party walls, even though they go beyond ordinary common-law rights. These include:

- Cutting into a wall to take a bearing beam or inserting a damp-proof course all the way through a party wall.

- Raising a party wall, while, if necessary, cutting off any projections that might prevent you from doing so.
- Demolishing and rebuilding a party wall.
- Underpinning a party wall.
- Protecting two adjoining walls by putting a flashing from the higher to the lower.

At least two months' notice in writing must be given of any intention to carry out these works and the recipient of the notice has 14 days to respond or issue a counter notice, after which a dispute is said to have arisen.

New building on the boundary line The Act does not confer any right to build any new walls or structures that bestride or intrude upon a neighbour's land, without their prior consent. However, and this is important, where a new wall or structure is to be built up to a boundary, the Act does confer the right for the footings for that wall or structure to intrude under the neighbouring land, subject to the payment of any compensation for damage caused during the construction. One month's notice in writing is required and once again, if the adjoining owner responds or issues a counter notice within 14 days, a dispute is said to have arisen.

Excavations close to neighbouring buildings You must inform an adjoining owner in writing, at least two months before the work commences if:

- You plan to excavate or construct foundations for a new building or structure within 3 metres of a neighbouring building or structure, where the excavations will go deeper than the foundations of those structures, or
- You plan to excavate or construct foundations for a new building or structure within 6 metres of a neighbouring building or structure, where that work would cut a line drawn downwards at 45 degrees from the bottom of the neighbour's foundations.

If a dispute arises over this, or any of the other works listed above, then an independent surveyor is appointed, with their fees paid for by the person wishing to carry out the work. The surveyor will make an Award, setting out what work can be carried out. They will also dictate how and when the work is to be done and they will record the conditions prior to the commencement of work, so that any damages can be properly attributed and made good. Either side has 14 days to appeal to the county court but this should only be done if an owner believes that the surveyors have acted beyond their powers.

Most importantly, where work is being carried out that is expressly authorised by the Act, and where the proper procedures have been followed, the Act gives the right of entry in order to carry out those works, provided that 14 days' notice of the intention to enter is given. It is an offence for an adjoining owner to refuse entry to someone who is entitled to enter premises under the Act, if the offender knows that the Act entitles the person to be there. If the adjoining premises are vacant then a police officer must accompany the workmen, surveyor or architect, as they enter.

Checklist: Site details	
PLANNING	
Outline planning permission (PP)?	Yes/No
Detailed/Full planning permission?	Yes/No
Expiry date of PP?	
Was PP gained at Appeal?	Yes/No
If so, was this because of local opposition or local-authority planning-department opposition? Has this died down?	Yes/No
If the land has no planning, what are the realistic chances of PP?	%
Is this the view of the Planning Officer?	Yes/No
Have you studied the local authority's Local Development Plan or Framework?	Yes/No
Is what you are proposing in accordance with this/these policies?	Yes/No
In particular is the land within an area where the planners will accept development?	Yes/No
Planning conditions (other than standard)?	Yes/No
Are they satisfied?	Yes/No
If no, what needs to be done?	
Are Permitted Development Rights (PDR) restricted or removed?	Yes/No
Any planning on neighbouring land?	Yes/No
Any planning blight?	Yes/No
If yes, what? Planning authority	
Name of officer	
Conservation Area/AONB/National Park/Listed Buildings/SSSI or higher?	Yes/No
Archaeological interest?	Yes/No
Archaeological survey required?	Yes/No
Special foundations to facilitate future surveys required?	Yes/No
Watching brief if necessary?	Yes/No
ACCESS	
Public Highway/Private access	
Is there a right of access?	Yes/No

If not, what arrangements have to be made?	
Any sign of a ransom strip?	Yes/No
Does the driveway need making up?	Yes/No
Is it suitable for construction traffic?	Yes/No
If not, is there an alternative/temporary site access?	Yes/No
Visibility splays required?	Yes/No
Obtainable within site curtilage?	Yes/No
If not, are the necessary Easements in place?	Yes/No
Levels right for gates/bellmouth?	Yes/No
Crossover made?	Yes/No
Pavement?	Yes/No
Grass verge?	Yes/No
Is this part of the Highway?	Yes/No
Parking space requirements	
Turning circles/need to enter and leave in forward gear?	Yes/No
Highways Agency local office	
Name of officer	
TREES	
Are there any significant trees on site?	Yes/No
Are there any on adjoining land?	Yes/No
Location plotted?	Yes/No
Species and sizes?	Yes/No
Any tree preservation orders in force?	Yes/No
If so, on which trees?	
Any sign of trees having been removed lately?	Yes/No
GROUND CONDITIONS/SUBSOIL	
What is the natural vegetation?	
Any signs of sedge or rush?	Yes/No

Ground water or signs of high water-table?	Yes/No
Has there been any flooding?	Yes/No
If so, what level did the water reach and is it possible to build above that level or take other precautions?	
Is the plot shown on any floodplain maps?	Yes/No
In the flowerbeds or disturbed ground, is there an indication of subsoil?	Yes/No
If yes, what do you see?	
Any trial pits dug?	Yes/No
Findings?	
Rock?	Yes/No
Streams/watercourses?	Yes/No
Radon gas precautions necessary?	Yes/No
Heavy clay?	Yes/No
With trees?	Yes/No
Any sign of local buildings employing special foundations?	Yes/No
If so, what type?	
Locals consulted?	Yes/No
Findings/rumours?	
Evidence of filled ground?	Yes/No
Any contamination?	Yes/No
Any existing foundations?	Yes/No
Local Building Control Department	
Name of the Building Inspector	
Any comments by the inspector?	
PHYSICAL CHARACTERISTICS/SITE DETAILS/SERVICES	
Level site/slight slope/severe slope	Yes/No
Levels survey available?	Yes/No

Datum point?	Yes/No

Key dimensions
    Width at building line (front)
    Width at building line (back)
    Triangulation measurements	

Ownership of boundaries
    North
    South
    East
    West
	
	Yes/No
	Yes/No
	Yes/No
	Yes/No

Sun/shade noted?	Yes/No
Exposure – none/moderate/severe	
Overhead cables/power lines	Yes/No
If significant, are they movable?	Yes/No
Drains on site?	Yes/No

Foul drains?
    Available?
    Location plotted?
        Invert
        Cover
	Yes/No
	Yes/No
	Yes/No
	Yes/No
	Yes/No

Surface water drains?
    Location plotted?
        Invert
        Cover
	Yes/No
	Yes/No
	Yes/No
	Yes/No

Public/private	
Legal right to connect?	Yes/No
Easements in place if necessary?	Yes/No

If no mains drains available, what system is acceptable/workable?
    Cesspit
    Septic tank
    Sewage treatment plant
    Other
	
	Yes/No
	Yes/No
	Yes/No

Environment Agency consulted and approvals given?	Yes/No
Is there space on site for these works or do you need to negotiate for it?	Yes/No

If no surface-water drains available, what system is acceptable/workable?
    Standard soakaway
    Sophisticated soakaway
    Aquifer
    Stream or ditch
	
	Yes/No
	Yes/No
	Yes/No
	Yes/No

Any sterile zones?	Yes/No
If yes, are they plotted?	Yes/No

Electricity available?
    Overhead/underground
    Connection charge
	Yes/No
	
	£

Gas available? Connection charge	Yes/No £
If not available, will you want to install an LPG (liquid petroleum gas) tank system?	Yes/No
If so, is there space for the LPG tank or can it go underground?	Yes/No
Or will you want oil?	Yes/No
If so, is there space for the oil tank?	Yes/No
Telephone available? Connection charge	Yes/No £
Mains water available? Connection charge	Yes/No £
If not, is a borehole possible?	Yes/No
Estimated costs	£
Comments	

LEGAL	
Rights of way established to plot's benefit?	Yes/No
Rights of way to benefit of others?	Yes/No
Covenants and Easements to plot's benefit?	Yes/No
Covenants and Easements to others' benefit?	Yes/No
Footpaths	Yes/No
Any sign of Adverse Possession?	Yes/No
If so, how long has it been established?	
Does any loss of land through Adverse Possession question the viability of the plot?	Yes/No
Land being sold with full title?	Yes/No
All or any part of the land being sold subject to a defective/incomplete/ Possessory Title?	Yes/No
Any protected wildlife, fauna or flora on site?	Yes/No

NEIGHBOURS	
Did the neighbours object to the granting of planning?	Yes/No
Is there a legacy of hostility or has it calmed down?	Yes/No
Will neighbours be able to obstruct site works?	Yes/No
Is there anything you can do to resolve the situation?	

ADJOINING SITES/SURROUNDING LAND	
What type of buildings make up the street scene?	
Are there any new dwellings in the area that give an indication of the planners' likes and dislikes? If so, describe.	
Is there a building line?	Yes/No
General characteristics of local architecture/design – mixed/uniform	
General architectural features on nearby buildings: 　Sizes 　Complex/simple shapes 　Brick/render/stone/black and white/tile hung/timbered/other 　Features, e.g. mullions/quoins/corbels/keystones/sills/heads 　Roof pitches 　Roof coverings, e.g. plain tile/profiled tile/slates/thatch/stone 　　　slate/other 　Roof treatment, e.g. gabled/hipped/barn-ended/tabled verges/ 　　　clipped verges 　Barge boarded verge/dry verges 　Soffit overhangs/soffits/exposed rafter feet/exposed purlins 　Window types, e.g. softwood painted or stained/hardwood/uPVC/metal 　Glazing, e.g. clear/all bar/leaded square or diamond	
Any sign of structural damage to adjoining buildings?	Yes/No
Any pollution/noise/smell/light from neighbouring properties?	Yes/No
VALUES	
What are the general property values within the area? 　Semi-detached houses 　Bungalows, 3 bedrooms 　Bungalows, 4 bedrooms 　Detached houses, medium, 4 bedrooms 　Larger detached houses/bungalows	£ £ £ £ £
What sort of property directly adjoins the plot? 　Houses/bungalows 　Detached/semi-detached 　Mixed	
What is the most appropriate type of dwelling for this plot?	
What is the carrying capacity(£)/ceiling value	£
Are there things in the offing that could affect local values (e.g. new roads, motorways, industry moving in or out/major infrastructure works)	

METHOD OF BUILDING/PRELIMINARY BUDGET	
Timber frame/brick and block/other	
Builder/subcontractors/shell building plus subcontractors/own labour £s per sq. metre/ft assumed £	

Preliminary Building Budge
    Site costs
    Fees
    Finance costs
    Other costs
    Total costs (A)
	£
	£
	£
	£
	£
	£

Value of finished house (B)	£
Equity gain (B minus A)	£

Buying the land

Purchasing land or property is not like buying any other goods or services, in that the purchase has to be evidenced in writing. Long traditions and practices have served to make this process a fairly complicated and obscure one that, to most people's minds, can only really be properly carried out and overseen by solicitors, assisted by their fellow professionals, the estate agents.

When you buy land or property, you are buying a long, legal history set down in documents or plans that form the deeds. The language in which these are written is sometimes quite archaic. There can be many clauses or covenants, some of which might seem obscure, some of which might seem benign, but some of which might well have a serious effect on your enjoyment or use of the land. It is the job of estate agents to identify this history and reflect its impact on the price. It is the job of solicitors to translate the almost impervious language contained in fusty old deeds and to explain to the purchaser the import of what they find. Are the professionals always up to the job? In many cases the answer is obviously 'Yes'. But in a few cases there is either a failure to spot the potential problem or an inability to understand the full implications.

Finding land is not easy. Finding a plot of land that does not have any problems or encumbrances is even harder. If you are not to lose a piece of land over a problem that is capable of being solved then you have to be aware of the potential pitfalls, the terminology and the solutions. If that means that you have, in certain instances, to augment or assist your solicitor in their work, then so be it – if it gets you the land, that's all that really matters!

In the United Kingdom, the process of buying land varies according to where you live. The law in England & Wales and Northern Ireland share one system, while the one in Scotland is substantially different.

England, Wales and Northern Ireland

By private treaty
The process of buying property or land by private treaty in England, Wales and Northern Ireland follows this sequence.

- You see a property or parcel of land that is usually advertised as being for sale through estate agents or others.
- If you are minded to do so, you make an offer, 'subject to contract'.
- If the vendors are agreeable to the offer, usually put forward through their agents, you will receive notice that they are willing to treat.
- Solicitors are then instructed and the purchasers' solicitors prepare a draft contract and a list of preliminary enquiries that they send through to the vendors' solicitors.
- The purchasers, if necessary or if they so desire, but there is no compunction, arrange for a survey.
- The purchasers make application for a mortgage, if required, and pay for the building society's or bank's mortgage survey and valuation, of which they are entitled to have sight.
- The solicitors exchange letters and enquiries, and the purchasers' solicitors arrange for and receive the local Searches.
- When all is in place and everybody is satisfied, the purchasers' solicitors will usually prepare a report on title and arrange to see the purchasers to discuss their findings.
- If, as a result of all these enquiries, it is decided to proceed, then each party's solicitor will arrange for their clients to sign copies of identical contracts and will then hold them until such time as their respective clients give them the go-ahead to proceed to exchange.
- Exchange of contracts, the first time that either party is bound to the sale or purchase, is effected by a simple telephone conversation or communication between the solicitors noting the time and date of the exchange. A deposit, usually 10 per cent of the purchase price, is paid by transfer at this point. Following this, each solicitor receives the copy of the contract that has been signed by the other party. This contract will detail the Completion date, usually 21 or 28 days thereafter.
- The conveyance, or addition to the title deeds noting the sale and purchase, is prepared by the vendors' solicitors and signed by the vendors.
- Upon the Completion date, the final monies are paid over in return for the keys and the purchasers take up occupation.

By auction or tender

In times when land or property prices are uncertain or rising many estate agents choose to make the sale by either auction or tender.

An auction room is a daunting place for a private individual. Professionals have long since learnt to stylise their procedures and deliveries in order to make it a hostile environment for those not in the know. If you are going to bid seriously make yourself known to the auctioneer beforehand. Sit somewhere in the room where you can be seen and, more importantly, where you can see all of the other potential bidders. Some of the professionals have ways of indicating their bid, such as the slight raising of an eyebrow, which the auctioneer recognises, and it might be necessary to study the direction in which he/she looks to pick up your opponent.

Be careful about 'spoof' bids given at the beginning of the offer, often made by the auctioneer staff or parties allied to the vendors in order to get the bids going and get them up to or past the reserve price. Don't join in down with increasingly small increments. Be careful not to get carried away, but, equally, if the bidding is nearing the limit of those in the room, don't lose the plot for a few hundred pounds.

In an auction the highest bidder when the gavel falls is the successful buyer, and you exchange contracts there and then. Therefore all legal work and Searches have to be done beforehand, and all finance must be in place. A number of properties fail to reach their reserve at auction and therefore, even if you aren't in a position to bid, it is worth attending. That way you can deduce the reserve price and might well be able to make an offer by private treaty shortly afterwards.

Tenders are similar except that sealed bids are sent in to the agents and, unlike at a public auction, you don't know the other bids or bidders. As if that weren't enough, there is usually no obligation on the part of the vendors to accept the highest bid and there is often a great deal of horse-trading afterwards. Be aware of this and be prepared to join in this process immediately after the tender date.

In England & Wales it became a legal requirement in June 2007 for those selling property to provide the buyers with a Home Information Pack (HIP), which must include an Energy Performance Certificate (EPC) containing advice on how to cut carbon emissions and fuel bills. It must also contain a sale statement and the Searches and evidence of title. There is at present no requirement for this pack to contain a structural survey. Apart from the sale statement and Searches, which the buyer's solicitor will in any case check out afresh, HIPs have little or no relevance to the purchase of vacant land or plots.

Scotland

The language as well as the use and meaning of legal terminology used in the purchase of land or property in Scotland is different from that employed in England, Wales and Northern Ireland. Details might refer to the Feu and go on to state that the sale will be by way of Feu Disposition, with reference to a Feudal Superior.

In England, all land was originally held by the Crown before being disposed of piecemeal in various forms of tenure that have all basically boiled down to Freehold. In Scotland, where huge areas are still held by the Crown, land was similarly parcelled and then re-parcelled out on the basis of patronage, and the Feu was the tenure or form of payment that allowed continued occupation. Over time these payments in kind have largely fallen away, and the Feu has come to mean the larger holding from which sales of land by division or subdivision are made. Feu disposition, from the word 'dispose', in essence therefore means the sale or alienation of land.

Real Burdens are quite simply the same as covenants in England and Wales and Northern Ireland, and the Feudal Superiors, often the original owners of the land, are the ones benefiting from those covenants, which can take all of the usual forms plus another that is not often come across in the rest of the UK, namely, the Right of Pre-emption. This gives the seller the right to buy back the property if you ever decide to sell, usually limited to allowing them to exercise their right to buy at the level of the highest offer within 21 days or at valuation. Servitude is merely the Scottish word for an Easement or Wayleave.

The process of buying land or property in Scotland follows this sequence:

- You see a property or plot of land advertised for sale, often by solicitors who, in the main, but not always, take the place of and combine the roles of the estate agents and solicitors south of the border.
- If you like it, you then have to decide on the price you would be prepared to pay, obviously taking your lead from the details and other discussions you might have.
- You then ask your solicitor to note an interest in the property, following which the sellers' solicitors or agents should not sell to another party without telling you first.
- You get a survey and valuation.
- You approach your finance source, remembering that your solicitors will not proceed further until they are satisfied that you have the purchase monies sorted out and available.
- Your solicitor then makes a written offer with an expiry date and a long list of other conditions and enquiries to which the purchase is subject. These are known as the Missives, and basically they are the same as the conditions and preliminary enquiries that go to and fro between solicitors in England, Wales and Northern Ireland. The offer will include an Entry or Completion date, which may be changed as the legal process progresses. If there are other interested parties then a closing date will be set, by when all interested parties must make their final offer. The best of these will be accepted, and the process will move forward with that party alone.
- Once a written offer is accepted, it is binding on both parties, unless something goes wrong on the Missives negotiations. A qualified acceptance may be issued, accepting some of the conditions in the offer but rejecting or qualifying others.
- At some point during this process your solicitors will obtain the Property Enquiry Certificates, which are really the same as Searches south of the border. These are often, however, provided by the seller's solicitors. The Date of Entry or Completion will be noted in the Missives.
- Following the Conclusion of the Missives, the purchasers' solicitors will receive a Draft Disposition.
- When all is agreed between the parties, the disposition is signed.
- With the monies paid over on the Date of Entry or Completion, the purchaser takes up occupation.

Advocates of the Scottish system point to the fact that once a sale is agreed there is a binding contract on both parties, one to sell and the other to buy. They point out that in England, Wales and Northern Ireland there is no legal obligation until exchange of contracts, and this allows either party to drop out at the last minute or engage in the practices of gazumping (raising the price at the last moment) or guzundering (offering a lower price at the last minute). In practice, the Scottish system also has its flaws, starting with the practice of having an Upset or guideline price, which basically turns the sale into a form of tender. Even when an offer is accepted the practice of hedging that offer or acceptance with conditions means that, in many cases, the obligation can be broken by either side.

chapter four

Getting the Design Right

B efore you commission your architect or designer and maybe even before you start to draw up your own sketches of what you want, there are some important questions that you need to ask yourself about the design of your new home, bearing in mind your lifestyle and life plan or intentions.

Design: step one

What are you hoping to achieve?

Examine your motivation for self-building. Is this the culmination of a long-standing desire to create something permanent of which you can be proud, which will be there long after you are gone, or merely a step on the ladder to your eventual dream home? Are you doing this in order to have a home that fits your own and your family's lifestyle and individual needs, or are you more interested in the possible gains in equity that are there to be made? Is it all about more accommodation, particularly more bedrooms, or is it more about quality? Is kerb appeal and instant attraction more important than having a home that grows on you or opens up in unexpected ways when you walk through it?

Have you properly considered the budget?

The budget is the most important piece of the design jigsaw. Have you worked out your finances and deduced just how much you can afford to spend? Are you aware that differing methods of building and the level of your own involvement with the build process will impact on the costs and therefore the proposed size of your new home? Are you going to go right up to or even slightly beyond the limit of your finances and trust to inflation sorting out any shortfall or are you going to play it safe? Have you considered whether a contingency sum would be appropriate? Have you put budget at the top of the requirements list that you will eventually be presenting to your architects/designers?

Are limited finances affecting what you're hoping to achieve?

If the plot is more expensive that you had hoped for and that has seriously eroded your ability to build just what you had wanted to build, could you look at things another way? Is it possible that you could think in terms of a design that could be built in stages or evolve as finances permitted in the future? Would it be possible to scale down your requirements? Could you cheapen the specification in some ways in order to gain more space on the understanding that at some time in the future you might strip out certain things and replace them with better ones? Could you think in terms of managing subcontractors for all or some of the trades rather than paying the higher price for a builder? Could you undertake one or more of the trades yourself?

How long are you likely to live there?

A home might not be for life, but it should be capable of evolving and adapting to changing needs. If you are going to be in the same house while you raise your children, will you need to think ahead for their accommodation requirements and the maintenance of your own sanity? What about visitors? Do you have family or friends who will often want to visit and, if so, do you have to design around the ability to put them up with relative comfort? If you opt for all of this extra accommodation, what use will it have when the family has left home? If you are planning to live in the home through to old age, should you make adjustments to the design to accommodate ground-floor living/sleeping or the possibility of physical disability in later life? Could part of the building provide either a granny annex or accommodation for a carer?

Are running costs important?

Have you examined your motives? Are you aware of the need to save money in both the short and longer terms? Are you conscious of the fact that in later life your finances might be limited and high fuel costs might make staying in your home untenable? Are your motives purely personal or are you trying to save the earth? Are you cognisant of the fact that many of the energy-saving devices and technologies have high capital costs that you might never recover by strict reference to your subsequent outlays? Have you considered which relatively cheap ideas such as extra insulation could lower your running costs and pay for themselves within a reasonable time-scale?

Ground floor beams ready to receive the infill blocks.

Design: step two

With those questions answered you can get more involved in thinking about the actual design and the way the dictates of the site are going to influence it.

Externally, what do you want it to look like?

It is a sad fact that external appearance is to a large extent governed by the planners and the general consensus that new homes should fit in with the local vernacular. Do you want to try to push the boat out in design terms? Are you ready for the extra work and cost that that could entail; are you also ready for the possibility that any departure from the norm might affect your chances of re-sale? Most self-builders stick to convention when it comes to design and almost all copy the houses of the developers that they purport to despise. Are you ready to buck that trend? Will your site lend itself to innovations and design ideas, or is this the wrong place or period of your life to buck the trend or conduct experiments of that sort?

'Kerb appeal' is what gives a property its value. Whatever the accommodation, if the property is not attractive from the road, few people will bother to stop and come in when you want to sell. Slim properties that are gable end on to the road are not always attractive although this way of doing things does help visually to distance the property from its immediate neighbours. Cheer them up by introducing a gable projection or by hipping the front plane of the roof to draw the eye backwards. If there is a garage door, try to face this across the plot rather then allowing it to become the dominant architectural feature. If this is not possible consider recessing the garage door to drag it back from the focal point. Another way is to detach the garage and incorporate it with walls and attractive gates to create an enclosed courtyard or mews effect.

All too often homes built on sloping sites fall into the trap of providing purely functional accommodation and pay little heed to the need to maintain a good visual impact. Sites that slope up from the road may well use the expedient of having the garage, entrance and utility accommodation on the lower floor. This can be boring especially if the remaining storeys then tower above with little or no break in regimented windows and walling. Try to break up the hard edges. Set garage doors back or beneath overhanging balconies to reduce their visual impact. Introduce doors as well as windows to upper floors and break up the front elevation by stepping parts back and introducing forward gable projections. Consider bolt-on balconies and consider also whether the ground has to be level at the front and whether stairs up one side to an entrance on the middle level might not look better.

Sites that slope away from the road suffer from being unable to advertise the full extent of their accommodation. If a five-bedroom house looks like a small bungalow from the road, potential buyers might be put off coming in; even if you do get them in, they might opt for a property with more obvious kerb appeal. There is little you can do apart from positioning the home so that even the casual observer can see from the front that it extends downwards. Alternatively, hint at additional accommodation by introducing roof lights, even if all they are illuminating is the unused loft space.

Sites with a slope from side to side are probably the easiest with which to gain kerb appeal, and there is often scope to create mezzanine levels that are visible from the road. But even here care has to be taken with the garage if it is not to dominate the frontage.

How much of the site can you cover?

Planning law and the Building Regulations are largely silent about this, although many local authorities have, within their Development Plans or Framework Policy documents, rules about just how much amenity space must be allowed for, with stipulations on distances between windows of different houses. Once more each application should be argued on its own merits.

Are building lines important?

These words of planning jargon have fixed themselves into the mindsets of much of the population, which is a pity because, to a large extent, there is no such thing. For a brief period in the 1960s and 1970s they were adhered to, but planners soon began to realise that in many cases they were an invention of the recent past and began to drop them.

Nevertheless, if you are building in a street of relatively modern houses or on an estate where to depart from established building lines would be a nonsense, they do become important. Each application will be assessed on its own merits. If it is appropriate for the property to come forward or go back beyond the established building lines, and it can be done without detrimentally affecting the neighbouring properties or interfering with the necessary visibility of adjoining driveways, then it may well be acceptable.

Overlooking and overshadowing

Within planning law there is an acceptable degree of overlooking and over-shadowing. The question comes with the interpretation of this phrase and, once again, each case will be considered on its own merits. Some authorities have a rule, at least to the rear of a property, whereby no building shall go back far enough so as to cross a line drawn at 45 degrees out from the edge of next door's windows. Others have no such rule and judge each application separately. Balconies can be a 'red rag to a bull' as far as both neighbours and planners are concerned, and it is better to avoid them if there is any question of overlooking.

Internally, could you go for freedom of expression?

The internal arrangements of most homes are remarkably predictable with a recognised progression of associated rooms. Do you feel the need to stick to conventional design formats? Does each area of your new home have to justify its existence by reference to a particular function or could you contemplate the idea of architectural space for its own sake? Could you envisage a layout or mixture of rooms that defied the accepted wisdom, yet fitted in with your own lifestyle, or would that seriously affect any re-sale values? Do you care? Do you want a strict division of living and sleeping arrangements? Do you want to create areas of your new home that are private from or even capable of being divided from other areas?

Sloping sites

In some areas, where the ground is predominantly flat, even a slight slope can bring on the jitters and cause builders to suck their teeth and mutter about extra costs. In other areas it's par for the course, and everyone accepts that most plots have a slope of some sort.

For the lay person looking at a site with a steep slope on it can be a daunting experience. But sloping sites are a unique opportunity. Adversity fires imagination. The very nature of these sites and the excitement that the design solutions create mean that the resulting dwellings become flagships for the flair and imagination of their architects. Here is the chance to create a home that has stepped outside the boring conformity into which most developers and many self-builders seem locked. It may be slightly more expensive. But there are ways of mitigating that and, if you are careful and follow a few simple guidelines, then the very uniqueness of the design will provide added value.

The advent of beam-and-block floors has had a significant impact on the costs of building on a sloping site. Prior to their use becoming almost universal, building on a site with even a slight slope necessitated considerable extra work to the oversite if differential settlement was to be avoided. With a beam-and-block floor the only significant extra costs to the superstructure relate to the need for a greater amount of walling below floor level. It would, nevertheless, be an oversimplification to say that these extra costs, amounting to only a few thousand pounds for even a slope as large as ten degrees, were the end of the matter.

Undoubtedly, a sloping site will make the design more complicated. It will mean extra hard landscaping, extra drainage, including perhaps the necessity for a pump, and extra work in stepping the foundations. All of this will cost money, although it is questionable whether it is safe to try to extrapolate this into sliding scales or costs per square metre relating to degrees of slope. Pounds per square metre is a rough-and-ready reckoner that you can use at the outset of your self-build project. It should never be employed beyond the detailed drawings or once work has commenced on site. Refer to the cost guidelines in the 'Beginner's Guide' in *Homebuilding & Renovating* magazine for the first assessment, but thereafter cost each project on its own merits.

The normal solution to a slope on site is to 'cut and fill'. This describes the process of carving out a level plinth on a sloping site in order to build a home that is essentially designed for use on a level site. Any spoil that is cut from the bank is reserved in order for it to be brought back to make up the levels on the lower edge. The foundation costs are always going to increase due to the slope of the land and the requirement that the foundations should find original subsoil bearing. If the spoil is piled up against the lower or built-up section of the new home then provision will have to be made for the oversite level within the building to be brought up to within 600 mm of the proposed external soil level in order to equalise the pressure on the walling. However, carting spoil away from a site is expensive and time-consuming and its retention on site is a cost benefit just so long as there is space to store it.

Could the hall, in particular, be given greater prominence?

The entrance hall is the window on to the rest of the home. Too pokey, and it gives a first impression of cramped and often untidy space. Too big, and it begs the question, could this space have been better employed? Could it indeed have some useful function other than just as an entrance and passageway? What about all or part of the hallway becoming a dining hall or great room? What about the idea of the hall doubling up as a communal sitting area? What about scrapping the idea of a hallway entirely and making the entrance though a conservatory or atrium or even directly into one of the living rooms? Does the staircase to the upper part have to go from the hall? Could you think in terms of the staircase being enclosed or off another room, or is the staircase itself part of the statement you want to make about your home?

What sort of living accommodation do you want?

Do you dare think in terms of open plan or is your requirement for open-plan living part of the reasoning behind your desire to self-build in the first place? If you stick to convention, will any large lounge be enjoyed by the whole family? If there's a snug, will it ever get used? Will that usage continue or will the need for the children to have separate space where they can watch and listen to their own choice of TV and music become apparent in years to come? Do you need family rooms, a music room or a television room? Do you require a study or an office? Could you think in terms of the various living rooms being interconnected or even capable of being opened up to each other?

Will the selection of certain external materials impact on your design?

The choice of external materials is dictated in many cases by the requirements of the local authority. Do you understand that if you are building in materials such as natural stone this may affect the design of your home, and as the walls will be thicker, you will lose usable area? Certain bricks, tiles and stone are no longer available, and alternatives can be very expensive. Could you use the argument that modern buildings can empathise with traditional architecture while making their own statement in terms of design and the choice of materials? Are you aware that some roof coverings have to be laid at either a minimum or maximum pitch and that this can affect not only the design but also the availability of loft space?

Could/should you think in terms of incorporating a basement?

To some extent you may already have thought about this when considering and evaluating the plot. Does the slope on your site dictate a split-level or partial-basement design as the cost-effective design solution? If there is a planning restriction on the overall size of the building, will the planners agree the basement as an extra or count it as part of the allowable area? Would it be extra living accommodation, play/rumpus space or a utility room? Are the soil conditions or water-table right for the building of basements in your area? Will you think in terms of a fully tanked basement or might you opt for one of the sump-and-pump systems?

Building a basement is always going to be costly. Nevertheless, on a tight site it can make sense. If at all possible, and particularly where they are going to be habitable rather than utility, try to give the rooms below some sort of natural light and ventilation. This can be achieved by high-level windows or by the use of light wells. If the planners are sticky about the overall size of the building and are insisting that the basement area be considered within the total area, indicate the lower floor as void or storage and occupy it at a later date under Permitted Development Rights or PDR (see Chapter 5, The Planning Maze). On a narrow site with adjoining properties close by, you will have to take extreme care with the construction and choose methods that are likely to cause the least disturbance, including noise and vibration, to your neighbours. Take

The suspended ground floor of beams and blocks.

detailed photographs of the adjoining properties before work commences to avoid arguments over any ensuing damage.

There are many different ways to build a basement. Massive blockwork, hollow blockwork with reinforcement, poured or pre-formed concrete and polystyrene blocks filled with concrete. All have their place and are suitable for different situations. There are also schools of thought about how to make the basement waterproof. The normal way is by 'tanking' – the application of a waterproof layer either inside or outside the structure or both. But systems are in place that allow moisture to be harmlessly channelled behind panelling and beneath the flooring to sumps, from which it is then pumped to a drain. One other way of achieving a watertight structure is to create drained voids between the external ground and the basement living accommodation, negating the need for tanking.

Retaining walls
When building on a level plinth beside a natural or carved-out bank, it may be necessary to construct separate retaining walls. Above 1200 mm in height these will have to be designed by an engineer. In certain circumstances it may be cheaper, and visually more attractive, to construct a series of lower retaining walls with the ground stepped between them. An alternative can be the use of wire cages filled with stone or interlocking concrete blocks that are subsequently filled with soil and planted.

Building on stilts
One way of building on steeply sloping land is to build out from it on a series of supporting stilts or columns. This gets away from the need to build extensive foundations on sloping ground, and it negates the need for tanking.. It also leaves the ground relatively untouched, allowing planting to take place over much more of the site. In certain situations it can be the cost-effective solution, and there is no reason why it cannot be employed with multiple-level designs.

Upside-down living

A sloping site often means that there is a view; one of the best ways of taking advantage of this is to reverse the accommodation to bring the living areas to the top with the sleeping areas to the lower floors. The garage can be a complicating factor in all of this. If the road is at the higher level then the solution is for the garage to move with the rest of the reception accommodation. If the road is at the lower level then there might be no alternative but for it to remain. However, it is likely that in those circumstances the entrance accommodation will also have to share the lower floor. Be aware that for every potential buyer who is excited by the individuality of the design, there are many who cannot accept departure from the norm. The house-buying public is incredibly conservative. They expect a natural progression of rooms. It may not devalue your home in real terms, but it will cut down the number of potential buyers and lengthen the time taken to sell.

Level changes and stairs

Level changes within the home can be visually exciting and allow the creation of architectural space for its own sake rather than the merely functional. Rooms can be divided by level without the need for walling. Multiple levels will mean that, unless you have the space or the inclination to install a lift, you are always going to be excluding the physically impaired from ever wanting to buy your home so there is really no sense in compromising. Use stairs to advantage. Like space they do not have to be merely functional and can be articles of furniture in their own right.

Could/should you plan to occupy the attic?

Now is the time seriously to consider the fact that attic space is cheap space and occupation of the roof space is likely to prove the most cost-effective way of gaining extra accommodation. But its use or eventual use has to be planned for. You cannot start cutting up ordinary trusses and you will have to think in terms of attic trusses or a purlin and spar roof. What will you use your attic for? Will it be additional bedrooms or bathrooms? Will it be office space and, if so, can you get heavy office machinery and equipment up there? Will it be used as a play area? If so, what are the implications for bedrooms immediately below?

How will you gain access? Are you content for an occasional use to have access via a pull-down staircase or loft ladder? If you want a permanent second staircase, is there room for its departure and arrival, and is there sufficient headroom? The landing must be at the full-height section of any roof space and not at the point of the roof slope, unless it is possible to take a dormer out to accommodate it. Try to keep all the stairs in the same well. Straight flights, all running in the same direction, take up the least space. Be aware also that with three floors, you will have to have self-closing fire doors, and the staircase will have to be a contained area.

Cooking and eating

In many homes the dining room is the least used yet most expensively furnished room in the house. Do you really need it? When you say that you couldn't have guests eating in the same area as the food preparation, are you thinking clearly? Whom do you have to dinner? Do you really have strangers to dinner or are they normally family or friends? Do you really entertain thoughts of having your boss for dinner or is it more likely that in those circumstance you would eat out? What about a kitchen–dining room or an archway between the two areas? At least the cook wouldn't have to be excluded from the dinner party. Kitchens are one of the biggest selling points. Is yours the right kitchen for your home? Have you chosen from the brochure or for fashion's sake without thinking how it will look in your home without showroom lighting? Would a breakfast area be useful and much used space?

Utility rooms and storage

What is the purpose of your utility room? Is its use allied to that of the kitchen and, if not, does it have to connect to it? If it is really a laundry room, why cart clothes downstairs, wash them and cart them back up again? Couldn't the room go upstairs? If it is a mud room, somewhere for dirty dogs and wellies, could it really just be a lobby and could it benefit from a toilet and/or shower room. If space is at a premium, could the utility room be scrapped altogether in favour of, say, a bigger kitchen or a breakfast area? If you are having underfloor central heating have you thought of where the necessary cupboards will go? Is there to be space for a central vacuum? Will the linen or airing cupboards be accessible to the communal areas, or must they be in one of the bathrooms or bedrooms? Have you already got wardrobes or will you want built-in and fitted ones?

What about the number of bedrooms?

You might only want two or three bedrooms. But adding that extra room to the design takes you into a completely different price bracket. A house with three large bedrooms compared with an identical-size house with four smaller ones might have considerably less value. Yet its build costs might be substantially the same. Could you plan for larger rooms to be sub-divided and if you sell on do you understand that it might be better for you to effect the change rather than relying on a prospective purchaser's imagination? What about sizes? It is your house, so are you going to insist that the master suite takes the lion's share of the space? Will you want dressing rooms? Do you want the remaining bedrooms to be more or less equal in size or could one or more of them be smaller and given over to occasional or some other use?

Bathrooms and toilets

Do you need a downstairs toilet by the front door or would it be more useful in the utility area or accessible from the garden? Might you not need both? An en suite is *de rigueur* in most large family homes. Do you want it to be a shower room or a full bathroom? With the communal bathroom, do you want the toilet to be separate or have you thought of a completely separate toilet in any case? What about en-suite accommodation for other bedrooms, or for at least one that you can call a guest suite? Could the idea of one bathroom being directly accessible to and serving two bedrooms fit in with your family arrangements? Have you thought through the family routines, especially in the mornings? Would doubling up the number of hand-basins help? Could you put hand-basins in some bedrooms?

Cranked ventilators allow air beneath the floor but impede light, therefore preventing the growth of weeds.

The method of construction

In most conventional designs the method of construction is secondary to the design. Certain specific construction forms do, however, facilitate or in some cases dictate the design. Are you sure that the construction method you favour will be able to provide you with what you want in design terms? Are you aware that to add in a fireplace to some of the sealed home systems might negate much of their energy-saving concept? Do you realise that some of the post-and-beam systems can provide clear open space that would otherwise be unattainable? Have you thought that open spaces and high or vaulted ceilings will require specific heating solutions if you are to maintain the same level of comfort as in other areas? Have you thought of running costs? Have you considered what the full-height glass wall will be like in summer as well as winter?

Passive solar gain

Using the sun to heat your house saves energy and makes it more pleasant. You don't need to increase the window area but the more of them that can face south the better, although you may need external blinds to prevent over-heating in the summer months. A conservatory can certainly help with the saving of energy, but in certain areas, such as Conservation Areas, Areas of Outstanding Natural Beauty and the National Parks, the planners will have a lot to say about their use and just how they look. In other areas they may be quite amenable but, even then, may balk at having them on the front of a house. Of course, some windows may always have to face north to ensure good daylight in all rooms. Any gain from any of the above is known as passive solar heating and the most important thing about it is that it is free.

A compact plan, without 'extensions', minimises the external wall area, reduces heat losses and reduces the shading of other parts of the house. A bungalow will lose more heat than a three-storey house of the same floor area. Rooms that are used most should be on the south side to take advantage of any solar gain. For rooms that are used mostly in the mornings, such as kitchens and breakfast rooms, a southeast orientation will get the best benefit from the sun. If possible halls, landings, staircases and less frequently occupied rooms such as bathrooms and utility rooms, should go on the north side. That's the ideal, of course, but when thinking about energy conservation, all of this has to fit in with the street scene and what the planners require. Additionally, there may be other factors that you may want to take into account, such as the specific views from a window or windows. As ever, the conflicting requirements have to be brought into balance, and that's the task facing you and your designers.

The garage, driveway and parking

Considered almost essential by the market, yet very rarely used for the housing of cars. Do you want one at all and, if so, will you ever use it and for what? Could you think in terms of building more house or incorporating the garage space within the home on the understanding that if it ever comes to re-sale, it can be put back to its original purpose? Could you have a carport instead? Should the garage be attached, integral or detached? Planners feel that detached garages reflect the rural character while attached and integral garages are an urban solution to the problem of what to do with the car. If the garage is detached or attached to the side of your new home, could it be left until later so as to concentrate available monies on the actual home?

Most local authorities will want to see a minimum of two car-parking spaces per property. There is usually no requirement for garaging, and in some cases and with smaller properties the general requirements will be eased. In urban areas on-street parking is often acceptable. Generally speaking, the busier the road the greater the requirements for off-street parking and turning will be. The Highways Agency and the local authority will assess each case on its individual merits with regard to visibility and safety. Where visibility splays are required on a narrow site, it might be necessary to come to a legal arrangement with adjoining owners. Where turning space is difficult to obtain the use of a turntable can be considered.

Most areas have maximum gradients for driveways, often 1:10. That can mean that the driveway may have to wind up or down the site, which, in turn, can mean that space is taken up that would otherwise be available for the home. However, a winding driveway is in itself a design opportunity. Straight driveways give no privacy and allow no mystery. Curved or winding driveways allow the home to shield behind planting or walls. Entrance gates opening on to a driveway that slopes up from the road may need to be set across the site or have a level area behind them in order to open. Once again this can add interest. Restricted sloping sites can employ a turntable to facilitate entry and leaving or, in extreme cases, a lift to transport cars up or down to the garage level.

Contents and furniture

Have you made a list of your favourite furniture? Most modern furniture is designed either to fit through door openings as narrow as 760 mm or be capable of disassembly; antique furniture certainly is not. How much space will that grand piano take up? Is the dining area large enough to accommodate your dining table at its full extension and is there room enough around it for chairs and circulation? Are the ceilings going to be high enough for antique wardrobes and dressers? If your snooker table is going in the loft, can you get it up there and, if so, will the floor take the weight?

Is there enough space to use it? A snooker or table-tennis table needs at least 2 metres all around.

Can you incorporate the garden into the home?

The garden should be an extension of the living space within the home rather than a separate entity and, weather permitting, it should fit into the natural progression between rooms. Can your access be via a sunroom or conservatory? What rooms do you want to have direct access to the garden? Are you worried about children and dogs bringing in dirt? In bad weather could the garden be brought into the home by means of raising flowerbeds and planting so that the eye is led through the window and beyond? Will the access be suitable for older people rather than serving to exclude them from the garden? Does the house design reflect the need for direct access between the garden and the street, negating the need for plants, mud and other garden materials to be brought through the living space?

If garden space is limited or is likely to be overlooked, consider the idea of an internal courtyard. On a very tight site, rooms that would otherwise not have light can then use this and obtain natural ventilation.

A garden that slopes away from the visual point within a home can be 'lost'. Think about raised decks or patios. Elevated wooden decks can be attractive and constructed in such a way as to allow light to filter down to the windows of lower storeys. If you want to build up a patio to a raised level, think carefully before you do that by the use of fill. It will always settle, and the slabs will become uneven. Instead, use floor beams to create a raised patio with an empty void beneath. You can then build walls at the edge with railings and steps down to the lower levels. And these walls can be made as planters, so that your garden is brought to the reception level.

A garden that slopes up from the home is one that can be seen to an even greater degree than a flat site. It becomes a three-dimensional space that can be terraced and planted so as to bring beauty to all levels of the home. However, if retaining walls are required, be careful that they are sufficiently distant from the house to provide suitable access and drainage. If they or any other pathways are north facing, be careful to select materials that will not become slippery when wet or attract verdigris.

How to find an architect/designer

A long march starts with the first step. When that elusive plot has been found, almost the first professional with whom the self-builder will need to make contact is the architect/designer. There is no doubt that finding the right person or architectural/design practice can be a daunting process that, if not dealt with correctly, can blight the whole project.

It is relatively easy to come up with names of architects/designers. But how do you assess who is best for you? How do you make sure that this relationship, which after all is probably going to lead to the biggest single expenditure and investment in your life, is going to be beneficial? There are organisations that will assist you with finding architects/designers.

Regional architectural bodies

All of the regional architects' organisations and associations, listed in Further Information (p. 205), have their membership data available on line, in hard copy or by telephone. It is important not to be overawed by any person or practice with which you make contact. They may be extremely highly qualified. They may have connections and social standing that is far beyond that with which you are used to associating. But in the end they are your potential employees, and it is you who should be calling the shots. They are only ever going to be on board in order to make your project succeed. They are the ones who have to demonstrate their ability.

National associations of designers

Once again these are listed in Further Information (p. 205). Architectural Technologists are not principally designers, although many of them are extremely good at it. Their main skills revolve around the technical aspects of a house design and making it work, which is why many architectural practices also have them within their employ.

Local papers, local guides and the Internet

Many competent architectural and design practices will actually take out advertisements in local journals or book space or display advertisements within local guides. All of the Internet companies that either specialise in or offer listings of building tradesmen and professionals have lists of architects and designers. These are listed by postcode. Sometimes the information given is just the bare bones of the name and address. But in some cases the listing extends to a brief résumé of the type of work that the practice carries out or in which it specialises, with a more personal description of the character and aims of the company.

The local authority

Travel around your area and make a note of all of the new homes that you like. Then, unless you are brave enough to knock on the door and request the name of the architect or designer, visit the local planning office and ask to see the files relating to that site. You will then be able to see who drew

The external walls start to go up.

the plans. Most importantly, you will be able to glean from the file just how cogent the designer was, how they presented their proposals and how they were received.

Some Planning Officers and Building Inspectors may agree to give out the names of architects or designers in your area. In all probability they won't want to give out just one name and will want to give you several. But it is often quite easy to see which ones they tend to favour. In some cases that might be a big plus point. In others, don't lose sight of the fact that this is your project. If you have a suspicion that the relationship might be a trifle too cosy, such that between them they might cook up an agreement that runs counter to your wishes, then go on to another name.

Other self-builders

If you see a mobile home on a site then you can bet your bottom dollar that it's a self-build site. Self-builders love talking and sharing their experiences with other self-builders. If you drop in and talk to them, you will get loads of useful information, among which will be the best and worst tradesmen with whom they have had dealings. Included within this will be their architect or designer. Apart from the obvious questions about design and how the planning went, make sure that you find out whether their architect's budget predictions were correct.

Package-deal companies

A large number of package-deal companies have grown up within the self-build market. Most of them are concerned with a timber-frame form of construction, but there are some that specialise in traditional brick and block.

Most package-deal companies will help you assess the site and prepare an initial drawing. Once this is done they will quote you for their service, including the supply of materials or a kit. Only when this is accepted will they then proceed with any applications for Planning and Building Regulations. If you accept their quotation and they get on with the work, you are legally obliged to purchase the kit or package deal of materials. You cannot cherry-pick the designs. Most of them know that the design is the hook. They largely offer a pretty good service and are reasonably knowledgeable about self-builders and their requirements.

Your architect/designer

So, what do you need to look out for when appointing any architect/designer?

Flair

No amount of training can make up for a lack of flair – you either have it or you don't. Architects train for seven years before they qualify, and technologists for a total of six years. But if you took the average decorator and trained them for 40 years, it still would not mean that they could paint the ceiling of the Sistine Chapel.

Willingness to listen

Nobody wants to employ an automaton. If you are engaging an architect or designer for their flair and imagination then it doesn't make sense to ignore all their suggestions. On the other hand, if they are unwilling to listen to you or incorporate your ideas within their concept then they are not the right person for you. If your proposals are not practicable then they should explain why and if possible vary the design to achieve the same effect.

A friendly and approachable manner

Whoever you deal with, it is not going to be a question of having one or even a few meetings and then leaving them to get on with the business. You are going to be entering a long-term relationship that may last for six months or longer and need frequent contact. If you don't feel comfortable in the presence of somebody or you feel intimidated in any way then move on to someone who makes you feel at ease.

Experience with one-off houses

Unfortunately, many architects tend to tick 'Yes' in the box on the question-naire that asks whether they do one-off housing, whether or not they actually do so. They do so for all the right reasons, of course, and they may well believe that they are capable or that it would even be exciting to deal with an individual project. However, it is important that the architect or designer has experience of one-off housing, where the criteria in dealing with you, the client, and with the whole planning process may be completely different to that used on, say, a large development or industrial complex.

Architects whose principal function is one-off housing have come together as Associated Self-build or ASBA Architects (Freephone 0800 387310). Those using a package-deal company will know that these companies have evolved around the ability to provide just what the self-builder wants in terms of both design and cost. Their presentation and literature will seek to reassure the prospective client of their abilities and understanding.

Portfolio

If you were going to employ an artist then they would arrive with a port-folio of their previous work. In just the same way, although it is not quite as easily portable, an architect or designer should be able to show you examples of their previous commissions. Design evolves. Fashions in archi-tecture, just like fashions in clothing, change as the years roll by. If you do get the chance to look back at previous jobs, look out for just how those changes were incorporated into the designs and ascertain; if you can, find out whether they were at the instigation of the designer or the client or both. Any lack in this area would indicate a total absence of flair.

Track record

Package-deal companies often trade on their track record with photographs within their brochures of previous clients, full details of their costings and testimonials. Architects and designers may not have such literature but it is still important to be able to track back to previous clients. If at all possible talk to them. Ask how they got on and, most importantly, ask if the cost predictions at the start of the project were adhered to. One television programme chronicled the despair of a client at the cost overruns experi-enced with a particular architect and then at the end introduced them to a previous client who could have told them all along that his predictions were invariably 100 per cent wrong. Don't let that happen to you.

Temporary frames or templates in place.

Professional membership

Architects will usually be members of one or more of the national bodies such as the RIBA, RIAS, RSAW, RSUA or RIAI, all of which are listed in Further Information, p. 205. In the UK they must also be members of the Architects Registration Board (ARB) if they are to practise under the name 'architect', which is protected by law. If things do go wrong, these bodies have dispute procedures, which are strengthened if the standard terms and conditions of appointment are imported into the contract between architect and client. Designers may be members of BIAT (the British Institute of Architectural Technologists).

It is important to verify any claimed membership and important also to make sure that the correct Professional Indemnity is held, something that in any case is mandatory for those practising under the auspices of the professional bodies.

A willingness to discuss fees

Many designers and architects will quote a fixed price for the job. You need to make sure that you are getting what you are expecting and you may need to establish a fee for each segment of their work; one for initial drawings, one for planning drawings, one for building-regulations drawings, one for working drawings, one for specification and tender documents and one, if it is required, for on-site supervision or inspection.

Many architects will quote percentage fees for each of these parts of their work. That is fine as long as you all agree of what, exactly, these fees are supposed to be a percentage. Sometimes it is as well to agree the build costs at the outset. Avoid having to pay extra fees as a result of increased specification. It costs the same to lay an expensive hand-made brick as it does to lay a standard wirecut. It costs no more to fit expensive kitchen units than cheap ones, and there is often no more work involved on the part of builder or architect. Why then should the fees be greater?

Above all do not be afraid to discuss fees and or take time out if you need to work out the implications of any fee structure that is asked for. If you come across an architect who is woolly about fees, is unwilling to discuss them or who attempts to brush the matter under the carpet, then stand back. And perhaps move on to someone who is not scared to set out and justify their charges.

Important criteria to look for

Once you have your architect or designer on board and their first drawings have arrived, how do you make sure they are on the right track? And, crucially, that they are up to speed on costs?

Can concept be translated into reality?
It is all very well having imaginative drawings with fantastic elevations and clear spans. Any good artist can produce a picture to stir the senses. But that is the essential difference between an artist and an architect or designer in that, when they make a drawing, they have to bear in mind the practicalities. They have not just to produce a pretty picture but also a representation of something that can be built and stand up and conform to all of the regulations and requirements that the various authorities impose.

If a drawing is unusual, ask the question, right at the beginning, 'Can this be translated into a buildable plan within reasonable cost parameters?'

Are construction drawings clear and precise?
Builders and subcontractors have to deal with a bewildering assortment of different plans and styles from each architect with whom they build. It is important that drawings are clear and that any special requirements or construction instructions are easily recognised. Too much detail on the drawings can be very confusing, leading to points being missed. Sometimes it is better for the drawings to be clear and simple with a separate written specification.

Is there detail and explanation where necessary?
Sometimes it is necessary for particular features to be expanded upon within the drawings in the form of details. Look to see if these are on the previous plans as a matter of course. Maybe there was no need for them. If there were a need and your drawings also share that need then you should be clear that any necessary explanatory detail will be included as a matter of course. You will also want to know that you will not be charged a whole load of extras simply in order to explain the reasoning and method behind a particular feature of the drawings.

Is there an understanding of your budget?
Beware of any designer or architect who gaily goes ahead with a drawing without fully discussing your proposed budget. The budget should be the prime consideration, and no drawing should take place other than within its parameters. The number of prospective self-builders who allow the drawing and planning process to proceed unchecked only to find, when the quotations start to come in, that it cannot and could never have been built within their budget is legion. Don't let it happen to you. If you meet

with an architect or designer who seems unwilling to discuss this aspect then move on to the next choice.

Is there an understanding of your building costs?

You might think that all architects would be aware of building costs – if you did you would be wrong. While there is no doubt that the reputable ones among them, and especially those specialising in one-off self-builds, are *au fait* with current costs of labour and materials, there are a significant minority who simply don't have a clue.

It is relatively easy to find out about rough build costs in various parts of the UK by reading the self-build magazines and by reference to the build-cost tables in the back of *Homebuilding & Renovating* magazine. Make sure that the architect or designer to whom you are talking also understands those costs and, above all, make sure that they believe them. Some have become so used to unquestioning clients and the acceptance of extortionate costs that they have simply left reality. They don't often trespass into the self-build world but when they do, they cause much grief.

Deal with the person or practice who is willing to talk prices from the start of the project and who demonstrates a shared desire with you that whatever gets drawn gets built within budget.

What can/should the self-builder bring to this contract?

A clear idea of your budget

Any designer worth their salt is going to be concerned that what they draw can be built within your budget. It therefore behoves you to make that clear at the outset and to be honest. Many architects assume that their clients have more money than they are being told is available. If they are right and they ignore the extra money available then there's the possibility that they might not achieve the full potential of the project. If they are wrong, and they assume the existence of money that you don't have, then the project will certainly go over budget.

Tell your architect exactly what your true budget is. If there is a limit then make it quite clear that it must not be breached and make that the essence of the contract between you. At each stage of the drawing process you must be able to ask the question, 'Are we still on budget?' And at each stage a responsible architect or designer should be prepared to answer honestly.

A clear and concise list of your requirements

Travel around your area noting and photographing your likes and dislikes in architectural terms. Study books of plans and make a list of those features that you want to have incorporated. If you are competent, draw out a rough sketch of what you want. Do not be shy about showing this to your prospective architect or designer. If they scoff because they feel that you have no business interfering in their job then they are not the right people for you. If they point out features that will be difficult or expensive to attain but then go on to suggest ways in which your ideas can be incorporated within a buildable plan, then perhaps a successful working relationship can be established. Most reasonable designers and architects will welcome an insight into your thoughts as a 'starter for ten'.

First floor joists.

The ability to compromise

You are never going to get 100 per cent of what you want. There are always going to have to be compromises. Be prepared for this and accept with good grace that sometimes you might have to give up on a cherished ideal in order to achieve the whole. On the other hand, do not let yourself be talked out of something simply because that makes it easier for the other person. If you are being told that something is unattainable then insist on a proper explanation of why, and if you need time to assimilate the information or make other enquiries, then insist on taking it.

When going through the planning process, the design may have to change in any event. Be prepared for this and don't waste time fighting an issue with your designer that may in any case be taken out of your hands by the dictates of the planners.

Understand that it is you, and not anyone you employ, however august, who should remain in control

Many things during the whole design process may seem to be outside your control. Architects may be telling you that such and such a design feature is physically or financially impossible. Building Control may water down a feature or even delete it altogether in order for your project to conform to the regulations. Builders may be reluctant to do things in certain ways – sometimes because they know best but sometimes, as well, because they know an easier way.

Don't be rushed into these decisions. Take time to digest them and their implications. Maybe they are right. Maybe there is no alternative but to conform. But equally, there might be a way around things and as you are the one paying for the project it should be you, upon good advice, who makes the final decision.

chapter five

The Planning Maze

Planning permission or consent is the key to whether land can be developed. Without planning permission, a piece of land is simply the corner of a field or part of someone's garden. With it, the land is a very valuable asset. Learning about planning permission is vital for the self-builder. Learning the mechanics is obviously important. But learning about the more intricate aspects of planning and about rights such as Permitted Development Rights (PDR) and Certificates of Lawful Use, which are detailed in this chapter, can be invaluable in the negotiating process. Simply demonstrating your knowledge of their existence can turn a negotiation around in your favour or make acceptable a decision with which you were otherwise less than happy.

You do not need to own land in order to make a planning application on it. You do not even need the owner's permission to apply for planning permission on their land. It is, however, necessary to serve the proper notice on the owners of the land, and this form of notice is proscribed in the application forms. Planning permission always runs to the benefit of the land rather than the applicant, so if you went around making planning applications on land that the owners subsequently refused to sell you, you would pretty soon be bankrupt. So if you did make an application on land that you don't yet own it would make sense to tie things up legally so that the owners are obliged to sell to you in the event of the application being successful. That can be achieved by either exchanging contracts on the land, subject to receipt of satisfactory planning permission, or arranging for a simple legal option that gives you the right to purchase within a certain time

Scaffolding at 'first lift'.

frame at either an agreed price or a price to be determined by a later valuation.

Planning consent

There are various forms of planning permission that range from Outline consent via Detailed consent (or Approval of Reserved Matters) to Full consent. There are also specialist planning applications, such as for Listed Buildings and Designated Areas. If consent is not given, you can consider a resubmission or an appeal. The rules vary within the UK. What follows relates to England and Wales (see p. 82 for Northern Ireland and Scotland).

Outline planning consent
This gives permission, in principle, for the development of land. It means that some sort of building or development may take place and it is what confers the value on the plot. Outline consent does not, in itself, allow you to commence work but, rather, it allows you to move on to the next stage of the planning process. It is always given subject to conditions. The first of these refers to the duration of the consent.

Up until recently most outline planning permissions lasted for five years with a condition that an application should be made for Approval of Reserved Matters (or Detailed Permission) within three years. The development had to be begun within five years of the original granting of outline planning permission or within two years of the date of the last granting of Approval of Reserved Matters, whichever was the later. These time-scales meant that it was normally possible to make several applications for Approval of Reserved Matters pursuant to the original outline permission. Scotland and Northern Ireland retain a five-year system for the moment, and in England and Wales many unused consents are still out there and will be until 2010.

Legislation enacted in England and Wales in August 2005, however, introduced a standard time limit of three years for all planning consents but, at the same time, gave local authorities the power to impose their own time limits. In future most outline consents in England and Wales will last for just three years, during which time approval of reserved matters must be obtained. Work must then be commenced within two years of the detailed approval. On the face of it you might think that nothing's really changed. Except that, and this is important, if your application for Approval of Reserved Matters runs beyond the three-year period and fails then the original outline consent could find itself out of time. If it succeeds, of course then the consent will last for another two years during which time, you must start work on site. All of this makes it all the more important that anyone contemplating buying land or property with a planning consent should study the conditions and, in particular, the dates in great detail.

Design and Access Statement
Legislation brought into force in June 2006 requires that the vast majority of applications for Outline planning permission, Full planning permission and Listed Building consent must include a Design and Access Statement.

For an Outline planning application, according to the legislation, the Design and Access Statement will:

play a part in linking general development principles to final detailed designs. A statement, accompanying an outline application, must explain how the applicant has considered the proposal, and understands what is appropriate and feasible for the site in its context. It should clearly explain and justify the design and access principles that will be used to develop future details of the scheme. Such information will help community involvement and informed decision making. The Design and Access Statement will form a link between the outline permission and the consideration of reserved matters.

Additional information required for an outline application must also include:

- The use or uses proposed for the development as well as an identification of any distinct development zones within the identified site.
- The amount of development proposed for each use.
- An indicative layout with separate development zones proposed within the site boundary where appropriate (effectively a site plan).
- An indication of the upper and lower limits for the height, length and width of any building (effectively elevation plans).
- Indicative access points – an area or areas where the access point or points to the site will be situated.

Approval of Reserved Matters or Detailed consent

This is the next stage in the normal planning process. It is sometimes referred to as Detailed consent, and it concerns itself with the final details for the development as listed below. In normal circumstances, it does not confer any extra value to the plot, over and above that already given to it by the outline consent. Within this application any conditions imposed by the outline consent have to be satisfied and it is possible that fresh conditions will also be imposed. An Approval of Reserved Matters never stands alone; it is always related back to and is a part of the original outline consent. It is necessary to understand, however, that even though the Approval of Reserved Matters cannot stand alone, it does not follow that it is a mere formality. Additionally, the granting of an Approval of Reserved Matters does not preclude further applications for quite different schemes relating back to the original outline consent. The refusal of an application for Approval of Reserved Matters does nothing to negate the original outline consent, so long as it has not expired.

Following on from the changes made to outline consents, the Approval of Reserved Matters is restricted to the following.

Layout The way in which buildings, routes and open spaces are provided within the development and their relationship to buildings and open spaces outside the development.

Scale The height, width and length of each building in relation to its surroundings.

Appearance The aspect of a building or place that determines the visual impression it makes, including the external built form of the development.

Access This covers all aspects of access and circulation to and within the site for vehicles, cycles and pedestrians and how these fit into the surrounding access networks.

Landscaping The treatment of public and private open space to enhance or protect the site's amenity through hard and soft measures such as the planting of trees, hedges or screening by fences or walls.

Full planning consent

This is really nothing more than a merger of the outline and detailed stages of an application, into the one consent. Full planning consent grants permission in principle and at the same time considers and approves the full details of the proposed development. A Full consent therefore confers value to the plot in just the same way as an Outline consent would do. Full applications granted before April 2005 may well last five years, but it is important to check the dates because full applications granted after that date are for just three years.

A full application must be accompanied by a Design and Access Statement that will explain and justify the following design principles.

Amount To include details of how much development is proposed including the number of dwellings and their proposed floor space.

Layout Detailing the way in which the proposed buildings are laid out on site, their relationship to open spaces, both public and private and their orientation and relationship to other buildings and open spaces surrounding the development.

Scale Detailing the height, width and length of any building or buildings in relation to its/their surroundings.

Landscaping Full details of what treatments are proposed for both public and private spaces to enhance or protect the amenities of the site and its surroundings by means of both hard and soft landscaping, including how the resulting landscape will be maintained.

Appearance To include the visual impression that the building will make, 'including the external built form of the development, its architecture, materials, decoration, lighting, colour and texture'.

The Design and Access Statement will also go on to:

Appraise the context According to the legislation, 'It is important that an applicant should understand the context in which their proposal will sit and use this understanding to draw up the application', which means:

- Assessing the impact the proposed development will have on the surrounding area, physically, socially and economically.
- Consulting various professionals involved in planning, Building Control, conservation, design and access.
- Consulting community members and local community and access groups.
- Evaluation of these consultations and identification of their principal findings to include balancing any conflicting issues.
- Understanding that the design should reflect the context in which it is proposed.

Explain access Lastly, the statement should explain how access arrangements will ensure that all users will have equal and convenient access to the buildings and spaces and the public-transport network. Access for the emergency services should also be explained including circulation routes, access and egress in the case of an emergency.

Listed Building consent

There are three grades for listed buildings in England and Wales: Grade I, major importance, Grade II*, particularly importance, and Grade II, most of the listings identified in an area as of historical or architectural value. In Scotland there are three buildings categories: Category A, national importance, Category B, regional importance, and Category C, local importance. In Northern Ireland, Grade A is for buildings of national importance, Grade B⁺ is similar but slightly degraded and B1 and B2 include buildings of local importance.

Listed-building consent is required for any alterations or extensions to listed buildings including gates, walls and fences. It is also required for any significant works, internal or external, and for the erection of any structure in excess of 10 cu. metres. There are considerable restrictions on Permitted Development Rights (PDR) and, if you carry out works that are permitted under these rights, you will still need listed-building consent.

An application for listed-building consent must be accompanied by a Design and Access Statement that will include all of the usual requirements listed above (see pp. 81–2) plus details of:

- The historical and special architectural importance of the building.
- The particular features that justify its designation as a listed building.
- The building's setting.
- An explanation and justification of how the proposals will enhance its special historic and architectural importance.

Northern Ireland and Scotland

In Northern Ireland planning will now be devolved back to local control, but for the most part follows the same pattern as the old five-year system of England and Wales. The Planning Service is split among eight divisional offices.

For the time being Scotland adheres to the old five-year principle with outline consents lasting five years within which application has to be made for detailed consent within three years of the granting of the permission. Full consents similarly last for five years.

Resubmissions

If you do get a refusal on your planning application, you can make a Resubmission, with no additional fee payable, within 12 months of the date of the refusal. This applies only to the first refusal and not to any subsequent or serial refusals, and it must be the same applicant and relate to the same site. If you choose to withdraw an application, you again get another free go, but this time it must be made within 12 months of the date of the original application.

Getting towards wallplate level, where the roof starts.

Designated Areas

Certain areas have a special planning status and are collectively referred to as Designated Areas. They comprise the National Parks, Areas of Outstanding Natural Beauty (AONB), Conservation Areas and the Broads. In these areas, either different planning rules apply or rights are modified in some way.

Unauthorised development and enforcement

If something is built without planning permission, and the planning authority does not challenge what you have done, then, after a period of four years, the unauthorised development becomes immune from enforcement procedures. Thereafter, the owner of the property can call for a Certificate of Lawful Use. It is mandatory for the local authority to issue this certificate, it confers all of the powers of a proper planning consent, and it may have conditions attached to it in just the same way. The four-year rule also applies to a change of use where a building is brought into residential use. But for all other changes of use the breach must go unnoticed and unopposed by the planning authority for a period of ten years in order for a Certificate of Lawful Use to be demanded. Breaches of conditions on a planning approval also fall under this ten-year rule. There is no time limit so far as unauthorised works to listed buildings are concerned.

Section 106 Agreements and Planning Gain Supplement/Statutory Planning Charge

Section 106 Agreements attach to the deeds of the property and are a legally binding agreement on the applicant or successors in title. They can be used by a local authority for a variety of reasons: to reinforce a planning condition, such as the requirement for a building to be occupied only by a person engaged in agriculture, or to prevent alienation of all or part of a holding and make sure that something is done before the planning permission is operated. They have also been used in recent years to require infrastructure payments to local authorities to cover schools, roads, affordable housing and suchlike. These payments are usually required at the point of development rather than on the granting of consent. Self-builders must be careful and, wherever possible, make sure that their requirement is reflected in the price paid for the land.

The government has long been committed to the idea of the public having a share of the uplift in value caused by the granting of planning permission and for several years have been committed to the idea of a Planning Gain Supplement that would have been additional to the locally imposed Section 106 Agreements. As this book goes to print they have changed tack somewhat and it now seems likely that a Statutory Planning Charge will be set by local and regional authorities as an extension of and in place of those Section 106 Agreements. The charge is ikely to be set at different rates according to the type of development, the size of the development and whether it relates to Greenfield or Brownfield land.

Tree Preservation Orders (TPOs)

The planning authority can place a Tree Preservation Order (TPO) on an individual tree or group of trees that they think worth protecting. This prevents the felling of any tree or trees subject to the order and limits any pruning to authorised work that will not harm their health or appearance. If the authorities feel that trees are in danger, they can place a provisional TPO on them in very short order, which remains effective for six months while the council considers whether to make it permanent. Trees in Conservation Areas are subject to special protection. Any work to fell, lop or prune a tree in a Conservation Area requires six weeks' notice in writing to be given to the local authority. If they then consider that the tree is of importance to the area, they can issue a TPO in the normal way. Removal of or damage to a tree that is the subject of a TPO can result in prosecution leading to a hefty fine plus a requirement that the tree is replaced.

The exceptions to this are where specific planning consent has been granted within which the removal of the trees is specified, where the tree has to be cut down or pruned by statutory undertakers such as the water and electricity boards or where the tree or trees are dead, dying or dangerous. Additionally trees on Crown land and fruit trees grown for the commercial production of fruit are exempt from these orders, although that doesn't mean that simply putting a bucket of apples for sale outside your gate would qualify you to call your tree 'commercial'.

In just the same way that planning conditions can be used to permit the felling of a tree that would otherwise be the subject of a TPO, they can also be used to protect them. Additionally, conditions within a planning consent can require the planting of further trees, and it is therefore possible for a TPO to be placed on a tree that has not yet been planted.

Any application for planning consent that involves felling trees always receives special consideration. If the trees are not subject to a TPO, it is sometimes advisable to fell any tree that is in the way straight away, although due thought must be given to the possible future effect on foundations. If the removal of the tree or trees is likely to create a rumpus, some people advocate doing it quickly and at a weekend, so as to prevent a provisional TPO being issued.

You can obtain details of TPOs in your area from the local authority and, in common with most areas of planning, there is the right of Appeal.

Permitted Development Rights (PDR)

PDR give consent for all sorts of development of land, without the need to apply for planning permission in the normal way. They are granted as part of the Planning Acts known as the General Development Orders. They are not a certainty; they can be varied or negated completely by the wording or conditions in a planning consent. They are severely restricted in National Parks, Conservation Areas, AONB and the Broads, and they can be removed or varied by the local authority over a whole area.

Permitted Development Rights can be withdrawn or modified over a whole area by means of an Article 4 Direction, an order by the local authority that has to be ratified within four months by the government, which, once confirmed, becomes permanent. They can also be withdrawn or modified by a condition within a planning consent.

Extensions
If your PDR are not impaired then you can build an extension to an original dwelling in England and Wales so long as:

- It is no bigger than 15 per cent of the volume of the original dwelling or 115 cu. metres, whichever is the greater, up to a maximum of 110 cu. metres or, if it is a terraced house or is in a Conservation Area, National Park, AONB or the Broads, the volume is no greater than 10 per cent of the original dwelling or 50 cu. metres, whichever is the greater.
- It does not protrude above the original ridgeline or is more than 4 metres high or closer to the boundary than 2 metres.
- The result of the extension does not mean that more than half of the area of land around the original house will be built upon.
- The extension does not protrude in front of the original building line, unless that would still mean that it was at least 20 metres from the Highway.

For Northern Ireland and Scotland, see p. 89.

Internal alterations
You can carry out development within the curtilage of the building, which means that you can alter walls or rearrange rooms and occupy the roof void, subject to the limits given in loft conversions below. However, if you live in a specially designated area, such as a Conservation Area, a National Park, an AONB or the Broads, you will need to apply for express consent for any extension to the roof or any kind of addition that would materially alter the shape of the roof. This would include roof lights or a dormer.

The new home beginning to settle into the street scene.

Loft conversions
In most areas loft conversions are allowed, so long as they do not add more than 40 cu. metres to the roof volume of a terraced house or 50 cu. metres to any other kind of house and the work does not increase the overall height of the roof.

Dormer windows or roof extensions
Any increase in the roof volume occasioned by the addition of dormer windows or extensions to the roof will count against the allowances for extensions listed above (p. 85). Planning is, however, required for dormer windows on the roof slope that faces the Highway.

Roof lights and solar panels
No planning permission is required for roof lights on any roof slope, and solar panels are allowed, so long as they do not project significantly above the roof slope.

Garages
You can construct a garage for a dwelling where none exists, so long as it does not go closer to the Highway than the nearest point of the original house, unless there would be at least 20 metres between it and the Highway and as long as it does not exceed 3 metres in total height or 4 metres to the ridge if it is a pitched roof.

You do not need planning permission to convert an integral or attached garage into living accommodation, unless, of course, this is prevented by a condition in the original planning permission.

Porches
You may erect a porch for a house, so long as it is at least 2 metres from the Highway, it does not exceed 3 metres in height, and it is no larger than 3 sq. metres.

New windows or doors
There is no requirement to seek planning permission for the insertion of new windows or doors, even if the effect of carrying out this work is to create an overlooking situation that would otherwise be unacceptable. This is an anomaly in the planning laws that might well be addressed at some future date. Once again, you cannot add new windows or doors if there is a condition on the original planning or a clause or covenant in the deeds preventing it, and of course you cannot carry out works of this sort to listed buildings or in the specially designated areas.

Boundaries and hedges
You can construct walls to the boundaries so long as they do not exceed 2 metres in height or 1 metre adjoining the Highway. Deciduous hedges are not covered by these restrictions, and you can plant and grow these to whatever height you wish, at present, unless there are special conditions in your planning consent or a covenant in your deeds preventing it. Moves are, however, afoot, to place restrictions on 'unfriendly' and, particularly, Leylandii hedges. Under the Anti-social Behaviour Act 2003 a homeowner can require, upon payment of a fee of £600, that the local authority acts as an intermediary to demand that a neighbouring homeowner cuts an evergreen boundary hedge to a height of no more than 2 metres. If they fail to do so there is a fine of £1000 with an additional £200 for every day that they disobey the order.

Outbuildings, sheds, greenhouses, conservatories, etc.
In most cases you can also construct outbuildings, sheds, greenhouses, conservatories, accommodation for pets, summerhouses, ponds, swimming pools and tennis courts, so long as they do not cover more than half of the garden and so long as any above ground structure does not exceed the height and size restrictions listed under Extensions, above. They must also be situated at least 5 metres from the house. In Scotland the outbuildings must not cover more than 30% of the garden area.

These outbuildings must be ancillary to and for the use and enjoyment of your home as a single dwelling. You cannot build specific sleeping accommodation or a 'granny flat' in the garden because that would be tantamount to building a separate dwelling. But you can convert existing outbuildings for use as sleeping accommodation, (although they would still have to satisfy Building Regulations). But if you build a 'gym' and that building happens to have a kitchenette and toilet/shower facilities then, once it is established as an 'existing outbuilding' you would have the right to convert its use to sleeping accommodation.

Replacement dwellings
Many local authorities have policies in place that restrict the size of any replacement dwelling by reference to the size of the existing property. The

amount of increase allowed is different from council to council but if their policy allows, say, a 50 per cent increase in size that means that if you find a 100 sq. metres bungalow on a one-acre plot, technically all you can replace it with is a 150 sq. metre property.

This is where your knowledge of the existence of Permitted Development Rights can come in handy. Simply demonstrating your knowledge of these rights could persuade the planners to approve a slightly bigger property of a homogenous design rather than be faced with a hotchpotch of extensions and outbuildings in the future.

Alternatively, you could, so long as the existing property has not used up its rights, argue that whatever you build should reflect the fact that the original building could have been bigger. You could actually extend the existing bungalow and build outhouses, garages, etc. and then argue that any new dwelling should be 50 per cent bigger than the extended building. But if you then knocked down what you'd just built in order to build again, that would be extremely wasteful.

But you could do things another way. You could first of all obtain planning permission for a 150 sq. metre property. Then, having got it, and before you operate the consent, you could address the existing bungalow and build an extension. You could also build a 'cinema room', 'games room' 'gym', etc. as outbuildings, 5 metres away from it. And then when you come to operate the planning consent you've previously obtained, so long as you've designed things accordingly, when you knock down the original bungalow, the new extension and the outbuildings should find themselves incorporated into and part of the new home.

Satellite dishes
Satellite dishes have come in for special attention. In most areas, only one dish per house is permitted, it must not protrude above the highest part of the roof and, if fixed to a chimney, it must not exceed 450 mm or stick up higher than the chimney itself. In some counties the maximum size of any dish is 900 mm, while in most others it is 700 mm. In Conservation Areas, AONB, National Parks and the Broads, the dish must not be fixed to a chimney or positioned on a roof slope that fronts a road, public footpath or a waterway.

PDR restrictions
The term Original Dwelling is important for it harks back to 1 July 1948 when the Planning Acts first came into force in England & Wales and Scotland and to 1 October 1973 in Northern Ireland. For any dwelling constructed since that date, it refers to the original dwelling that was given planning permission. Any extensions undertaken since either 1 July 1948 or the original consent have the effect of soaking up the PDRs. In some circumstances the volume of other buildings that belong to the house, such as a garage or shed, will count against the volume allowances, even if built at the same time as the house or before 1 July 1948. These are where an extension comes within 5 metres of another building belonging to your house and where a building has been added to the property that is more than 10 cu. metres in volume and, again, closer than 5 metres to the house.

In addition if you live in a Conservation Area, a National Park, an AONB or the Broads, all additional buildings that are more than 10 cu. metres in volume, wherever they are on the plot in relation to the house, are treated as extensions of the house and reduce the allowance for further extensions. In all these cases, the volume of the buildings concerned is deducted from the volume limits given for the extension of your house.

Normal home maintenance, including re-roofing a house, so long as the roof profile is not altered, and external painting and decoration, unless of course there is a prohibitive planning condition, is allowed. In Conservation Areas, National Parks, AONB and the Broads you will need planning permission to alter the external appearance of a building or to clad it in stone, plastic, tile or timber and so on, but in all other areas there is no such restriction.

Northern Ireland In Northern Ireland, perhaps as precursor to forthcoming changes in England & Wales, PDR can be affected by the need for an Environmental Impact Assessment if the property to which they relate is in a sensitive area, a Site of Special Scientific Interest (SSSI), an ANOB, a National Park, a World Heritage Site or a specially protected area such as a nature reserve or bird sanctuary.

Scotland In Scotland the rights to an extension to an existing house that has not been previously extended are related to size with a limit of 24 sq. metres or 20 per cent of the floor area up to a maximum of 30 sq. metres. In a Conservation Area this is limited to 16 sq. metres or 10 per cent of the original floor area. Extensions must be no higher than the original ridgeline and must not be forward of the original building line. Porches are considered extensions.

Outbuildings of more than 4 sq. metres, closer than 5 metres to the house, are treated as enlargements to the home and will use up Permitted Development allowances. Equally, when considering the size of the house for the purposes of finding out what Permitted Development Rights are available, they can be included in the whole. New outbuildings must not cover more than 30 per cent of the garden.

Dormer windows do not come within PDRs in Scotland.

Demolition
Demolition is classed as Permitted Development, so long as the building to be demolished is not greater than 50 sq. metres, measured externally. If you intend to knock down an old or substandard dwelling and replace it with a new one, then you might be tempted to demolish it during the planning process, in order to save time. Be very careful! Once the old building is gone, there is technically nothing to replace. If the site is in green belt or in any situation where the planners would prefer that a house wasn't there, they could simply refuse what would be tantamount to a new dwelling. Never take the old building down until all the consents have been received.

If the building is listed you will need to apply for Listed Building consent if you want to demolish all or part of it. If it is in a Conservation Area, you will need Conservation Area consent to demolish a building with a volume that exceeds 115 cu. metres or any part of such a building. You will also need consent to demolish a wall, gate, fence or railing over 1 metre high adjoining a Highway (including a footpath or bridle-path) and over 2 metres high elsewhere.

Planning Appeals
If you receive a refusal of a planning application, you have three months in which to lodge an Appeal. You can also Appeal against failure by a local

authority to determine, or make a decision about, an application and against conditions on an approval. The entire Appeal process will probably take five to nine months.

Against a refusal

A written Appeal against a refusal starts off with your written submission explaining why the reasons for refusal are inappropriate. You do not have to set out why your application should have been granted. You must deal only with the reasons for refusal listed on the refusal certificate and explain how they are unreasonable. It will require considerable mental discipline to restrict your submission to this simple formula, but anything else you might want to write is irrelevant.

A copy of your opening broadside is sent to the local planning authority, which then has four weeks in which to produce its own written reply. If it does not respond within four weeks, then the Appeal carries on without the council having a say. It is quite amazing the number of times a local authority fails to reply and, instead, relies only upon the terms of its original rejection. Sometimes this is due to pressures of work, personnel change or holidays, or simply because the local authority has nothing to add to their original reasons for refusal. You will receive a copy of the council's written statement, and you have two weeks in which to submit your replies.

Following this exchange of statements there is a long pause – and then after some months you will receive a letter from the Planning Inspector saying that they propose to visit the site on such and such a date. The site visit is important. The local authority will be represented, and of course you will go along yourself, accompanied by any professionals working for you. You will be told that at the visit the inspector will not allow either party to make any further submissions, nor will they discuss written submissions. The inspector's purpose in visiting the site is simply to see the situation on the ground, and you, your agent and the Planning Officer are simply there to answer queries. With some inspectors this will take the form of fairly perfunctory questions such as, 'Is this the brick wall you will be removing in order to create the visibility splays?' But, with others, the conversation can widen out to a quite detailed discussion of each aspect of the Appeal that they identify.

It is important to realise that the Planning Inspector is in the driving seat. If you try to browbeat them and launch into a detailed speech about your application and why you feel that they should support you, you will be doing little other than harming your case. Respond to their questions quietly and get your points across within your replies. Stay close enough to the group as they walk around to be able to hear the answers given by the representative from the local authority so that, at an opportune moment, you can counter anything that you feel to be untrue. Avoid any display of enmity between yourself and any other representative, and at all costs avoid any direct argument with any other party. If any other representative gets angry remember that your very calmness contrasted with their anger is probably doing your case a lot of good. Above all, let the inspector make the running in much the same way as you would a judge in court and defer at all times to their conducting of the Appeal.

Finally, about a month after the site visit, you will receive the inspector's findings, and these are final. If you have won, the findings act as your planning consent. If you have lost, you must realise that you have come to

The 'guide' trusses go up as a template for the gable ends.

the end of the road with that application. Only if there is a major change in the local planning situation, or if a substantially different scheme is adopted, is any further planning application likely to be successful.

Against conditions on an approval
If there are conditions on an approval by the local authority that you feel are unfair or unreasonable, and the local authority refuses to vary or remove them, then you can appeal against the imposition of those conditions. Beware! The inspector will consider the whole of the application again; they can change other conditions that you had not previously objected to and they can impose new conditions! They can even reverse the local authority's decision altogether, although if they are thinking of doing so, you will be informed and given an opportunity to withdraw the appeal and stick with the local authority's original approval and conditions.

Against a failure to determine
An appeal against a local authority's failure to determine is all well and good on paper, but the reality is that most of them, faced with such an appeal, will move to determine the application prior to the appeal being conducted.

How to handle planners and a planning application

Your project is important to you. It is one of many for the planners. It helps to learn to speak their language.

Study the Local Development Plan/Local Development Framework
The Local Development Plan/Local Development Framework is the local authority's planning policy, containing all of its intentions regarding planning

in its area. They are lengthy documents, but if you want to find out specific policies or whether a piece of land is included or excluded within the settlement boundary and for what use the land in question is zoned, they are invaluable. Most can be viewed on line via the website of your local authority.

The Local Development Plan (LDP) is a five-year plan containing the Structure Plan, produced by the County Council to deal with strategic county issues, the Local Plan, prepared by each District Planning Authority, covering more detailed and site-specific policies, plus a Minerals and Waste Plan prepared by the County Council. Unitary authorities, where the local and county authorities are combined, have what is known as a Unitary Development Plan (UDP).

Scotland and Northern Ireland retain this five-year LDP, but in England and, to a lesser extent, in parts of Wales where there is no unitary authority, the Planning and Compulsory Purchase Act of 2004 scrapped the old system in favour of a new system of Local Development Frameworks (LDFs). These documents will contain the local authority's planning policies. Each local authority will prepare a Local Development Scheme (LDS), which must then be approved by the Secretary of State. It will specify which documents are to be Local Development Documents (LDDs) and what they will cover – effectively, a loose-leaf planning policy. Additionally the local authority's policies for development must include a Statement of Community Involvement (SCI) detailing how the public can be involved in plan preparation and decisions on planning applications. This SCI will once again require the Secretary of State's approval.

Not all authorities in England have changed to the new system as they are having difficulties in preparing their LDFs and getting them ratified. Some have reverted to the old-style plans and intend to keep them going for another two years (2010).

If your application goes against the local authority's adopted and approved policies, then the truth is that in most cases you are on a hiding to nothing. Before considering any application, find out just how your plot has been zoned and what the local authority's attitude to its development will be. Study the plans and follow the planning guidelines if you want to maximise your chances. Be aware that all policies can be interpreted in different ways, so be prepared to use the policies themselves to support your application.

Be prepared to compromise

Planning is law translated by opinion. Opinion can vary from authority to authority and, indeed, from officer to officer. If there is a personnel change during the course of an application then the outcome can be different. Remember that a Planning Officer has to juggle what you want with what he perceives to be the policy of the authority and the interests of neighbours and the environment. Remember, also, that what you want to achieve is your new home and if you need to make compromises to achieve that goal, then do so.

Keep tabs on progress

Too many applications are just made and then left to run their own course with little or no intervention or support. Keep tabs on just what stage your application has reached. If you do need to short-circuit something in order to speed things up, then do so. If you need to make changes, then by finding out about them in good time you will have time to effect them; if you need to reconsider of even pull out an application in order to re-group and avoid the stigma of a refusal, then do so.

Use the lobby

Lobbying is an important and long-established part of the political life of this country, and planning is basically a political process. It is perfectly legal to ask elected representatives for their support so long as there is no bribery involved. Lobby the parish councillors and ask your local district councillor for support. Ask them, also, for the names of the influential members of the planning committee and then lobby them for support. If you are so minded, ask your local MP for support. After all, come election day, they want you on side.

Avoid contentious proposals

Unless you are up for a crusade, it is always best to avoid a contentious application. If you must, then it is preferable to present anything unusual in as least contentious a way as possible. The easiest way to obtain planning permission is to make sure that an application contains all the established criteria for approval. Although a Planning Officer does have some discretion to make recommendations that are at variance with planning policy, this is highly unusual.

Consider the appropriate form of application

If the principle of whether there should be any kind of planning permission on the land is at stake then, in most cases, it makes no sense to try to force through a full application. In such a case it is often best to make a relatively cheap outline application and then to lobby and argue for its support. In cases where the principle is not at issue, it can be a waste of everybody's time and money to go through an application for both outline and Approval of Reserved Matters, and it is often best just to make a full application.

Ensure all drawings are clear and concise

Nothing is going to detract more from your application than unclear or unattractive drawings. Planning drawings do not have to be as detailed as those for Building Regulations and some artistic licence is allowed. Nevertheless, too much ambiguity will cloud the decision-making process. Try and ensure that drawings are attractive. You might think that you have been clever in producing drawings on your computer, but these amateurish efforts are unlikely to have the same impact as properly drawn-out plans.

'Softly softly catchee monkey'

Consider whether it might be a good idea to think in terms of a design that can evolve by extension. You can extend most properties under PDR. Although these can be removed or varied, if they are still in place, they can allow for things like an extension of up to 15 per cent of the volume of the house or 70 cu. metres, whichever is the greater, together with the construction of ancillary outbuildings and garages. If you feel that the planners might object to your full design aspirations then you might consider thinking in terms of starting with a smaller house that can be extended under these rules.

Think in terms of negotiating tactics

In some cases it can pay to make an application for a larger house than you would otherwise want and then substitute it for a smaller one that will then be more favourably considered. In other instances, it is possible to make separate applications for differing schemes that reflect well on the property you actually want to build. Developers often gain consent by negotiating trade-offs such as the setting aside of a playing field or the construction of a road in return for planning. If you can demonstrate a specific improvement to the immediate environment within your control then this can help.

Prepare a detailed photo dossier

Planners and conservation officers, although in positions of power, might well be quite new to an area and relatively unfamiliar with many of the local design details. In a meeting, if you can illustrate what you are aiming at by means of a detailed photo dossier of local architectural detail and features then you could have the edge. Consider also the preparation of an elevation plan showing the street scene. In some cases the use of a model can help. These are not cheap but they can be helpful in persuading a wavering committee, made up, essentially, of lay people, who might well be plan blind.

Consider an Appeal or the threat of one

All of the advice given is that an appeal should be the last resort and that, if at all possible, a negotiated solution should be sought. Appeals take a

With the gables in, the purlins have support. They, in turn, will support the rafters.

great deal of time and only about half of them are successful. However, they also take up a lot of the local authority's time, and officers are aware that they might lose control of a planning situation. In some cases where the officers recognise that they have a slim chance of having a refusal upheld, the gentle reminder that you are prepared to take an application through to Appeal can bring them back to the negotiating table.

Consider an independent report or the use of a planning consultant

In contentious cases it can pay to use a specialised planning consultant to argue your case. Make sure they have a good track record. Beware those who used to work for the local authority in question. They will feel that they have a better-than-average chance with their erstwhile colleges. They will not; in fact quite the reverse might be the case. In farming or rural-enterprise situations always back up any application with an independent report that details your full business proposals, financial expectations and future development plans. For an Appeals inquiry, consider the use of a barrister versed in planning law to present your case.

Don't lose your temper

Try not to get upset when dealing with officers and, whatever you do, don't lose your temper. There are panic buttons in many meetings rooms. Don't be the cause of their use. Whatever the popular conception, Planning Officers are rarely 'out to get you'; they are only doing their job, interpreting the rules and guidelines laid down by the local authority's planning policies. A weak Planning Officer who finds it difficult to say 'No' in face-to-face contact can be more trouble than one who tells you exactly what the local authority's position is regarding your application.

Consider engineering a deferral or site meeting

It is Planning Officers who negotiate an application and, in many cases, those same officers are delegated to determine it. Sometimes it may seem that they have set their minds against your application and that you are faced with them being both judge and jury. If your local councillor cannot arrange to have the application taken to the full committee, then engineer an objection, which will result in it doing so. If all does not go well at the committee meeting, see if that same councillor can arrange for a deferral to a site meeting, at which you will, more often than not, be invited to express your case.

Offer to accept conditions

If the planners fear that your application will be used as a Trojan Horse, you could consider offering to accept conditions within the consent. If you are planning accommodation for granny that they feel could be hived off as a separate dwelling, then you could allay their fears by offering to accept a condition within the consent or even a legal arrangement, known as a Section 106 Agreement, preventing this. Similarly, if you wish to include land outside the village envelope as garden land only, you can come to an agreement that is legally binding on you and your successors in title that it will not be built upon.

Get the neighbours on side

When a planning application is made, letters are sent out to interested parties, including your neighbours. Try and talk to them beforehand about your proposals and get them on side. Too many objections can sway a planning decision. If your neighbours express reservations, then try to take their concerns into account with your drawings and tell the planners that you have done so. Consult the Highways and Environment agencies, and make sure that you have conformed with all or as many of their requirements as possible and, if you can't, then prepare your arguments in advance as to why you don't need to do so.

Look for precedents
Many Planning Officers will tell you that they will not be held hostage to their own mistakes. Nevertheless, if you can show via a detailed dossier and photographic record that what you are proposing accords with other successful applications in your area, then they could find it difficult to argue against your proposals. If you have to go to Appeal, then while the Planning Officers might not consider what has gone before to be important, the Planning Inspector certainly will. In most cases an inspector will take note of any precedents that you quote and take time to visit them before coming to a site meeting.

Be prepared to go to the top
Just as you can go over the heads of the Planning Officers by enlisting the support of elected councillors, you can also go over the head of a case officer assigned to your planning application and request a meeting with the senior Planning Officer. If you feel that the junior is perhaps inexperienced or unfamiliar with your area, then this can be a good idea. It is not unknown for applications just to stall and for the applicant to feel that they are being stonewalled by the officers. Although there is provision to Appeal against non-determination, this is protracted, and you can often get things moving by talking to the chief executive of the authority.

Pick the professional with the best track record
Although employees of the local authority, such as Planning Officers and Building Inspectors, aren't allowed directly to recommend individuals or companies, it is, nevertheless, possible to glean names from them. They will probably give at least one and maybe more than three names, but if you listen carefully you can ascertain which are most in favour. Alternatively, look in the planning register for the names of those individuals or companies who are consistently successful. If you are using a package-deal company, enquire about their track record with your particular local authority.

Be aware of time-scales
For you, this project is of paramount importance and may well form the central pivot of your life. For the professionals and those in the local authority dealing with your application, it is one of many in their normal day-to-day job. Be aware of the time-scales involved in the preparation of plans and in their consideration. If the architect or designer needs more time to get it right then, within reason, let them have it. If the planners need longer to consider the application then they will request a time extension. In normal circumstances it makes no sense to deny them, as you could otherwise attract a refusal.

chapter six
▌Building

P lanning permission is subjective and governs whether you can build at all and, if so, what your new home will look like. Building Regulations consent, on the other hand, is objective and confines itself to the structural aspects of the build by reference to the regulations themselves. An application for approval under the Building Regulations either conforms to those regulations and is approved or fails to conform and is rejected – unless, in special circumstances, a relaxation can be negotiated.

What are Building Regulations?

Building Regulations cover the structural and safety aspects of any construction and draw together a mass of other health and environmental issues. They are set out in denominated parts (see table, 'Building Regulations in the UK' p. 98) that deal with each aspect of building. Scotland has the Scottish Building Standards listed in seven numbered documents, which do not directly compare with the

With the roof underfelted and battened, it's in the dry.

English/Welsh lettered equivalents. Northern Ireland has lettered sections that, once again, do not directly match those of other regions.

The regulations are changed from time to time, and it is the job of architects, designers and other professionals working within the industry to keep themselves up to date with those changes and to incorporate their requirements within any plans that they prepare or process. It is also their job, by inference, to make themselves as aware as possible of any impending changes to the legislation, of which they are usually warned in advance via published discussion papers and consultations.

If you want to read the regulations themselves then they are almost certainly available, probably with explanatory leaflets, on your local authority's website or on the government website www.communities.gov.uk. It is also a good idea to read the 'Standards' manual of the National House Building Council (NHBC) and/or Zurich Municipal's 'Technical Manual and Builder's Guidance Notes'. These are not the Building Regulations, but an expansion of them, and the explanatory detail and drawings within them are extremely helpful. By the way, trees are probably the major reason for trenches having to go deeper or other foundation systems being adopted; perhaps the best tables to determine the relationship between foundations and trees are to be found in these handbooks.

Building Regulations in the UK

England and Wales

Approved Document A	Structure
Approved Document B	Fire safety
Approved Document C	Site preparation and resistance to contamination and moisture
Approved Document D	Toxic substances
Approved Document E	Resistance to the passage of sound
Approved Document F	Ventilation
Approved Document G	Hygiene
Approved Document H	Drainage and waste disposal
Approved Document J	Combustion appliances and fuel storage systems
Approved Document K	Protection from falling, collision and impact
Approved Document L1	Conservation of fuel and power
Approved Document M	Access and facilities for disabled people
Approved Document N	Glazing – safety relating to impact, opening and cleaning
Approved Document P	Electrical safety

There is also an Approved Document to support Regulation 7 – materials and workmanship.

Scotland

Section 0	General: introduction, exemptions, changes of use, durability and workmanship, building standards and security of buildings
Section 1	Structure: introduction, structure and disproportionate collapse
Section 2	Fire: introduction, compartmentation and separation, structural protection, cavities, internal linings spread to neighbouring walls or buildings, means of escape, lighting and communication, fire-service access, water supply and facilities
Section 3	Environment – introduction, site preparation and protection, flooding, ground water and moisture, drainage, surface and waste water, precipitation, sanitary facilities, heating, ventilation, condensation, natural lighting combustion appliances, oil storage, solid waste storage
Section 4	Safety: introduction, access, stairs and ramps, protective barriers, electrical safety and fixtures, danger from accidents and heat, LPG storage
Section 5	Noise: introduction, resisting sound transmission to dwellings
Section 6	Energy: introduction, policy, building insulation envelope, heating system, insulation of pipes, ducts and vessels, commissioning building services, written information
Appendix A	Defines the terms
Appendix B	Lists the standards and other publications
Appendix C	Cross-references the new numbered regulations to the old lettered ones

Northern Ireland

Part A	Interpretation and general
Part B	Materials and workmanship
Part C	Preparation of site and resistance to moisture
Part D	Structure
Part E	Fire safety
Part F	Conservation of fuel and power
Part G	Sound insulation of dwellings
Part H	Stairs, ramps, guarding and protection from impact
Part J	Solid waste in buildings
Part K	Ventilation
Part L	Combustion appliances and fuel storage systems
Part N	Drainage
Part P	Sanitary appliances and unvented hot-water storage systems
Part R	Access to and use of buildings
Part V	Glazing

The regulations no longer contain tables of timber sizes and spans as these have been devolved to the Timber Research and Development Association (TRADA), and details can be viewed on their website, www.trada.co.uk. However, the NHBC and Zurich handbooks do contain tables that specify timber sizes in relation to the spans and purposes for which they are to be used.

Who administers the Building Regulations?

The Building Regulations are usually administered by the Building Control department of the local authority, which has a statutory obligation to enforce them and oversee their function within its boundaries. However, the government has also devolved the authority to inspect and certify compliance under the Building Regulations to other bodies, such as the NHBC. In addition it is open for architects with the appropriate Professional Indemnity insurance to register to carry out this work.

In most local authorities the Planning department and the Building Control department are situated in close proximity to each other and are usually lumped together as Technical Services. Make no mistake, though, these are separate departments operating and receiving their powers through and from completely separate Acts of Parliament. Although they can, and usually do, co-operate with each other, there is no certainty of this, and it is possible to fall between conflicting legislation and interpretations. Planning says you *may* build something – it does not say that you *can* build something. If you get express planning permission for something or it is implied that you have planning consent for, say, Permitted Development, then it does not absolve you from having to seek Building Regulations approval for that development, either expressly or, by implication, due to exemption.

In like manner, if you achieve Building Regulations consent for a structure, it does not mean that you can build it without planning permission, again, either expressly or implied. A porch, for example, may well be exempt from the Building Regulations in some circumstances, and in many locations its construction could take place under the Permitted Development Rights (PDR) laid down by the planning laws. In a Conservation Area those PDR could well be curtailed or removed, and the fact that the porch could be built under a Building Regulations exemption would do nothing to change that situation. See Chapter 5, for more on PDR.

Building Regulations approval

When is approval required?
You require Building Regulations approval if you intend to carry out any of the following works.

- Erect a new building or extend an existing building (unless it is covered by the list of exemptions below).
- Make structural alterations to a building, including underpinning.
- In certain cases, introduce a change of use.
- Provide, extend or alter drainage facilities.
- Install a heat-producing appliance (with the exception of gas

appliances installed by persons approved under the Gas Safety regulations (see p. 102).
· Install cavity insulation.
· Install an unvented hot-water storage system.
· Electrical works to domestic premises.

When is approval not required?

You do not need Building Regulations approval for any of the following works. However, if you are in any doubt, it is as well to contact the Building Control department for advice.

· Carry out certain very minor works to electric wiring.
· Replace a roof covering, so long as the same covering is used in the repair.
· Install new sanitary-ware, so long as it doesn't involve new drainage or plumbing arrangements.
· Carry out repairs as long as they are of a minor nature and replace like for like.

Exemptions

In addition to the exclusions listed above there are common types of building work that are exempt from the regulations:

· The erection of a detached single-storey building with a floor area of less than 30 sq. metres, so long as it does not contain any sleeping accommodation, no part of it is less than 1 metre from any boundary and it is constructed of non-combustible material.
· The erection of any detached building not exceeding 15 sq. metres, so long as there is no sleeping accommodation.
· The extension of a building by a ground-floor extension of (a) a conservatory, porch, covered yard or covered way, or (b) a carport open on a least two sides, so long as, in any of those cases, the floor area of the extension does not exceed 30 sq. metres. In the case of a conservatory or a wholly or partially glazed porch, the glazing has to satisfy the requirements of those parts of the Building Regulations dealing with glazing materials and protection.

You may still need planning permission for any of these works. If there is any doubt, you should consult the planning department of your local authority.

How to apply for Building Regulations

A Building Regulations application has to be accompanied by the necessary fees for the approval stages, after which the local authority has five weeks to process and determine the application. In practice, many applications cannot be determined within the statutory period and it has become almost commonplace for applications to be rejected several times, with each fresh, and happily free, application dealing with different points raised. Such a system, which often seems almost incredible to the lay person, would not have evolved were it not for two important points. Firstly, the legislation is worded such that it is necessary to have *made* an application for Building Regulations approval or issued a Building Notice prior to commencement of works; secondly, the fees for the necessary inspections stages are separated and, with a Full Plans or Building Notice application, payable *after* the issuing of an approval.

This means that, as long as 48 hours' notice in writing is given of your intention to start work on a site, following an application for Building Regulations approval or the issuing of a Building Notice, then there is nothing to stop you doing so. The building does, however, still have to be inspected and approved as it proceeds, and the Building Inspectors will, therefore, come along and inspect at the relevant stages. If they approve the work, you may then carry on to the next stage in the normal way. If they do not approve or cannot sanction what you are doing, then you have to stop until either the approval is granted or the necessary information is received that will allow them to agree to your continuing work.

Effectively, this means that although you will be advised that by working prior to the formal approval of the plans you are proceeding at risk, so long as you do not go beyond whatever the Building Inspector has agreed and approved on site, you aren't really in any different a position to anyone who does have Building Regulations approval. The essential rule is that nothing is built that fails to conform to the regulations and if, therefore, the inspector feels that the work is contrary to the regulations then, whether or not you have a formal approval, they will stop you and have legally enforceable powers to do so. Perhaps as many as 60 per cent of new self-build dwellings commence work without formal Building Regulations approval. In Scotland the approval is referred to as a Warrant, and there is no facility for making the application and then commencing work. An application for the building Warrant has to be made, and no work must commence until such time as it is granted.

'Competent persons' and Building Regulations

The principle of having to use 'competent persons' for certain works is becoming more and more integral to the Building Regulations, as the table detailing such works shows below.

Works that Require Building Regulations Approval to be Carried Out by Competent Persons

TYPE OF WORK	COMPETENT SCHEME TYPE
Installation of a heat-producing gas appliance	A person or an employee of a person who is a member of a class of persons approved in accordance with Regulation 3 of the Gas Safety (Installation & Use) Regulations 1998
Installation of a heating or hot-water service system connected to a heat-producing gas appliance or associated controls	A person registered by CORGI Services Limited in respect of that type of work

TYPE OF WORK	COMPETENT SCHEME TYPE
Installation of: • an oil-fired combustion appliance that has rated heat output of 100 kW or less and is installed in a building with no more than three storeys (excluding basement) or in a dwelling • oil-storage tanks and the pipes connecting them to the combustion appliances • heating and hot-water service systems connected to an oil-fired combustion appliance	A person registered by Oil Firing Technical Association Limited (OFTEC), NAPIT Certification Limited or Building Engineering Services Competence Accreditation Ltd (BESCA) in respect of that type of work
Installation of: • a solid-fuel-burning combustion appliance with a rated heat output of 50 kW or less, installed in a building with no more than three storeys (excluding basement) • heating and hot-water service systems connected to a solid-fuel burning combustion appliance	A person registered by HETAS Limited, NAPIT Certification Limited or Building Engineering Services Competence Accreditation Limited (BESCA) in respect of that type of work
Installation of a heating or hot-water service system or associated controls in a dwelling	A person registered by Building Engineering Services Accreditation Limited (BESCA) in respect of that type of work
Installation of a heating, hot-water service, mechanical ventilation or air-conditioning system or associated controls in a building other than a dwelling	A person registered by Building Engineering Services Accreditation Limited (BESCA) in respect of that type of work
Installation of an air-conditioning or ventilation system in an existing dwelling, which does not involve work on systems shared with other dwellings	A person registered by CORGI Services Limited or NAPIT Certification Limited in respect of that type of work
Installation of a commercial kitchen ventilation system that does not involve work on systems shared with parts of the building occupied separately	A person registered by CORGI Services Limited in respect of that type of work
Installation of a lighting system or electric heating system or associated electrical controls	A person registered by the Electrical Contractors Association (ECA) in respect of that type of work

TYPE OF WORK	COMPETENT SCHEME TYPE
Installation of fixed-low or extra-low voltage electrical installations	A person registered by BRE Certification Limited, British Standards Institution, ELECSA Limited, NICEIC Group Limited or NAPIT Certification Limited in respect of that type of work
Installation of fixed-low or extra-low voltage electrical installations as a necessary adjunct to or arising out of other work being carried out by the registered person	A person registered by CORGI Services Limited, NAPIT Certification Limited, NICEIC Group Limited or Oil Firing Technical Association (OFTEC) in respect of that type of work
Installation, as a replacement, of a window, roof light, roof window or door (being a door that has more than 50% of its internal face area glazed) in an existing building	A person registered under the Fenestration Self-Assessment Scheme by FENSA Ltd or by CERTASS Limited or the British Standards Institution (BSI) in respect of that type of work
Installation of a sanitary convenience, washing facility or bathroom in a dwelling, which does not involve work or shared underground drainage	A person registered by CORGI Services Limited or NAPIT Certification Limited in respect of that type of work

Inclusive access

The objective of Building Regulations on inclusive access is to make sure that entry is available and accessible for everyone, including disabled people, to the entrance storey, all habitable rooms in that storey and, most importantly, the toilet. These rules apply to all new dwellings and are covered by approved document M in England & Wales, section 4 in Scotland and part R in Northern Ireland.

Externally, the rules require that access ramps for slopes up to 1:15 should not be longer than 10 metres and those for gradients up to 1:10 no longer than 5 metres. Steeply sloping sites can, in the absence of a ramp, employ steps at least 900 mm wide with a rise no greater than 150 mm and a distance between landings of no more than 1800 mm. Additionally, if there are more than three risers, handrails must be provided to one side at least. However, the regulations require 'reasonable provision for disabled people to gain access to a building'. Building Inspectors are usually pragmatic people, and if a steeply sloping site made this interpretation impossible and threatened to render a site incapable of development, a reasonable solution can often be negotiated. This could entail the use of a lift, a spiral ramp or, in the final analysis, a complete relaxation on what would probably, and in any event, be a site that was never going to be suitable for disabled people.

The entrance door, and in certain other circumstances that can be another door other than the front entrance door, should have a clear opening width of at least 775 mm. It should also have a level sill, but if a step up into the dwelling is unavoidable then the rise should be no more than 150 mm. There should be free access and circulation within the entrance storey. The relationship between doorway widths and the approach passageway width is as follows:

Width of doorway, clear opening	Width of corridor/passageway
750 mm or more	900 mm when door approach is head on
750 mm	1200 mm when door approach is not head on
775 mm	1050 mm when door approach is not head on
800 mm	900 mm when door approach is not head on

There must be a WC compartment on the entrance storey. It is recognised that it is not always practicable for a wheelchair to be fully accommodated within the compartment. Access must, however, be as easy as possible, and the provisions are usually satisfied if the door to the compartment opens outwards with the wash-basin positioned so that it does not impede access. There is no stipulation on the wash-basin size.

Power sockets must be set no lower than 450 mm from the finished floor level. Light switches must be no higher than 1200 mm from the floor.

Electrical installations

In January 2005 a new section concerning electrical safety (approved document P) was added to Building Regulations in England & Wales, for the first time bringing electrical works to domestic premises and their ancillary accommodation into the Building Regulations. So far there are no dedicated sections on electrics in Scotland or Northern Ireland. Approved document P applies equally to buildings such as conservatories, porches, detached garages, sheds and greenhouses, where the construction or alteration of such a building would be exempt under all other parts of the regulations. It also applies to electrics installed on land associated with dwellings such as garden lighting, pond pumps and sewage-treatment plants.

If the electrical works are being carried out in conjunction with a new build, extension, conversion, material alteration or change of use of a building where a Full Plans application has been made, then the works will be covered and dealt with within the principal application. But to ensure compliance with the regulations, a copy of an electrical-installation certificate from a competent person must be provided to Building Control in order to obtain the Building Regulations Completion Certificate.

If works are being carried out only to the electrical system, then as long as they are carried out by a competent person registered with an approved document P self-certification scheme, no separate Building Regulations application needs be made so long as the self-certification certificate is provided to the customer and a copy forwarded to the authorities within 30 days. If the works are carried out by an unregistered electrician, who must be a competent person as defined in (ii) below, then, as well as making a separate Building Regulations application, they must provide a written statement that the works have been designed, installed and tested to ensure that they comply with BS7671 requirements for electrical installations.

A competent person is defined as either:

(i)   A competent person registered under an electrical self-certification scheme, or
(ii) A competent electrician who could be considered competent for the purposes of signing a BS7671 Electrical Installation Certificate but is not registered with an electrical self-certification scheme.

These definitions create grey areas but would almost certainly exclude a DIY self-builder and most general builders. This puts the onus on the Building Control department to inspect and legitimise the work and, quite frankly, most Building Control departments do not have the time or expertise. Some are accepting established but unregistered contractors as competent. Others, in the absence of qualified inspecting staff, are insisting that only registered contractors are employed. The various self-certification bodies and schemes are listed under Further Information on p. 206.

Bringing electrics into the regulations means that there is an interaction with other parts of the regulations and, in particular, approved document M. New buildings must obviously comply with the requirements for positioning of sockets and switches within the 450–1200 mm zones above

Internal studwork partitions come under '1st fix' carpentry.

floor level. Extensions to dwellings built after July 1999 must also comply with approved document M. Extensions to dwellings built before that date can either have the switches and sockets in conformation with approved document M or at the same heights as the existing, so long as access to them is not made worse. If an older house is being re-wired without removing the plaster it is considered reasonable that the sockets and switches should be put back in the same place as they were before. If a complete renovation is being undertaken with plaster removed, then, in most circumstances, the outlets should conform to the approved document M regulations.

For the frustrated DIY-er there are a few electrical works that need *not* be notified to the building-control bodies, although the requirements of approved document P still apply and the installation must comply with BS7671, a list of which follows.

- Replacing accessories such as socket outlets, control switches and ceiling roses.
- Replacing the cable for a single circuit only, where damaged, for example, by fire, rodents or impact.
- Re-fixing or replacing the enclosures of existing installation components.
- Providing mechanical protection to existing fixed installations.
- Adding lighting points (light fittings and switches) to an existing circuit, other than in a 'special location or installation'.
- Adding socket outlets and fused spurs to an existing ring or radial circuit, other than in a 'special location or installation'.
- Installing or upgrading main or supplementary equipotential bonding, other than in a 'special location or installation'.

A 'special location or installation' is defined as:

A kitchen
Locations containing a bathtub or shower basin
Swimming and paddling pools
Hot-air saunas
Electric floor or ceiling heating systems
Garden lighting or power installations
Solar photovoltaic (PV) power-supply systems
Small-scale generators such as microchip units
Extra-low voltage lighting installations, other than pre-assembled, CE marked lighting sets

There are, in addition, certain conditions imposed on the works that can be carried out without notification.

- Any replacement cable must have the same current-carrying capacity, follow the same route and not service more than one sub-circuit through a distribution board.
- The circuit's protective measures must be unaffected.
- Any increased thermal insulation must not affect the circuit's protective measures and its current-carrying capacity.
- The existing circuit protective device must be suitable and provide

protection for the modified circuit with all other relevant safety
provisions being satisfactory.
- All work must comply with other applicable legislation, such as the
Gas Safety (Installation and Use) Regulations.

Much consternation has been expressed in the media at the perceived
infringement of rights that this legislation entails. But in truth it was always
going to happen. Even where objections to these rules have been most
vociferous, it has always been policy never to encourage DIY electrics in
recognition of the fact that if you get your plumbing wrong, you'll get wet;
if you get the electrics wrong, you'll kill yourself or others. In the self-build
world, most who expressed an intention to carry out one or more of the
trades used to list electrics as the one they would do. There was never any
great saving, and the sense was that it was more for the sense of achievement than anything else.

Electrical energy efficiency

The Building Regulations also concern themselves with electrical energy
efficiency, stipulating that energy-efficient light fittings must be provided to
various rooms in accordance with the table below. The fittings must be
dedicated to the use of low-energy bulbs, which have a greater efficiency
of 40 lumens per circuit watt and must not accept screw or bayonet bulbs.

Rooms created	No. of energy-efficient light fittings reqd
1–3	1
4–6	2
7–9	3
10–12	4

External lighting fittings must either automatically extinguish when there is
enough daylight or when not required at night or else have sockets that only
accept bulbs or fittings with an efficiency of 40 lumens per circuit watt.

Conservation of fuel and energy

The increasing cost of fuel and modern awareness of environmental issues
have meant that insulation has become an increasingly important element
in the design and construction of new homes. However, insulation is just
one part of the whole equation that goes towards the energy requirements
for your new home. In April 2006 the regulations and requirements for
thermal insulation to new houses was beefed up in England & Wales by the
introduction of a new approved document L1 (Conservation of fuel and
power) and F (Ventilation) of the Building Regulations. These were
extended to Northern Ireland in the same year. Scotland followed in May
2007. The new regulations provide for an increase of at least 20 per cent
in the thermal efficiency of new buildings and of extensions and alterations
to existing buildings over the 2002 regulations. These changes are occasioned

by the need to comply with a European Directive, to which all EU governments have signed up.

The SAP (Standard Assessment Procedure) is the government's standard system for home energy rating. It estimates the space and hot-water heating costs per sq. metre of the floor area of a house (based upon such factors as its size, heating system, ventilation characteristics and standard assumptions such as occupancy and heating pattern) and converts it into a rating from 1 to 100. The higher the number, the lower the energy consumption. A SAP calculation is a requirement under approved document L1 of the Building Regulations for England & Wales, section 6 in Scotland and part F in Northern Ireland, and it is necessary for one to be provided before a Completion Certificate is issued. The SAP scales have been revised to a scale of 1–100, where 100 will represent a zero energy cost. Each element of the building's fabric will also have to conform to minimum U values (the heat loss in watts for every sq. metre of any material in relation to each degree of temperature difference between the inside and the outside – the lower the figure, the better) with an avoidance of thermal bridging plus certain levels of air tightness. The design will be required to balance window sizes with orientation and the achievement of maximum solar gain.

Although elemental U values are used in the calculations, they cannot be the sole method of compliance with the Building Regulations for new dwellings. Instead a system of calculations measures the target CO_2 (carbon dioxide) emission rates for all buildings to give a Target Emission Rate (TER) based on a notional building of the same size and shape, constructed according to the reference values set out in the government's Standard Assessment Procedure (SAP, 2005), taking into account the choice of fuel to be used.

To comply with the regulations additional calculations, based on the actual design elements of the new home must be carried out in order to arrive at the proposed Dwelling CO_2 Emission Rate (DER). This DER must be no worse than, and hopefully better than, the TER. In the main these calculations will need to be carried out by a competent person possessing the correct software, who will also provide the local authority with the SAP value of the proposed dwelling. You can see for yourself how changes to the specification and to the U values of the various elements that go into a building affect the DER and SAP values by visiting www.playtheregs.com.

External lighting must meet set standards with a maximum power of 150W per luminaire, and either sockets that can only be used with low-energy bulbs or a Passive Infrared (PIR) system that automatically turns them off after a short period.

Extensions to existing dwellings must comply with certain target U values:

External walls	*0.30*
Concrete ground floors	*0.22*
Suspended timber floors	*0.22*
Ceiling joists to a cold roof void	*0.16*
Pitched warm roof	*0.20*
Flat roof	*0.20*
Glazing (timber or plastic)	*1.8*

Renovations or upgrades to the thermal elements of an existing house and changes of use must conform to the U values set out below:

Cavity walls	*0.55*
Other wall types	*0.35*
Ground floors	*0.25*
Ceiling joists to a cold roof void	*0.16*
Pitched warm roof	*0.20*
Flat roof	*0.25*
Replacement windows	*2.0*

These requirements may be reduced if their implementation is uneconomical, affects the historical integrity of the building or reduces the floor area by more than 5 per cent.

Ventilation
The regulations also contain a tightening up of approved document F, dealing with ventilation. This requires that homes should be airtight; it should be demonstrated that there is no air leakage. For those building a single new home, there is a get-out clause to the requirement to demonstrate air tightness in new homes, so long as the Robust Details needed in order to comply with approved document L1 are used.

Heating and hot water
Since April 2005 all new gas boilers, whether installed in a new home or as a replacement, have had to achieve a SEDBUK rating of A (90 per cent efficiency and upwards) or B (86–90 per cent). In January 2006 oil boilers installed in new homes had to achieve the same ratings; in April 2007 this extended to replacement oil boilers. You can view the ratings of any boilers by logging on to the website www.sedbuk.com and selecting the type of boiler about which you are enquiring. Certificates will have to be signed confirming that the heating and hot-water systems have been properly commissioned, and all these details, together with all operating instructions, SAP ratings and the building's energy performance certificate must be available within a Home Information Pack (HIP).

LZC technologies
The government will not be prescribing the use of solar panels or other low- and zero-carbon (LZC) technologies, such as wind generators, heat pumps and wood-pellet stoves. However, the revisions to approved document L1 will, it is hoped, raise performance standards to a level that will provide a strong incentive to designers, taken alongside the various grants available, to consider these systems.

Existing dwellings
Apart from the issue of boilers, the government has brought in no new legislation requiring existing properties below 1000 sq. metres to be made more thermally efficient. However, they do have obligations under the European Directive on the Energy Performance of Buildings to bring in these and other changes, and it is quite likely that they will revisit the idea. The Sustainable and Secure Buildings Act 2004 enables the Building Regulations to be used to improve the energy performance of existing dwellings, and these powers could be used at any time when it is considered politically acceptable to do so.

The requirement under the Directive for all buildings that are built, sold or rented out to have a certificate detailing their energy performance, including a summary on just how that performance could be improved, came into force in August 2007 with the introduction of Home Information Packs.

Types of insulation

Mineral wool or fibreglass can be used in suspended ground and first floors, in walls and in roofs and ceilings. Rigid foam boards made from expanded polystyrene, extruded polystyrene and polyurethane can be used above and below solid ground and first floors, in cavity walls and with pitched and flat roofs. Cellulose fibre made from recycled newspaper and sheep's wool can also be utilised, specially blown into cavities. Radiant heat barriers, a blanket of mineral wool within shiny, reflective outer sheets have had their accreditation withdrawn. They may get it back, but until they do it is best to give them a miss. There are also many products on the market to prevent 'cold bridging' (the passing of heat from a warm structural element to a cold one) and to close and insulate cavities around windows and door openings.

Active solar power/green energy

Increasing emphasis is being placed on the harnessing of natural energy, expressed in terms of direct solar energy, wind and wave power and the latent heat of the earth, water and air. Photovoltaic (PV) cells and wind turbines are used in the production of electricity, and solar panels can be used for the production of domestic hot water. But there are other forms of geothermal harvesting, the first of which is the use of a heat pump to extract the latent heat from the air, a water source or the ground. The government does not yet recognise the value of the first two within the grants, but it is quite keen on the idea of ground-source heat pumps. These work using a series of coolant-filled coils or 'slinkies' laid within the ground, and effectively the heat pump acts like a refrigerator in reverse, extracting the low-grade latent heat from the ground and upgrading it for use in the home. They are very expensive, and even with the grants that are available you are talking in terms of £8500–£10,000 for what is essentially the firing source, as against £1500 for an all-singing all-dancing condensing oil boiler. They also rely on electricity (essentially they are an electric central-heating system) and are therefore hostage to electricity prices with a payback of around 10–15 years.

Bio-mass, or the burning of renewable fuels, is becoming increasingly popular as it is 'carbon neutral', that is, the carbon released during its combustion is equalled by the carbon that is soaked up in its growth. The fuel is usually wood pellets, but some boilers can handle diverse materials such as grain. Most of the boilers have an augur and hopper system, so that they are semi-automatic. This does of course require quite a bit of space. The cost of the pellets equates to more or less the same price as oil, but the capital and installation costs are around £5000–£8000 dearer.

While many of the systems available to harness 'free' energy cannot, at the moment, claim to be economically viable, their time will obviously come. In an effort to increase their take-up, the governments have introduced grants. In England and Wales, these are administered by the Energy Saving Trust under low carbon buildings programme of the Department of Trade and Industry (DTI) (www.est.org.uk/housingbuildings/funding/lowcarbonbuildings). In Scotland the grants are administered through www.est.org.uk/schri and in Northern Ireland you will need to contact www.niesmart.co.uk.

The levels of grant are constantly changing and the take-up for each trench of available grant is always oversubscribed. To qualify for a grant, systems must be approved within the schemes and be installed by an installer who is approved by and registered with the scheme.

Even with these grants, there is still a long payback time for many of these 'green' systems, and if you are looking for immediate savings then you're bound to be disappointed. The trouble is that the capital costs are too high at the moment, and the grants don't seem to be doing anything to bring them down. In fact they may even be sustaining them.

Ventilation

Ventilation is important to provide both fresh air and prevent condensation. The Building Regulations require that there should be extractor fans or passive stack ventilation (PSV) in all kitchens and bathrooms. With PSV, air is drawn out of the house, without the need for electric fans, through a combination of the effect of the air flowing over the roof and the natural buoyancy of the warm, moist air. In order to prevent over-ventilation, humidity-controlled dampers can be fitted, which need no electrical connection. Permanent ventilation must also be provided to all other rooms using trickle vents that are fitted to all windows.

Mechanical ventilation with or without heat recovery may offer benefits such as filtered air and reduced noise intrusion. The systems use fans to supply fresh air and extract stale air in a very controlled manner. The heat-recovery options recover much of the heat from the extracted air and add it to the returning air using a heat exchanger, so that the two air streams do not mix. Filters can be fitted to the supply air to remove dust and pollen and they can, therefore, provide very good quality air. There is no need for trickle ventilation with such a system, and this may be an important factor in reducing the noise from outside in certain locations. Mechanical ventilation will not work properly unless the house is well sealed, and sealing of the house can only really be done at the construction stage, involving very close attention to detail and a close watch on workmanship. Unfortunately, open fireplaces are incompatible with these systems. The running costs are also significant and may outweigh the energy saved, so, while they will provide good ventilation and good quality air, they should not generally be seen as an energy-saving or -efficient feature.

Roofs

Cold roof voids need to be ventilated to prevent condensation. With a pitched roof where the insulation is at ceiling joist level there is a requirement that there should be ventilation at the soffit level equivalent to a continuous gap of 10 mm with ridge-level ventilation equivalent to a 5 mm continuous gap. Where there are rooms in the roof, there must also be ventilation at soffit and ridge levels with a 50 mm continuous air gap between the insulation following the rafters and the underside of the sarking. Effectively, this

Starting electrical first fix or carcassing.

means that the insulation at this point must be either rigid foam slab or a radiant heat barrier type.

Flat roofs should really be of the 'warm deck' type, where the insulation is on top of the decking with no requirement for ventilation beneath. Cold-deck roofs are still allowed but much frowned upon. It is necessary to maintain a 50 mm space above the insulation and to make sure that this space is adequately ventilated. They are not allowed in Scotland.

Soffit and eaves ventilation may be omitted if a 'breathable' underfelt is used beneath the tiles or slates.

Trees

The Building Regulations and all of the warranty providers will be concerned about the presence of trees on site as they can affect the foundations of houses in the following three ways:

- The roots may push into or invade the foundation brickwork and crack it.
- Roots can rot, leaving voids under the foundations when the tree is felled.
- In clay soils, when a tree is felled and no longer takes hundreds of gallons of water out of the subsoil, the ground may heave and rise.

The minimum distance between a new house and a tree depends on the species of tree, potential height and the nature of the ground. There are strict rules for this, and they are, most conveniently, set out in the NHBC handbook. As a rule of thumb it is unwise to build closer to a tree than 4 metres or one-third of its mature height, whichever is the greater. On some soils this distance may be increased, and with tree species particularly harmful to buildings, such as poplar, elm and willow, the distances may be quite considerable.

Sewage and drainage

Where there is no mains drainage the disposal of sewage comes down to three main methods. The Environment Agency, often using the local authority as its agent, has strict guidelines regarding the disposal of sewage effluent into the subsoil or a watercourse. Often the method of sewage disposal is determined by a percolation test, which determines the porosity of the ground and the water-table.

Disposal of sewage

Septic tanks These are miniature sewage works that require no external power, involve no pumps and house millions of friendly bacteria that break down the sewage into non-sterile effluent, which is discharged into the ground via a system of land or weeper drains. Septic tanks are quite small, requiring a hole about 2.5 metres across and 3 metres deep, and they can cost under £500. They are easily installed. They need to be pumped out by a small sludge tanker once or twice a year, at a cost of just under £100 a time, and all that you see of them, above ground, is the manhole, which gives access to the interior. New and innovative versions that increase aeration and speed up the bacteriological process are coming on to the market all the time. The prices are obviously higher, but the principles remain essentially the same.

A septic tank relies on the fact that its final effluent will be discharged into the subsoil. That's why the percolation test is so important. If the subsoil is of an impermeable nature, such as heavy clay, or the water-table is too high, then the effluent will not be able to get away, and it will back up into the tank and stop the entire process.

If the ground conditions are not quite right or there is a requirement for extra refinement of the effluent because of, say, proximity to a watercourse, then the authorities may require that a septic tank discharges into a filter bed of some sort before the effluent is then passed on down the weeper drains.

Mini treatment plants A mini treatment plant works like a septic tank insofar as it receives raw effluent and then processes it into a sterile effluent that can again be passed into the ground. Where it differs considerably is the fact that it is electrically powered and the quality of the effluent is such that, while it is not exactly drinking water, it is often good enough to be discharged into a ditch, stream or other watercourse. In certain circumstances this can happen as a direct discharge but, more often, it is effected through either weeper drains or a filter bed of some sort. Whereas a septic tank utilises mainly anaerobic bacteria (those that live without oxygen), the mini treatment plant utilises both these and the aerobic bacteria (those that live in the presence of oxygen) to break down and neutralise the sewage. This is effected by either a paddle or turbine system alternatively exposing the effluent to air and water, while all the time passing it through towards the outlet or by the introduction of a stream of air to the settling effluent. The merits of each type of machine will be trumpeted by the various manufacturers, but the essential factor is not how they work, but the quality of the treated effluent. The prime cost of one of these units for a single house is in the region of £3000, and they may also have to have the sludge pumped out more often. In addition they do require a power source and regular maintenance.

Cesspools A cesspool is simply a great big tank that holds the raw sewage until a vehicle comes to pump it out and take it away. If the ground isn't suitable or the plot is in a built-up area, where mains drainage is either not available at all or is available but any further connections are banned until such time as either the drains themselves have been upgraded or the local sewage-treatment plant has extra capacity, then this is the third option. The normal size of a tank for a single dwelling is 18,000 litres; it has to be emptied quite frequently at a cost of up to £250.

A modern fibreglass cesspool will cost about £3000, and the cost of the excavation and installation may be significant. A cesspool is the solution of last choice, and many of the factors that make the use of a cesspool necessary, such as waterlogged or rocky ground, are also the factors that tend to increase the cost of its installation.

Sloping sites

A sloping site may involve extra costs with drainage and sewers, though not necessarily. If your site slopes down from a road in which the sewer is fairly shallow then you may have to think of using a pumped sewage system. This can add at least £2000 to the drainage costs but, having said that, there may be a corresponding saving due to the fact that the 50-mm flexible pipe may well be cheaper to lay than conventional drains. If your site slopes down from the road, within which the sewer is quite deep, then the slope may actually represent a saving in cost as the resulting house drainage will not have to be as deep.

Sites that slope up from the road and sewer may seem more attractive so far as drainage is concerned. But if the slope is too steep then it might be necessary to install tumble bays within the manholes in order to slow off the fall so that the effluent can enter the sewer at a reasonable rate.

Surface water

Most authorities will not allow surface water or rain-water to discharge into the public sewers and require on-site soakaways. In heavy clay these may not work, and you may have to use a combination of filter beds or concrete ring sections with a pump to lift the water into the vegetable zone. A lawn constructed on a gravel or stone bed can then be employed to percolate and soak up the water. Alternatively, one of the rain-water harvesting systems can be utilised, meaning that a large quantity of surface water, once used within the home, can be disposed of through the foul drains.

Precautions need to be taken to ensure that surface water does not flow on to the road. Where a site slopes away from the road it may be necessary to install a drainage channel.

Grey-water systems

Grey-water systems are coming on to the market, whereby the less harm-ful waste water from baths and wash-basins can be recycled for use in flushing toilets. While that may not seem much, there are estimates that up to one-third of domestic water usage is involved in flushing the toilets. The water is of course filtered and does require chemical dosage from time to time, and there is, therefore, no question of nasty soapy water coming out of the cistern. The tanks used for grey-water recycling are fairly small. They are probably not cost-effective in strict cash terms at the moment.

Composting toilets

Old-fashioned chemical toilets are not acceptable under current regulations, but composting toilets in one form or another have been around for some time, and they can be. The toilets that do not use water to flush and require shovels of sawdust to be sprinkled over each deposit do not bear thinking about or discussion. Of more interest, but still only for the hardy few who cannot connect to the main sewer, are the centrifugal systems. In these the toilet is flushed in the normal way and as the effluent descends the down-pipe to a basement, it is whirled around in such a way that the water and the solids are separated. The grey water is taken to a soakaway, and the solids fall into a composting bin that is shovelled out and put on the garden every so often. Not everyone's cup of tea, but useful in certain circumstances.

Reed beds and ponds

Reed beds and ponds can soak up and neutralise an extraordinary amount of effluent and, space permitting, a reed bed can often solve a problem with effluent quality. In some cases a septic tank can discharge, probably with the aid of a pump, on to a series of flat reed beds and in others an even more satisfactory system can be devised using floating beds of reeds growing on mats. With a series of baffles such a system can return perfectly good water to the environment and at the same time provide a magnificent habitat for all forms of waterlife. The drawback is that most self-build plots simply don't have the space for such enterprise.

Rain-water harvesting

Rain-water harvesting can be used for things like flushing toilets and for washing machines in order to save on water charges. Rain-water harvesting to provide drinking water is not quite so common but is possible. It relies on having a large enough roof-collecting area with the water being stored in an above- or below-ground tank before being pumped up to a header tank. Rain-water is actually less prone to pollution than ground water, but it will still need filtration or treatment to satisfy the authorities.

Siting of storage tanks

Oil tanks

Oil tanks below 3500 litres do not need a bund or retaining wall unless they are within 10 metres of a watercourse. They must also be stood on a hard surface. However, if they are situated closer than 1800 mm to the wall of a building, you must either provide a fire wall or make certain that the affected wall has a 30-minute fire resistance. If they are sited less than 760 mm from a boundary, you will have to provide a 30-minute fire wall at least 300 mm higher and wider than the top and sides of the tank.

LPG tanks

The regulations governing the siting of an LPG (liquefied petroleum gas) tank are somewhat more complicated, but they boil down to the fact that a 1.1-tonne capacity tank must usually be sited at least 3 metres from the wall of a building or boundary. This is reduced to 2 metres if there is an inter-vening 30-minute fire wall sited 1–1.5 metres from the tank, at least the height of the pressure-relief valve and wide enough such that the shortest path from the tank to the house remains 3 metres. It can be further reduced to 1.5 metres if the wall of the building is constructed as a 60-minute fire wall in an inverted T. At the ground floor, and as high as the pressure-relief valve, this wall should be wide enough such that the distance from the end of the tank remains 3 metres with any openings a further 1 metre away. Above this level the fire wall should extend at least 1 metre either side of the pressure-relief valve with any openings a further 1 metre away.

The provider companies renting out the LPG tanks and the oil supply companies have rules regarding the siting of tanks and distances from the carriageway.

Construction methods

All construction techniques for house building in the UK have to conform to Building Regulations, to the thermal and structural requirements within those regulations and those imposed by the warranty providers. In the UK most homes are built with brick and block; in Scotland, however, the majority, both within and outside the self-build market, are built using a timber frame with a significant proportion still built using brick and block.

This may well change quite rapidly. Severe skill shortages mean that more people and companies are looking longingly towards the concept of greater off-site prefabrication. New systems of building and cladding are being introduced to the market, and many within the self-building industry see prefabrication as the future. They may well be disappointed. Self-builders are an experimental lot. Many of the innovations that have become standard items in building technology, such as underfloor central heating and thermal stores, were first tried out and accepted within the self-build market. Many of the newer methods of construction really exist only within the self-build market. But self-builders are also an anarchic bunch. Most have decided that they don't want to have a house or design that somebody else has devised. They want to feel that the choices have all been their own, even if, in the end, those choices lead them to building a house that is indistinguishable from the very houses they originally purported to despise. If they feel that they are being corralled into some kind of conformity, they may well walk away.

The various methods of construction that you are most likely to come across are traditional masonry (brick and block), timber frame, green oak framing, structurally insulated panels (SIPs), insulated concrete formwork (ICF), steel framing and thin-joint masonry.

Traditional masonry (brick and block)
Most modern masonry construction is built as a cavity wall consisting of an outer facing or cladding leaf, a cavity that usually contains some form of insulation and an inner leaf of blockwork.

The outer leaf can be brick, stone or blockwork. If it is blockwork then it is usual for this to be harled or rendered, but it may sometimes be clad with either timber or uPVC. This outer leaf is not loadbearing, although it does provide much of the stability for the wall as it is tied to the inner leaf with stainless-steel or galvanised wall ties.

The cavity was originally devised to prevent damp crossing through the wall into the interior of the building. Nowadays it is used to provide much

Putting in the stair-case means that access to the upper levels is much easier. It will, however, need some protection.

of the insulation for the walling. Full-fill cavity insulation uses mineral or glass-fibre wool batts that are built into the cavity as work progresses. The wider the cavity, the more insulation, the greater the thermal efficiency. Partial-fill insulation is used in high-exposure situations, where it is advisable or necessary to maintain a clear cavity. This form of insulation uses dense and rigid foam boards that are held against the inside edge of the inner leaf of the wall by means of special clips on the wall ties.

The inner leaf of the wall is constructed using blocks. These can be either dense aggregate blocks, which have a high load-bearing capability but a low thermal rating, or lightweight aggregate blocks, which have a much higher thermal efficiency but are not quite as strong. The inner leaf of the cavity wall supports the main loadings and takes the roof weight.

Openings within the walls have to have lintels above them to support the upper brick and blockwork. These lintels are usually steel and either contain insulation or allow the normal cavity-wall insulation to be maintained over the gap so as to avoid cold spots or 'cold bridging'. The bridge in the cavity, down the side of each reveal, is insulated using a cavity closer that also prevents damp crossing the cavity.

Masonry walls are strong enough to support beam-and-block or concrete suspended floors at first and other floor levels.

Timber frame
Most of the timber-frame companies that you are likely to come across are also package-deal companies, though such companies provide much

more than just a timber frame. They usually offer help and support in choosing and buying land. They can assist with design and often have standard designs to offer, and they will usually undertake to make and prosecute the planning and Building Regulations (Warrant)] applications. In addition they will often help with the finding of builders and sub-contractors, and generally be on hand to provide support and assistance during the build. The client pays for this service in the mark-up on the timber frame and erection. Most times they get value for money and having a company literally to hold their hand means the difference between being able to self-build or not.

There are other timber-frame manufacturers who work within the self-build industry, providing and erecting timber frames for private clients. They do not offer the services of the package-deal companies, they do not 'hold hands' or help with planning and, instead, they simply take the plans that the self-builder's architect has drawn and produce a manufactured product to suit. They will, however, help in the provision of calculations and information necessary to obtain Building Regulation (Warrant) approval. Naturally, their prices are considerably cheaper than the package-deal companies, some of whom, in any event, buy from them and simply 'brass plate' the items.

The various forms of timber frame include open panel, closed panel and aisle frame.

Open panel The panels are made up in the factory from treated softwood studs or framing, over which a structural material or sheathing is fixed to give the frame 'racking' strength or stability. A vapour-permeable but waterproof breather membrane is fixed to the outside face of this sheath-ing. A soleplate is fixed to the oversite, and the panels are erected on to this with the sheathing and membrane to the outside. The panels are fixed together, and if there is an upper floor the flooring or decking is put down before the upper-part panels are erected and the trusses put on top. The panels are open on the inside, hence the name.

In this form of timber frame, as with most others, the frame usually becomes the inside leaf of a cavity wall with the outside leaf being constructed in brick, block or stone, tied to the inner leaf with special ties. The timber frame bears the main loads and the roof loads. The cavity is always kept clear.

Windows and door-frames are fitted on site, and once the roof is tiled and the electrical and plumbing carcass has been completed, the gaps between the studs are packed with insulation. A vapour-proof barrier is then tacked up before the plasterboard is fixed.

Closed panel This is similar to open panel, except that much more is done in the factory and the panels are delivered to site in a more finished form with the insulation already in place, the windows and doors fixed and all ducting in for services. The Scandinavian companies use this method where much more work is devolved from the site to the factory floor.

Aisle frame Essentially, this uses the same open panels as for a normal timber frame, but here a massive timber skeleton takes all of the main loads and the roof load, leaving the panels free to act independently. It can be used with an outside cladding skin or left as a single skin that is rendered to receive timber plants.

Green oak framing

This is Middle Ages technology brought into the modern age. Although often included within the various methods of timber-frame construction, it does really stand alone. Huge oak timbers are cut, planed and shaped to form a massive skeletal frame, held together with mortise-and-tenon joints and dowels. The gaps between the frame are then filled with urethane panels, made waterproof by a complicated system of perimeter trims and water bars before being rendered. The huge oak timbers are exposed both inside and outside, making this a single-skin form of construction.

This method of building can also be employed as an internal skin with external cladding either as a separate leaf or fixed to the frame.

Structurally insulated panels (SIPs)

This construction material is formed by bonding rigid foam insulation between two sheets of structural boarding in a sandwich. The result is light, strong panels that can be used either as walling or roofing in their own right or in combination with other systems. They can have openings cut into them for doors and windows.

Insulated concrete formwork (ICF)

This method of building uses hollow polystyrene blocks that fit together rather like a giant Lego set. The blocks are then filled with concrete, often with reinforcement bars running through the structure. In some ways it is similar to the concrete formwork that is put up to make motorway bridges except that here the formwork is left as the insulant for the wall. The filled blocks can be rendered on the outside and plastered on the inside.

ICF seems deceptively simple, and many self-builders are attracted to it by the thought that they can do it themselves. It is, however, very complicated – the work of pouring is a skill in its own right – and it is not cheap.

Steel framing

Steel-framed buildings follow almost exactly the same principles as the main methods of timber framing. It is expensive but with new lightweight C-sections that can easily be cut to size it could become more popular. If it doesn't catch on for 'whole-house' construction, there could still be a use for this system in internal partitioning.

Thin-joint masonry

Thin-joint blocks are highly engineered lightweight aggregate blocks that are glued together with a special adhesive rather than being laid with a thick mortar bed. These blocks can be used as a traditional cavity wall or, in thicker section, as a single-skin construction. Their advantage is that they can be laid very fast without the need to wait until lower levels have 'gone off', and the speeds with which experienced labour are able to build with them can rival timber frame. Take-up has not been huge, mainly due to the fact that the 'bricklayers' have to have special training in the use of these blocks, and many are reluctant to take the time off or spend the money to attend the courses.

chapter seven

How to Work with Builders & Subcontractors

I t is not easy choosing a builder or subcontractor, and it is made all the more alarming by all the horror stories featured in the media. Can you trust this man or that company? Are they going to do all that they say? They may be nice as pie when they are trying to get the job, but how will they behave when you have made your choice and are more or less stuck with them? Although this chapter is divided between builders and subcontractors, it is as well to read both sections because many of the recommendations, descriptions and traits apply to both. Equally, if you want to know exactly who does what in the building trade, so you are aware of exactly what to expect, see Chapter 11, Costs, Cashflow and Who Does What, for how building work is generally allocated among the trades during the building of a typical house.

How to find a builder

Builders are only as good as their last job. There is nothing you can do to make sure of the quality of their next job other than look at their track record. However you find your builders, before you contract with them, do some research on their previous clients and work. Go and see the work. Study it carefully to look for obvious faults. Talk to the clients and find out if they did what they promised, whether they came in on budget or if there were massive extras.

Contact the local NHBC or Warranty Inspector when you register your property and ask them for their opinion of your impending choice. Do the same with the Building Inspector. Strictly speaking, they are not allowed to pass comment, but there are ways of letting you know how they feel and forewarned is forearmed.

The various ways to find the names of builders in your area include via trade associations, the *Yellow Pages* and local newspapers and Internet sites as well as generally asking around.

Trade associations
A builder's membership or listing with a warranty provider should give some indication of a certain standard of workmanship because the warranty company is taking it upon itself to police its work. The best known of the warranty providers are of course the NHBC and Zurich Municipal, but the Federation of Master Builders also has a warranty scheme. The NHBC publishes its membership lists on its website (www.nhbc.co.uk), but the details it gives are sketchy, useful for checking if membership is current but little else. The Federation of Master Builders

also publishes details on its website (www.fmb.org.uk). Zurich Municipal on the other hand, does not. It is worth emphasising that membership is a good clue to performance and ability, but it is not a total guarantee. While the warranty company will be there to pick up some of the pieces if it all goes wrong, it will still involve you in a good deal of heartache and worry. So don't forget to make all of the advised checks.

The Yellow Pages and local papers
A quick scan through the classified sections of your local paper or the *Yellow Pages* may well reveal the names of local builders and tradesmen offering their services. There is little to be gleaned from these apart from the names and the fact that they are there is no guarantee of their probity. Avoid, or at the very least be suspicious of, those with mobile telephone numbers only and no indication of permanent address. Display advertisements, however, can be some indication of permanence; something that is a small, but not conclusive, clue to their abilities. Whatever you do, make all of the normal checks and track back to previous clients and work.

Internet websites
A number of companies have tried yet failed to provide a comprehensive on-line register of builders and tradespeople. The problem has always been the transient nature of those participating in the building industry and the way that partnerships continually form, break up and re-form under different names. The companies that are left within this section are those whose lists are based on slightly different criteria.

The yell website, www.yell.com, has lists of various trades, including builders and professionals working within the industry, but it is little more than an extension of the *Yellow Pages*, with no recommendations or information other than that which the companies themselves provide. HomePro (www.homepro.com) has lists of builders and tradespeople by postcode and discipline. They all have to pay an annual fee in order to appear in the lists, and there are quite stringent reference requirements with subsequent monitoring and rating. Members are encouraged to offer an insurance-backed guarantee, covering the work, loss of deposits and the possibility of the company going out of business. www.house.co.uk is a site run by British Gas with the assistance of HomePro. It gives similar information including a rating system and a brief résumé of the company's legal and credit history. BuildStore (www.buildstore.co.uk) has a Trades Referral Service that provides the names of various contractors and tradesmen together with details of on-site services including project co-ordination and insurance-backed guarantees. The lists are based on details provided by the major site and employment insurers, augmented by approved and vetted applicants.

TrustMark (www.trustmark.org.uk) is a scheme that is backed by the government. When you log on to this site you are directed to the site for the Federation of Master Builders. It claims to be the only scheme of its kind, enjoying the support of government, industry, consumer groups, local authorities and trading standards. There are, however, very few names on this site.

Asking around
The first and best place to ask for builders' names is on the building site of another self-builder. These are usually, but not always, recognisable by the

presence of a mobile home. Other self-builders can provide a wealth of information on the best architects, the best merchants and, of course, the best builders or tradespeople. They will be able to advise you about their costs and on how helpful and reliable they were, and report back, above all, on the quality of their work.

Building sites in general are a good source of names. Be careful not to infringe Health & Safety legislation, but talking to site operatives can be beneficial. Be aware that it is never a good idea to try to get a recommendation from a tradesperson within their own discipline; they never have a good word to say about their competitors. On the other hand, a good tradesman won't like following a bad one, and so they are usually quite keen to recommend trades who work before, alongside or after them.

It is all highly irregular, of course, but it is possible to glean from a conversation with a builders' merchant or tool-hire company whether a particular builder is financially sound and whether they have a reputation in business.

Finally, anyone using an architect or package-deal company can also benefit from names provided by them. They will be careful to make it clear that they are acting in an introductory capacity only and are in no way recommending them, unless of course they are party to the contract. But the truth is that no one would put forward a company or tradesman who might cause them bother.

The qualities of a good builder

An ability to keep jobs running
Few builders worth their salt can survive on just one job at a time. Very few tradesmen can expect to be continually employed on one site. The measure of a good man or company is their ability to keep continuity and progress on all sites. Watch other jobs on which they are working before yours and check that work is always ongoing and schedules are kept to.

Tidiness on site
It may seem pedantic, but it is a fact that a tidy site is one that runs smoothly and normally comes in on time and on budget. Messy sites are where accidents happen, where materials are lost or spoiled, and where progress is slow and laborious.

An ability to relate to the self-builder
Self-builders are a peculiar bunch. They have deliberately set out to circumvent the normal channels to house ownership. They have chosen to become involved in things that are sometimes at the limit of their knowledge or at the start of a new learning curve. Yet at the same time they may have fairly rigid opinions. It takes a very special sort of professional or builder to recognise these qualities and to accommodate them.

Forward thinking
The key to successful management on site is the ability to think ahead and anticipate requirements. Self-builders may miss some of the triggers, and builders or tradesmen who take it upon themselves to prompt, in the interest of site continuity, are invaluable.

Helpfulness
You would think that this would go without saying. But it is an important and often overlooked quality. The best builder in the world who is unhelpful to the lay person self-building their own home is worse than many of lesser ability who are prepared to be helpful.

A willingness to pass on knowledge
Much of what happens on a building site may be new to the self-builder. A builder who is prepared to show how things are done and discuss alternative ways of doing things on site is an invaluable tool for that site and for future projects.

A need to be 'up to speed' with modern innovations and new regulations
Many builders are so busy working that they have little or no time to investigate innovations or to acquaint themselves with changes to regulations. Many self-builders, with just one project to consider, have the time and the inclination to investigate such things. Never use a builder or tradesperson who is not up to speed with modern innovations. If they cannot understand or have no knowledge of what you are proposing, then move on to someone else. It is not your job to be the teacher. On the other hand, if they show a willingness to adapt to new technology and innovative techniques and are clearly excited at the prospect, then you might take a different approach.

Looking up through the joists at the first fix plumbing or carcassing.

Particular points to watch out for

Cavity trays
Many external claddings are porous to one extent or another. A cavity wall is designed to allow any moisture that finds its way in to pass harmlessly down to ground. However, where an opening or abutment interrupts the cavity, unless precautions are taken, moisture can find its way into the building. Cavity trays need to be correctly positioned to interrupt and divert this moisture to the outside by means of weeper holes. They need to be built in at the right height above any opening or abutment, and they have to be used in conjunction with cover flashings.

Neat brickwork
You don't have to be an expert to know whether brickwork is generally good or bad. Watch out for mortar smudges on brickwork, for uneven beds (horizontal joints) and for perps (the vertical or perpendicular joints) that line up neatly. Stand to the end of a wall and look along it to see if there are any bows in it. Pay particular attention to the pointing and make sure that weeper vents are built in at the lintel ends. Check that all cavity trays and damp-proof courses are in, and pay particular reference to chimneys or brickwork that protrude through the roof.

Sound first-fix carpentry
One way to sort the good guys from the bad is to watch how they treat timber joists. Make sure that they lay the joists to a stringline set on a batten so that the top edge is level on them all. If necessary they should be firmly packed up with slate or similar. Check that all mid-span strutting is in correctly. Failure to do these simple things is the most common cause of squeaking floors

Neat second-fix carpentry
A good measure of a carpenter's ability is the cut and fit of the doors and the surrounding architrave. Make sure that all doors show the same gap all around and that the gap at the bottom is the same open and closed. Make sure that sets of double doors line up correctly. Make sure that architraves are neatly cut and fit at the mitres (corners).

Watch out for undulations in the roof
Badly sitting tiles or slates or undulations in the roof can often be attributed to the person laying the roofing battens. If there is the slightest discrepancy in the plate or the roof trusses or timbers then the cross battens will multiply this. Make sure that the battens are packed up where necessary.

How to cope when things go wrong with your builder

The avoidance of problems should be at the forefront of every self-builder's mind. Careful project planning, scrupulous attention to detail and strict criteria in the choice of both labour and materials should mean that most are indeed avoided. But sometimes things go wrong. Sometimes this means a change of course or a different choice having to be made. Most times the problem can be replaced by a solution. But sometimes it is difficult to see a way forward, and a major problem can even appear to threaten the viability of the whole project. Even then it is unlikely that all is lost. There are usually warning signs. There may have to be some compromises and maybe some hard swallowing of pride. But usually there is a way forward.

Careful investigation can tell you if a builder has been reliable in the past, which should be a pretty good guide to how they will perform in the future. However, every builder is only as good as their last job, and there are lots of things that can bring about a fundamental change.

Warning signs to look out for are long periods when nothing is happening. Follow-on trades fail to arrive or plumbers and electricians fail to turn up to carry out the second fix. If a builder's personal problems are to blame then the problem is an organisational one. In which case maybe you can step in and help by judicious calls to subcontractors and/or suppliers. Don't expect a reduction from the builder. You are helping him to help yourself and that should be reward enough.

Cashflow problems

But if the problem is money then you need to think carefully. A builder in financial difficulties will often ask for money ahead of schedule. It will invariably be accompanied by a story that so-and-so hasn't paid up on the previous job and it's causing cashflow problems. Whatever you do resist this request. It may come to the point where, with the builder's agreement, you have to make direct payments to subcontractors or suppliers or both; but for now take time to take stock of things.

Most builders have cashflow problems. Many have overdrafts that are considerably bigger than your eventual mortgage, and they learn to live with them and to juggle the money from one job to pay for another. Usually it works. Occasionally it gets stretched and the result is that one job or another has to stop. It doesn't necessarily mean that they are heading for bankruptcy. You need to find out what the situation is. Talk to the subcontractors. Be very careful not to be antagonistic. What you don't want is to create rumours that become a self-fulfilling prophecy. Be circumspect in your questioning. 'Is everything all right between you and Bloggs Builders?' is a better question than, 'Is Bloggs going bust?'

If materials are failing to arrive you may be told that there has been a mix-up somewhere. Equally, they may not have been ordered or the builder's account might be on stop at the builders' merchants. You need to know what the problem is. Strictly speaking, the merchants are not at liberty to discuss their client's account details with you, and in any case you don't want your enquiries to make matters worse. So the question that should be posed at the merchant's is, 'What's the situation on those materials that Bloggs Builders have ordered for my site?' And the answer might be that they are not yet ordered or they might give you a hint of trouble with the account. Bear in mind that Bloggs Builders might have told them that one reason he can't pay his bills is that you haven't paid him.

Think and act calmly. The last thing you want is to have to switch contractors. While that is technically possible, it is fraught with legal and organisational difficulties. If you have paid for half the job and half the job has been done, a new builder will want much more than the remaining 50 per cent to finish another's work. One reason for that might be the fear that when the first builder began to get into trouble they started to cut corners and skimp on the job. That shouldn't happen. You, the Building Inspector and the Warranty Inspector should always be insisting on quality of work, whatever else is going on.

Pragmatically, if you find that your builder is in trouble with cashflow, you might decide to do one of three things. You can either move to sever the contract on a quantum–merit basis, in which case you are faced with finding a new builder or dealing directly with the subcontractors and effectively becoming the builder yourself. Alternatively, you can agree to pay weekly according to an agreed schedule of work that makes sure that you are never paying for more than you are getting. Or you can agree that the original builder continues to manage the project and that you pay directly for all materials and labour.

If you are one of the very few who entered into a written contract before the work commenced then that document will almost certainly detail the arrangements by which a dispute or the severance of the contract is settled. But for most self-builders the solutions will have to come from within their own resources.

The builder goes bust

If your builder does go bust you need to be the first to hear of it, and you need to act fast. Buy strong chains and padlocks and secure the site's security fencing. Change all of the locks on the house and if necessary arrange to camp out there or maintain a presence. Builders' merchants will arrive at the site and pick up everything and anything that they can. They will be assured that they have the right to do this; that legal title has not passed in the goods until such time as they are paid. And they will be right in many respects. Except that the goods are on your land and they have no legal right of entry.

You need to prevent them gaining access and you need to inform them that the goods were supplied to you by the builder and that their problem is one for the liquidator. Strictly speaking you may at some stage have to negotiate with them before you can actually use any of the materials, but your first task is to keep them on site.

The other danger is subcontractors, some of whom, highly aggrieved, will want to storm on site and rip out everything of value. Once again they have no legal right of entry and no right to cause damage to your property. If goods are fixed they have become part of your property. That does not mean that they do not have to be paid for and that the title in them continues to rest with others. It does mean that their removal will be detrimental to your property and your rights and that their removal, or not, is something that will have to be negotiated. Goods such as a boiler supplied by a plumber but not yet fixed might legitimately be considered the property of that subcontractor. So that may prove, but for now it is in your interests to keep them on site; you should prevent them being removed even if that means that you have to promise to negotiate for them when the dust has settled a little.

As long as you can keep these people off your site you have the upper hand. If you have stuck to the payments schedule with the builder you will either be well in front in monetary terms or at the very worst you have only paid up to the preceding stage.

Immediate action to take when your builder goes bust

- Get to the site and secure all gates and fencing
- Post a notice denying access to any person not directly authorised by you
- Change the locks on the house
- Camp out or engage a watchman
- Inform the police
- Contact your warranty provider
- Contact your insurers
- Make an appointment with your solicitor

Things can get pretty unpleasant. Some subcontractors may be facing ruin, and they may be determined to get their rights or at the very least revenge. You need to make them understand that you are not the problem and that you might indeed be the solution. As a precaution you should also inform the police. They won't be concerned about the nature of the contract or the dispute but they will be concerned to prevent a breach of the peace and if things get out of hand you might need them fairly quickly.

If the builder's insurance policy was the principal cover on site then you will need to make alternative arrangements quickly. In any event a self-build insurance policy is always a good bet, because many of the items at risk on your site might not have even been purchased by the builders. Self-builders do a lot of their own shopping, and a builder's policy won't cover goods that they did not buy.

Help from your warranty provider when your builder goes bust

You will need to inform the warranty providers of your situation and, eventually, you may have to come to an arrangement with them to vary the policy or change the name of the providers. Most of the warranty companies will offer little but sympathy. The exception is the NHBC, which offers quite considerable help in that it will either:

- Pay you the amount that is needed to complete the home substantially in accordance with its requirements, together with the cost of putting right any defects or damage, or
- It will reimburse you any amount you have paid to the builder for the home under a legal obligation but cannot recover from him, or
- Instead of either of the above, it may also, at its own option, arrange for the works to be carried out.

The maximum liability of the NHBC is 10 per cent of the original purchase price (house value) up to a maximum of £100,000.

The NHBC will only be liable for what was in the original contract. It is not concerned with extras. If you have retained any part of the original contract price this will be deducted from the sum that it pays out and if it arranges for the work you will be required to pay it the amount still owing on the original contract.

The liquidator If your builder goes bust, you must be aware that whatever you do will come under the scrutiny of the liquidator whose job it is to make as much as possible from the builder's assets and distribute them fairly to all of the creditors. If you have not already come to an arrangement with suppliers, it might be necessary for you to make the liquidator an offer for materials on your site. This offer may well be below their face value as the goods will have been unwrapped and will therefore be deemed second-hand.

If you owe money to a builder under your contract then the liquidator will want to know why you should not pay it. It is no good saying that he was a dirty rotten scoundrel for letting you down; you will have to address the situation properly by preparing a counter claim. This will detail the expenses to which you have been put, the amount it has cost you to rectify the situation, including payments to other builders and subcontractors. It can also include a sum for the consequent distress and wasted time.

The builder The builder may try to come to a private arrangement with you. If you owe them money under the contract, they may attempt to get you to pay this. Do not do so. That money, if it is payable, should go to the liquidator. In similar vein the builder may try to get you to employ them under a different guise. This is not always a good idea. It could put you in the wrong with the liquidator and cause friction with the other workers on site who have lost out as a result of the builder's misfortune.

The subcontractors If a subcontractor goes bust on your site then it is unlikely that it will jeopardise the project. In all probability, the payments to a subcontractor will be on the basis of work done, and there is therefore little chance that their going broke will leave you at a disadvantage.

The subcontractors who worked for a bankrupt builder are a different matter. After their initial anger they may well seek to come to an arrangement with you. If that means you paying them directly for any future work then that is all right. But you have no liability for paying them for work that they did while working for the builder. Now, that is the strict position. But if you are a stage in hand with the builder then, strictly speaking, you haven't paid for their services. Your goal is to get your new home built. If that means that you have to negotiate a figure with them to finish the job that doesn't leave you out of pocket, then surely that is the best option.

Choosing and working with subcontractors

Always take people on by recommendation
Wherever possible obtain subcontractors by recommendation. Many are in any event reluctant to take on work unless it comes through or by a previous contact. Seek out other self-builders, who love to talk about their experiences and no more so than in connection with tradesmen. Ask about reliability and timing as well as quality of work. Try to find out at which bits of the trade the guys are best and on which bits you need to keep a close eye. Ask at local builders' merchants or tool-hire depots for the names of reliable subcontractors. They are hardly likely to recommend the chap who doesn't pay his bills or who returns tools or plant in bad order. Beware of recommendations for, and especially against, guys from

the same trade. Tradesmen are notoriously critical of others' work. See for yourself or get the opinion of other subcontractors working either side of a particular discipline.

If you are looking for a particular trade then there are quite a few associations, most of whom have lists of their members available on the Internet. Of course, the fact that somebody is on a list merely means that they have kept up their subscription and, to certain extent, have not done anything to warrant being struck off. One factor that may influence your decision is whether, by being a member of such an organisation, they are able to offer an insurance-backed guarantee.

There is a statutory requirement for plumbing and heating engineers installing or working on gas appliances to be CORGI (Council for Registered Gas Installers) registered. But membership of the similar NICEIC (National Inspection Council for Electrical Installation Contractors) is purely voluntary, although, with the inclusion of electrics into the Building Regulations, persons carrying out electrical work to a new home must be competent, which usually means that they must be registered with one of the bodies that allows them to self-certify. Persons carrying out work to an oil-fired installation should be OFTEC (Oil Fired Technical Association) registered or similar.

Being a member of one of these bodies does not tell you just how good they are or how suitable they might be for your purposes. So it behoves you to carry out all of the checks, to ask all of the questions and, effectively, create your own recommendation. You must not be afraid to ask where and for whom they have worked before, and you must be prepared to knock on front doors and ask their previous clients about them.

Make sure the work is actually their own. Even if they worked on that job, were they the actual tradesman or were they labouring on others? Ask to see other work they have done and if at all possible try to speak to their previous clients. Watch out for untidy work. With face work, it is obvious and apparent, but with hidden work, such as plumbing, you need to look at the quality of the jointing and pipework runs. On brickwork, check that the perps (the vertical joints) line up and look along the beds (horizontal joints) to see that they are straight. Check for smudged mortar or dirty cavities if you can. On carpentry, check the standard of joints, first fix and second fix. Check the hanging of doors and their correct opening. With plasterwork check not only the finish but also the adherence and that the correct angles and beadings have been used and all joints are properly filled.

Check prices and extras
Make yourself as aware as possible of the prices and rates for each trade. Wherever possible get three prices for each trade and try to ascertain the rates at which they have priced. On the other hand, don't beat your head against a brick wall trying to make up the three prices if the ones you have got are within your expectations and from recommended or reliable contacts. Above all, don't miss the window of opportunity and availability for a good tradesman in an academic exercise. Talk about the possibility of extras with a potential tradesman before you take them on, and agree the procedure and the costing basis for any that might occur. In any gang of men there is a leader. Never talk to the underlings about extras or additional work. Always talk to the person with whom you formed the contract.

With the ceilings tacked, the walls can be plastered or, in this case, dry lined.

Almost always agree a lump-sum price

If you can't get a lump-sum price, go for measured rates instead. Wherever possible, avoid the subcontractor who wants to carry out the whole of his trade on the basis of daywork or time taken. You might be told that there are too many uncertainties and that it is impossible to know just what the job entails. While there are specific cases involving renovations or refurbishments where this might be true, it is certainly almost never true for new build. That is not to say that there are no instances where daywork is applicable, but it should certainly be avoided for the whole trade. Discuss daywork rates and just how and when they will be appropriate before work starts.

Don't try and argue down prices

Negotiation is a large part of management but do be careful about trying to knock down a price. There is nothing wrong in telling someone that you had particularly hoped to use that their price was a little high in comparison with others. If they offer to look at things again and if they find out that they had made incorrect assumptions or a mistake then you can congratulate yourself on your successful negotiating skills. On the other hand, if they reluctantly agree to come down in price you might find that they claw back what they perceive as having 'lost' by finding extras or skimping on the job itself.

Be careful about detailed contracts

Do not imagine that many subcontractors will accept or sign up to long written contracts. Most will run a mile and those who do agree will have added in a 'buggeration factor'. In any event many subcontractors are 'men of straw', and it would be difficult or impossible to enforce a contract. Many subcontractors are more than happy to undertake a job on the basis of either a verbal quotation or something scribbled on the back of a fag packet. While that often works it is not really suitable, and you should endeavour at least to confirm the arrangements in writing, referring to specific plans and specifications.

Nevertheless, much of the advice that you will receive exhorts you to enter into a formal contract with whomsoever you choose to employ in any capacity. Architects and package-deal companies will probably be prepared to proceed only on this basis. But there is no doubt that the vast majority of building contracts between self-builders and builders and self-builders and subcontractors go ahead with no formal contract other then perhaps an exchange of letters. For some this is an anathema. They cannot countenance the idea of not having a long and formal document detailing every part of the contract. Perhaps they are right? Perhaps if things go wrong they will be covered and if it goes to court they will win. But will it be a pyrrhic victory? Perhaps the person who carefully manages things, who pays for nothing that is not done and approved of, has the edge?

Perhaps a halfway house in all of this, and one that all but the most bloody-minded of subcontractors or small builders will accept, is the simple four- or five-page contract such as that available from the Joint Contracts Tribunal (JCT) entitled 'Building Contract for a Home Owner/Occupier'. The JCT can be contacted via its website (www.jctcontracts.com). A similar contract can be downloaded free from the HomePro website (www.homepro.com). Both of these contracts are only a few pages long, written in plain English to cover all of the major details and with most of the points dealt with by simple tick boxes.

Don't become the teacher

As a self-builder, you can often find yourself way ahead of the subcontractors in respect of your knowledge about innovations. This is perfectly under-standable: for you, this is a one-off project, and you are reading and find-ing out all about the latest technology. For you, the project is of paramount importance, whereas for the subcontractor it is just another job. If you find yourself talking to a subcontractor who seems not to be able to grasp what you are hoping to achieve, then pull away and move on to the next one. Whatever you do, don't let your job become part of a learning process for the subcontractor unless you are certain that they are as interested in the end result as you are. Otherwise you might just find that you end up being a conduit of information between them and the manufacturers as the costs and time spiral out of control.

Beware trying to list the tasks

The temptation is to try and tie things down as tightly as possible by listing all of the tasks that the various subcontractors are expected to perform. An architect or quantity surveyor preparing a specification for a tender docu-ment could be expected to think of everything. A lay person might well forget something; even if they didn't, most subcontractors would run a mile from a hefty document. It is often better to keep the wording fairly minimal and, for example, with the carpenter refer to all first-fix, roof and second-fix work. That way they can't turn around and claim that a partic-ular task is not in their remit. Always tie the quotation and acceptance back to the plans that form the contract and the written specification on them, and make a note of the date and number of all plans issued.

Make sure of insurances

Some subcontractors will carry professional insurance. Most will not. It is vital that any self-builder should have appropriate self-build insurance covering them for Contract Works, Public and Employers' Liability. Contract Works covers for most site risks, such as vandalism, theft, storm, fire and flood. Public Liability covers for damage or injury to a third party as a result of your building works. Employers' Liability you might suppose, as these are self-employed men, isn't necessary. You would be very wrong. Although there is no requirement for you to collect taxes or stamp documents, you are deemed to be employing the subcontractors working on your site. If one of them has an accident then as a self-employed man he doesn't get sick pay as an employee would, and his solicitor might well advise him to seek recompense from you.

If circumstances change the specification, stop and renegotiate

It is not always possible to anticipate every eventuality in a self-build. Sometimes, even despite a full survey, difficult or entirely different ground conditions can manifest themselves. If this is merely a matter of a little more concrete, a bit of extra digging or more brickwork or blockwork, then it can be dealt with as an extra. If it entails a completely different form of foundation or construction then you may need to stop and establish a revised contract or price, almost as if you are starting again. Be careful not just to drift on thinking that it will all come out in the wash. Wait until the new drawings are ready and approved, and then establish a completely fresh contract based upon them. Be prepared to have to pay for any abortive work but think carefully before paying waiting time.

Project management

Building with subcontract or direct labour means that someone has to be responsible for the management of the site and the co-ordination of materials and labour. In most cases this is the task of the self-builder. If, however, you do not have the time to spare for this, there is an alternative to the more expensive option of using a builder for the whole project.

It is possible to source your own project manager using perhaps a retired Building Inspector, an architect or somebody with knowledge of the building industry. Do be careful that they are experienced in one-off housing and aware of the current on-site regulations and requirements. Do also be careful that they are of the right temperament. Somebody whose experience is factory- or office-based might well alienate self-employed subcontractors. If a package-deal company offers you a project manager, do make sure that they are completely independent. If the project manager is also a representative of the company or exists in expectation of continuous work from the company it will be difficult for them to be able to act independently on your behalf.

Qualities of a good client

Building your own home puts you in the driving seat in more ways than one. For many this first taste of real power can be daunting, because power brings with it absolute responsibility, the exercising of which may need training and self-discipline. While knowledge of the technical aspects of building or, at the very least, the sequence of events, is useful, what is undoubtedly of far greater significance to the successful self-builder is the ability to handle people and situations. Acres of print are devoted to choices of materials and the selection of suitable contractors, subcontractors and architects. But very little is devoted to the qualities that the self-builder should bring to these partnerships.

Can it be said that certain classes or types are better or worse suited to self-building? Not really. Self-builders come from all social and economic backgrounds. It used to be claimed that teachers made poor self-builders despite the fact that they had long holidays within which they could devote themselves to management or even to working on site. For many teachers of the old school, a bricklayer was someone who had flunked school and ended up in manual labour. For a bricklayer, a schoolteacher was just somebody who earned a third of the amount they did. But as the boundaries between white- and blue-collar workers have blurred, so too has this feigned antagonism.

What remains true is that many of the practices and attitudes of the factory floor or office do not easily translate to the building site. The engineer who boasts an ability to work with micrometers and looks forward with eager anticipation to 'teaching these guys how to do things properly' will come a cropper. The self-builder who stands like a factory inspector, clocking people in and out, will soon find themselves with an empty site. There is no need to be a bad client, and if you follow a few simple rules and observations you can get the best out of people by getting the best out of yourself.

Tacking (plasterboarding) around the dormers, on the top attic floor.

Adopt the right attitude

Building with subcontractors, also known as direct labour, often demonstrates a considerable saving over using a builder. You 'don't get owt for nowt' in this world, though, and the reverse of this coin is that you have to be prepared to take on the role of the builder. A builder is really a manager. That is the job you are taking on: the management of various trades and individuals together with the proper co-ordination of materials, services, relevant authorities, inspectors and plant. In all likelihood, you are going to be the person on site who is least experienced in matters of building, but that should not and does not prevent a successful outcome. An ability to manage people and situations is what's required; far more important than technical knowledge, which after all, you are buying from the professionals.

Keep a sense of proportion

You could almost say a sense of humour. You are never going to get 100 per cent of what you want. You are going to have to learn to make many compromises in order to keep continuity and achieve the end goal of your new home. Always look at the big picture. If a compromise might blight your eventual occupation or the value of the home then dig in your heels and don't give way. On the other hand, if it is really not going to make that much difference or is going to be hidden anyway, why jeopardise the whole project?

Most self-builders will find themselves spending money in amounts and at greater speed than they had ever envisaged. The project can take over lives. At times it might even seem that nothing is more important than this new home. Keep things in proportion. It is vital but not more so than family life, and it certainly should not be more important than your business life. After all, what you do for a living is what is going to pay for this new home and, without an income, it is unlikely that you will be able to sustain what you are trying to achieve.

Don't make the mistake of believing that you and the tradesmen are an equal partnership. This is your project. It is not theirs. You will enjoy the house afterwards. You will reap the benefit of any increase in equity. For them, it is just another job. Talk of partnerships is naïve, and if you try to involve them in such talk, they will pay lip service to the concept, laugh at you behind your back and take advantage of your obvious inexperience.

One thing you will notice on building sites is a sort of gallows humour among the tradesmen. Life can be difficult on a building site. The work can be dangerous, and in the winter months it can be pretty uncomfortable. Like all men in those situations they find relief in humour, and it has to be said that a site where there is plenty of laughter often goes better than one with miserable faces.

It is not always going to go right. Things will go badly at times. Be prepared for them and keep things in perspective. Very few things that go wrong on a building site spell absolute disaster, and most can be remedied. The solution may soak up your contingency fund, but that is what it's there for. It may eat into your projected equity increase but it is unlikely to swallow it up entirely.

Choose whom to deal with

It is no good taking on someone in the supposed belief that they are members of an august association if their membership has lapsed and nobody has had the foresight to check its currency. It is no good taking on someone in the belief that they were responsible for certain other works unless you have checked that their involvement was crucial. It is no good taking on someone who, even though they might be the very best at what they do, is not going to be helpful. Do you have the gumption to check things out? Do you have the nerve to walk up a pathway, knock on a door and ask a complete stranger for information on somebody who carried out work for them in the past? If not, then maybe you need to examine your own abilities in this man-management project upon which you are about to embark, if you are not to rely on mere blind faith.

Remember, when a builder, architect or tradesman is keen to get the job they will be your new best chum. You will be bought drinks in the pub, given all sorts of helpful advice and may even be invited to their annual barbecue. But what are they going to be like at the fag-end of the job or when things go wrong? You need to know that, and the only people who really have the answers to these questions are the people for whom they have worked before. You need to have the ability and the boldness to search out those answers.

Be careful about your management style
Subcontractors are self-employed men who have deliberately stepped outside the system, opting for the insecurities and uncertainties that go with the 'hire and fire' world of the building site. Each one, including the one-man band, is therefore a representative of his own company and they need to be treated as such rather than as employees or servants. Avoid the 'white coat' syndrome. Don't stand behind them pointing out each broken brick or questioning each move they make. Don't attempt to clock them on or off unless the work they are doing is based on daywork or time taken. Judge them by their performance as a whole. Watch out for grey areas between trades. As the builder it is your responsibility to find out whether the plumber or the roof tiler is responsible for the lead-work or whether the plumber or the electrician will be wiring up the boiler.

Get to grips with the timings
Make yourself as aware as possible of the general sequence of operations and timings on a building site. If possible, prepare a schedule of works and a programme. Check with each tradesman or ask others how long each discipline is likely to take and make a note on the schedule of the dates when you need to be gearing up the following trades. Make notes on the same schedule of the dates when you need to have made important decisions or choices. Understand that tradesmen have to go away at certain points in the construction and that they will go off to other sites from time to time. The indicator of a reliable man is his ability to juggle the various jobs in order to maintain continuity on them all.

Understand the other guy's problems
Why should you worry about the problems of the people whom you employ? Because if their problems impact upon your site, you will suffer in the end. Whenever a builder quotes for a job, they do so on the basis of certain assumptions. Usually there is enough 'fat' in the price to cover for unknown eventualities. Sometimes things will not be quite as presupposed and if the changes are minor then you would be right to think that a decent tradesman might shrug them off. But make a distinction

between somebody trying it on for a bit more money and somebody who is faced with something major that neither they nor you could ever have envisaged.

In the end, you want your project finished and you want it done properly. If the unforeseen problems mean that a respectable tradesman or contractor has no alternative but to walk away from the job, then that is not going to help. If they decide to stay but are forced to skimp on the work then that is no good either. A contract is a contract, and you could stay on your high horse and insist upon its fulfilment. And you would be perfectly within your rights. But you can't force people to work, and any attempt to do so might be more expensive than renegotiating.

If that all sounds like a recipe for financial anarchy, then you are right – if, and only if, you fail to spot the difference between genuine hardship and somebody just trying it on. Any builder is only as good as his last job. That is why when you have made all the checks it is no good just resting on your laurels. You need to keep abreast of things. Look for warning signs. Look for lack of attendance, materials not arriving on time or subcontractors failing to turn up. They might be warnings of financial problems.

Or they may just be personal difficulties. Is it the self-builder's job to worry about the marital problems of his builder? No, of course, it isn't in the sense of becoming a marriage-guidance counsellor. But if sympathy with their problems and a willingness to step into the breach and take over, albeit on a temporary basis, some of the site management means that your site keeps going, then it is well worth while.

Get your cashflow right

Many builders work with an overdraft that would eclipse most self-build mortgages. Many subcontractors operate on a hand-to-mouth basis, spending up to and beyond their income every week. Builders regularly get into financial troubles, not because they are technically insolvent but because their cashflow is so bad. If your failure to pay them on time is the reason for your builder getting into financial difficulties then it will certainly impinge on your own job. If the problem is outside your control or not of your making, then be careful about bailing out a failing enterprise.

In reality a builder's financial weakness is probably something to do with the job before yours or the job before that. But here again if you made the in-depth enquiries at the beginning, this might be something about which you know. You might decide, in the light of this information, that you are going to employ them on a labour-only basis so that you are only ever paying for work that has already been done and all materials on site remain your property.

It is important for you to get your cashflow right and vital that you have the money available at the right time if you are going to keep continuity on site. Most subcontractors will want paying in cash at the end of the week. If you haven't got it then they will not be there on the Monday and will slip off to another job where they think or know they will get paid on time. If there is any doubt, discuss it with them beforehand; don't just leave it until they are standing there with their hands open.

A positive cashflow is the principal advantage of the Accelerator or Advance Payment mortgages available within the self-build lending market. But even with these mortgages it is important for the self-builder to exercise restraint and watch out for overspending. Running a building site is like running a business, and if you do nothing else then careful management of the finances, by means of a running check on a daily basis allied to a meaningful cash projection and programme, is essential.

Never pay in advance
Always pay for work in arrears when the relevant stage has been reached and when you and/or your advisers are happy with the quality of the work. Never pay in advance of work being done. If you are paying weekly, then ascertain beforehand just how long the job is expected to take. Take off 10 per cent and divide the remainder by the number of weeks, leaving an incentive to complete. Avoid falling into the trap of paying by reference to materials used, even if the price is based on measured work. Many jobs, such as bricklaying for the gable ends, use small amounts of material but take a very much longer time to do.

At times there may be circumstances where expensive materials need to be purchased by builders or subcontractors and they might admit that they haven't got the money. Don't make an advance payment. Purchase the materials yourself; that way the title in the goods will be yours.

Always pay promptly
Subcontractors expect to be paid promptly and in cash. If you do not do this you are asking for problems and running the risk of the labour going off to another site, never to return. If you have a cashflow problem then that is your problem, not the tradesmen's, and they cannot reasonably be expected to shoulder your financial burdens. If you anticipate that you are going to have a cashflow problem and you cannot raise the cash by other means then you should consider stopping the job until such time as you are in funds. Alternatively, depending on your relationship with the tradesmen, you could tell them in advance and leave the decision to them. You might find that if they know that the money will be forthcoming by certain construction stages they will accommodate you.

Be willing to listen and learn
You may have fairly strong ideas about what you want. However, be aware that the builder and the tradesmen are all much more experienced than you and may have an important contribution to make. Listen to what they advise. But then be careful to sift from that advice what is merely designed to make their job easier versus what might mean you having to make a compromise too far.

Most self-builders are entering a new field. Even experienced self-builders might have something to learn and, indeed, most builders and subcontractors are on a constant learning curve with new regulations and methods coming on stream. As the self-builder you are the instigator and the final arbiter of everything that happens on site. You chose the site. You chose, with the help of the architect and the planners, the design. You chose the materials and the specification. So here you are on site with men who have done all this for years and who know far more than you about how it all fits together, and they are asking you what to do!

If a subcontractor asks you if they should do something one way or another, then they might either be just testing you or aiming to show you

Some of the rooms can get a bit messy – tidy them up as soon as possible.

just how knowledgeable they are. If you don't know the answer, respond with a question, 'I'm not sure. What would you normally do?' Almost invariably they will have the solution on tap and the 'problem' will be solved. If not, then ask around. Maybe the Warranty Inspector will know. Almost certainly the Building Inspector will have a view, as will your architect or designer. Don't be afraid to stop and ask. Building a new home is just about the most regulated and overseen activity there is, and it pays to make full use of all of the available and relevant professionals.

Don't hold things up

Many self-builders using subcontractors will opt to undertake all or part of one particular trade themselves. Tradesmen are busy people who have learnt their skills including how to allot a time-scale to each individual task. Beware of holding them up or interfering with their progress. If you can't hold your own with the rest of the tradesmen then you should perhaps consider whether you might be better employed standing back and concentrating on the management of the site. Whatever you decide, you can't expect the tradesmen to be responsible for your on-site training, and you certainly can't expect them to lose money waiting for you to finish a job that others could do more quickly.

Avoid changing your mind too often

The *bête noire* of all tradesmen is the constant changing of minds that requires work to be taken down or done again. If you come home at night once or twice and decide that perhaps a door should be moved to one side, then your bricklayer might well be prepared to accommodate you, albeit at a cost. But do it too often and the relationship will quickly break down. Once again, the job has lost momentum, and it always seems harder to re-build a wall than to do it in the first place. Self-building is all about choice, but you have to strike the right balance. Make your choices by careful prior consideration wherever possible. Don't work on a 'suck it and see' basis and always be prepared to understand that the tradesman is usually not at fault for things not turning out just as you had envisaged them.

Nearly all jobs that run over time get blamed on the builders. Yet in many cases it is the clients who are at fault. Simple changes of mind during the job can put days on to the schedule.

Know when to compromise/be pragmatic

Most people don't know one end of a brick from another. Then they come into self-building, and they are faced with a myriad of choices. They make those choices and then they defend them zealously against any attempt at change. But building houses isn't like that. Too many other interested parties are involved and if you insist on getting 100 per cent of what you want, rather than the 80 per cent that you are likely to get, you will probably be disappointed.

Be pragmatic. If the planners don't like your choice, then be prepared to compromise. If the bath taps on which you have set your heart fail to turn up on time or are no longer manufactured then there are thousands of alternatives, most of which are probably just as good or even better. Be aware that a failure to compromise can be damaging to the entire concept. Always keep the bigger picture in mind, which is finishing the project as a whole and on budget. Details that seem important at the time will always, with the passage of time, pale into insignificance.

Learn how to judge tender prices

One of the biggest problems can be deciding which contract to take. Many people who come into self-building for the first time are astonished at the differences that there can be between quotations for essentially the same job. Sometimes these differences are as great as 100 per cent! You need to learn to look at these things analytically. Are the quotations given on the same assumptions? Were the same tender documents and plans sent out to each party? Were they clear in their requirements?

Quite often they were and the reasons for the differentials have more to do with whether they wanted the job or not. Here it is important that you make yourself aware of what the price should have been, and there are plenty of references in *Homebuilding & Renovating* magazine and self-build books that can help with the broad detail. Understand that the high pricers either didn't want the job or, if they did, may be working to a different scale of costs. The big builders with offices and fleets of vans have huge overheads, which mean that they can never really be competitive against the smaller builder who uses the kitchen table as his office and works on site himself.

Beware the lower prices that you know are less than even you'd been hoping for. Your greed may be your undoing. Maybe the builder or subcontractor was inexperienced? Maybe they have made a mistake? Either way, if you take on someone at an uneconomic price it will be you who loses out in the end when they fail to finish, go bust or simply skimp on the job. Go for the middle ground and then, before you enter into a contract, do all of the checking that has been talked about throughout this chapter.

Terminate the contract quickly if you make the wrong choice of subcontractor

It is unlikely that bad workmanship by one trade will spoil your whole project, although it could set it back a bit while you sort out alternatives. Keep a look-out on site to make sure that you are getting what you picked the tradesman for. If you are in any doubt then consult with others or your architect. If despite your best endeavours the tradesman seems incapable of providing you with a good job or if they prove unreliable in any other way, then move quickly to terminate your contract with them. Do not be persuaded to change your mind. A bad subcontractor is used to being 'finished' and there is no need to consider their feelings. Pay them in full for the work done. Your choice of subcontractor is what is at fault, and you will have to pay for your mistake.

Be careful about the day-to-day relationship

Building sites are not terribly formal places. Keeping relationships on a strictly formal basis might work in some instances but it will engender hostility in others. On the other hand, joining in as a mate can just as easily lead to advantage being taken. Be friendly but always keep that little bit of reserve. You are not one of them. This is their job, but it is your project. You are the ones who are going to gain from it and live in it, and they will be gone some day. You may need them again, presuming you are satisfied with their work, and you might make good friends. But never lose sight of what it means to be a good client.

Snagging

Perhaps the biggest bone of contention for anybody moving into a new home, self-built or not, relates to snagging or the putting right of things that go wrong. The only difference with a self-build is that it is the self-builder who must put in place the correct mechanisms to remedy things. Many think in terms of retention clauses. They work well with the reputable and the bigger builders. They work badly with smaller builders who will often agree to having them in the contract, add them to their original worked-out figures and then discount them, assuming that they are never going to get them.

It is about relationships but even more about money. Snags that are obvious before Completion can be put right before final payments are made. But snags that appear six months later, as they almost certainly will, are not easy to accommodate without a formal retention or agreement for the builders to come back. Those building with subcontractors may choose to carry out later snagging themselves because, almost certainly, most subcontractors will not agree to a retention. On the other hand, most reputable plumbers and electricians will agree to come back for little or no charge if faults arise. In the end, for most self-builders, the most they can do is insist on things being done properly in the first place and accept that in six months' time they will have to redecorate.

Golden rules for engaging and working with builders and subcontractors

- Always try to take up references or talk to previous clients.
- Wherever possible, go by recommendation.
- Check that memberships of organisations or trade bodies are current.
- Get as many quotes as you can. But don't lose a good builder simply because you are waiting for quotes that might not come in and could be higher.
- Be careful about beating down builders in price – they will always feel that they have been robbed and may claw it back in extras or by skimping on the job.
- Don't push too hard to get them to work for you – if they don't seem interested, then probably they are not and won't do a good job, and you should move on to someone else.
- Wherever possible, insist on a warranty or insurance-backed guarantee.
- Don't become the teacher – if they don't understand what you are trying to achieve, move on to the next guy.
- Make sure all site insurances are in place.
- Tie up contracts as much as is possible or feasible, either by using standard forms of contract or by confirmation in writing with reference to plans and specification.
- Negotiate prices for extras before they are enacted.
- Don't be afraid to put your own interests first.

Health and Safety

Although the Factory Inspectorate is unlikely ever to have time to send an inspector to visit your site, that does not absolve you from a duty of care to those who are employed to work on your new home. If you are employing more than five people on your site at any one time, then you could find yourself running foul of criminal rather than civil law in the event of an accident. The Management of Health and Safety at Work Regulations 1999 require that all reasonable precautions are taken and that adequate risk assessment takes place regarding every aspect of work.

Keep a few hard hats in the shed together with sets of goggles and pin up a notice requiring that they be worn at all times on site. Make sure that scaffolding is only erected or altered by qualified professionals with adequate insurance cover. Provision of latrine facilities, a hut for meals, protective clothing, a first-aid box and an accident register are required. Employers and the self-employed must identify any hazards involved with their work, the likelihood of any harm arising and the precautions that they feel are necessary. In particular the self-employed must ensure, so far as is reasonably practicable, their own health and safety and that of other workers or members of the public. There are various methods and suggestions contained in the regulations, which can be obtained from the Health and Safety Executive or HSE (details are available via its website: www.hse.gov.uk), but they all really boil down to a common-sense attitude to safety at work.

Employees covered by the Employers' Liability section of a self-build site's insurance policy are defined as:

- Direct employees
- Labour-only subcontractors, whether working directly for you or someone to whom you have given a subcontract
- Persons hired or borrowed from another employer

This does not include family who are working on site without any charge for their services, nor does it include friends who are giving you a hand. However, these others who may be hurt on the site are covered under your public-liability section of the policy, and this includes those who are on the site in connection with some sort of business arrangement made with you (the architect making a routine inspection), those invited to the site by you (your friends and family), and trespassers on your site (the child who climbs your scaffolding while you are not there). If you have children you will have to do some careful thinking about the extent to which you are going to let them visit the site. Having your kids help by clearing rubbish is happy family togetherness and a good thing. The moment one of them is hurt it becomes an irresponsible disregard of safety legislation. There is no doubt at all about this: in law they should not be there. New European safety legislation emphasises this. Unfortunately, in most family situations your children are likely to become involved with what you are doing. You will have to make your own careful decisions, decide what the rules are going to be and see that everyone sticks to them. If you are living on the site in a caravan this will involve you deciding to fence off the caravan and family area from the building site. Remember that, besides more obvious hazards, children are at risk from toxic materials on a building site. The worst of these, and certainly the one that gives most trouble, is cement. Cement dust, mixed concrete and wet mortar are highly corrosive and lead to concrete burns.

As far as you personally are concerned, the self-builders' policy gives you no help at all if you are injured. For this you have to take out personal accident, death, and permanent injury insurances if you do not already have this insurance cover in some other way. This has been discussed on p. 14.

Valuable as these insurances are, they should not encourage you to ignore common-sense precautions. Not only is the food in a hospital unlikely to be up to the standard that you normally enjoy but your inability to manage the job while you are recovering from your injuries is also going to be very expensive; this loss is not covered by any sort of insurance. Most of the precautions you should take are common-sense matters, but please do take serious note of all of this and use the 'Checklist for self-build site safety' on pp. 144–5. Site safety is an aspect of site management that is every bit as important as any other; a well-managed and tidy site is often the one that has the best safety record.

Checklist for self-build site safety

· Get into the habit of wearing a hard hat on site and make sure that there are some spare hats in the site hut with a notice on the wall that they should be worn at all times. When accepting quotations from subcontractors, slip a little paragraph in about expecting them to wear theirs on site.
· Wear protective footwear. Wellies and boots with steel toecaps are readily available – look under 'Safety' in the *Yellow Pages*.
· Buy two or three pairs of plastic goggles and always use them with cutting or grinding tools, etc. Encourage others on site to wear them when appropriate by hanging the spare sets up, next to the hard hats, with a suitable notice.
· Use specialist and bona fide scaffolding contractors only and make sure that when you accept their quotation you confirm that the scaffold is to be erected and maintained in accordance with all of the Health and Safety legislation and by reference to best-possible practice. If scaffold boards are, quite rightly, turned back at night by the bricklayers, make sure that they are properly replaced each day and that no 'traps' are formed by the boards failing to run to a putlock (see below).
· With conventional scaffolding the short lengths of scaffolding that carry the boards are called putlocks. They project beyond the scaffolding at head level and building professionals know that they are there, almost by instinct. Self-builders, however, bump into them on a regular basis. Tape some empty plastic bottles over the ends – it looks funny but is very effective.
· Whenever you hire equipment from a hire firm, ask if instruction leaflets and safety manuals are available. You may feel rather self-conscious about doing this, but most hire firms will welcome your enquiry and will probably be pleased to give you the benefit of their experience. They will all have stories of the wife returning the tool that put the husband in hospital.
· Keep petrol for mixers in a locked hut, preferably in the type of can that is approved for carrying petrol in the boot of a car. Do not let anyone smoke in the hut where you keep the petrol. Better still use diesel equipment.
· Professional electric power tools from a plant-hire company will normally be 110 volts and equipped with the appropriate safety cut-outs etc. If you are using 230-volt DIY power tools or any other 230-volt equipment, including lighting, take the supply through an RCD contact breaker.
· If trenches for services or your foundation trenches are more than 1 metre deep, treat them with respect and go by the book with shoring. If they show any tendency to collapse, deal with them from above, in company with another person. Never work in a deep trench alone.

- Packs of bricks and blocks that are crane off-loaded, with or without pallets, must always be stacked on stable ground and never piled more than two high. Take great care when cutting the bands and re-stack them by hand if packs are in any way unstable. Stop children from climbing on them and sheet them up if at all possible.
- Concrete burns are a self-build speciality. Bad ones can leave the bone visible and require skin grafts. Never handle concrete or mortar with your bare hands and, in particular, do not let it get down your wellies or in your shoes. If it does, then wash out the offending footwear or clothing immediately. Remember, cement burns do not hurt until after the damage is done. If you get cement dust in your eyes, flood your face under water immediately. Do not let children or animals play with or walk through wet concrete.
- Do not get involved with work on roofs unless you are used to and confident with heights. Do not take risks and never go on to a roof without the appropriate scaffolding.
- Self-builders regularly fall down stairwells. If they do not, then their visitors do. Use rough timber to form a temporary balustrade until you fix the real one.
- Do not use old-fashioned wooden ladders. Always tie the ladder on at the top, and if there is any danger of the feet slipping, fix a cross board at the bottom.
- Be obsessive about clearing away any loose boards or noggins with a nail sticking out of them and, in case you miss one, never wear thin-soled shoes on site.
- Put together a first-aid box containing plasters and antiseptic and fasten it on the site hut wall. You will suffer your fair share of cuts and abrasions and a poisoned finger is a nuisance.
- Watch your back when unloading heavy items or if you are handling more weight that you are used to. This also applies to digging work. The risk of straining yourself is very real. The most scrawny-looking professional builders can handle heavy weights without any risk of injury. If you try it, you could put yourself out of action for a week or more.
- Watch out for machinery moving about on site and be aware that the driver might not be able to see everything behind.
- Always be careful when walking on joists. Many inexperienced people fall through joists either because they are considerably less skilful at balancing than they supposed or because the joists were not fixed. Use scaffold boards laid across the joists and make sure that the joists are either built in firmly or held in place by battening, nailed across and to each one.
- Cover up old or new drainage manholes and pay particular attention to the backfilling or covering over of disused septic tanks and the like. If dumpers or other site vehicles are likely to go near these, then hire a metal plate rather than trying to trust to a sheet of ply.

chapter eight

DIY: The Dos & Don'ts

B uilding your own home means different things to different people. For many it is simply a matter of origination and choice; the thought of actually getting their hands dirty and stuck in with the building process is an anathema. But for many more there is a deep, almost primaeval need to be hands on. They need to know that they have contributed physically to the building of their own home and maybe, although this is never really admitted, they want to be able to regale friends and family in the future with tales of their heroic deeds.

Perhaps it is because they really do possess the necessary skills. Perhaps, and this may be the key, it is because for many self-builders the building site is quite suddenly a new and more exciting world, far from the humdrum of office or factory life. The craic on site is great. The work is often hard and physical. In winter it is freezing cold, but in summer there is a tan and muscles to be had, the like of which could never be obtained from an ordinary holiday. And at all times there is that odd gallows humour and sense of camaraderie that can only otherwise be found in adversity.

But whenever a self-builder makes the conscious decision to undertake all or part of a trade, they need to think very seriously and carefully about what they are taking on. Maybe the decision is driven by the need to save money. But is the saving of money at the expense of time? Is the saving of money on the building site itself at the expense of money elsewhere in the form of job or promotion prospects? For most self-builders, by the very definition of the words, however important the project is to them while it is ongoing, it is an adjunct to their 'normal' lives. When it is all over, they will slip back into the job and, to all outward appearances, be no different to their peers apart from the fact that they will often be driving home at night to a much better house.

What follows is a list of points and questions. If you understand the motive behind the points and if you answer the questions honestly then your DIY input to the site will be worthwhile.

To DIY or not?

Do you understand the sequences and the timings on a building site?

If you are going to slot yourself into the building process then it is vital that you understand how each trade relates to the others. It is all very well understanding the point at which each trade comes in, but it is also necessary to understand just how various trades overlap each other. Electricians and plumbers both have to be involved in things like firing up the boiler and the cross bonding and earthing of pipework. Plumbers, roof tilers and bricklayers all have to mesh in with each other for lead-work to roofs, dormers and chimneys.

Can you maintain continuity?

One house cannot sustain any trade on a continuous basis. All tradesmen have to be able to go from job to job doing their bit and then leaving while the next trade takes over. Tradesmen have to juggle many different jobs, and the mark of a good man, aided by good management, is his ability to maintain continuity on all sites.

If you have decided to carry out all or part of a trade, ask yourself whether, by doing so, you are going to be able to keep up with the programme. Not just the programme you have set but also the programme that the other tradesmen have assumed. It might be all right for you if there is a long time gap between first fix and second fix for a trade such as the plumber. But does that fit in with their cashflow expectations? Will they want to get on with the job and move on to the next one rather than having it hanging over?

Above all, might you risk losing following tradesmen? If you are doing the electrical first fix and your plan is to finish over the weekend so that the plasterers can get in on the Monday and then it all goes pear shaped, you might miss their window of opportunity. And it could be weeks or even months before they can get back to you if they go on to other jobs that are ready and where they were expected to be.

Do you possess the skills?

The odd bit of DIY can bring one to the belief that simply to scale things up into a whole-house situation should be quite easy. In some respects that is right. Hanging one door is no different from hanging a series of ten. Fitting a run of kitchen units is not so different from putting in a new unit at home. But is that so? When you realise in the middle of it all that the floor is uneven or the walls aren't square and that you are going to have to scribe in or line up all the worktops, then suddenly the time frame slips, and the job becomes so much more complicated.

Do you possess the right tools?

DIY tools that have served you well for the odd job at home might well not be man enough for the work that is required to build an entire house. Most tools can of course be hired, but some of them are fiendishly complicated and others, despite instructions and the accompaniment of safety equipment, can be downright dangerous in the hands of an amateur. Round-edge worktops need Pythagorean skills that you have probably long forgotten and never dreamed a mere carpenter could possess in order for them to fit kitchen worktops into each other at the corners. And don't be fooled by gadgets that purport to make seemingly impossible trades easier. Devices for laying bricks in neat courses might be fine for the odd garden wall but you cannot expect that to translate to building a whole house.

Have you accurately estimated the scale of a job?

Many self-builders choose to take on the trade of decorator; most that do make a pretty good job of it. But don't be fooled into thinking that just because this is one of the last trades, time doesn't matter. That may of course be true with a task such as internal decoration but it is certainly not true when it comes to painting the outside. The time slot for decoration of the fascias and bargeboards sits between the tiling of the roof and the fixing of the guttering before the scaffolding comes down. It is very small, and if you miss it then the job is not impossible but considerably harder to do, and you will never make such a good go of it. It pays as well to understand that although the painter is quite near the bottom of the hierarchy on a building site, it is their responsibility to 'snag' many of the ills that other trades have left behind. The trade is two-thirds preparation and one-third finish. No amount of paint will cover up rough plasterwork or unprepared timber.

Can you do it physically?

You may indeed possess the skills. You may be good at gardening and see no reason why you can't muck in and take responsibility for the ground works. After all they are not that different. All it is, surely, is a question of shifting muck one way and replacing it with concrete? But do you possess the physical stamina? People who work full time on building sites have mostly done so since early life. They develop the knack, the muscle forma- tion and the bone structure to cope with prolonged physical exertion and the carrying of heavy weights. Those whose life has been spent in the comforts of an office may have the enthusiasm and the self-belief but that can quickly be brought down to earth by strains, hernias or worse.

Is DIY your most effective use of time?

Most self-builders have to hold down a job of work at the same time. For many it is the money supply for the whole thing that will continue to pay for it when the build is all over. There is a limit to how much time can be taken without compromising your future position and prospects. Analyse just what time you can make available and then husband your resources to the greatest effect. If you are going to work on site be honest about what time it will take. Be honest about how that time, used up by your physical involvement, is going to impinge on all of the other things you could and should be doing to make sure that continuity is maintained.

Floor tiled and the beginning of the kitchen fitting.

Project management Understand that of all the DIY skills that you can contribute, effective project management is the most important. Very few self-builders can ever hope or even wish to do all of the work on site them-selves and most who do actual physical work limit it to a few trades or parts of trades. In doing so they undoubtedly make some savings. But if while the self-builder is busy with any or all of those trades, they allow the management to slip then they stand to lose far more than they could ever seek to gain. Choosing to manage a self-build site by employing subcon-tractors instead of putting the whole job out to a builder can bring about a saving of at least 27 per cent and may be even higher. But to achieve those kind of savings it is vital that the management is kept tight. If there is one maxim that self-builders should understand it is that project manage-ment is king. It is essentially the difference between a good and a bad builder. Those who let things drift from crisis to crisis see costs spiral and the project run way over time. Those who think and plan ahead bring in sites on time and on budget. Learn the sequences of the workings of a building site. Plan ahead and gear up labour for your expectations and requirements. Choose materials on time and order them ahead so that no trade is held up. Keep a tight rein on expenditure and watch the cashflow.

Keeping a tidy site If you must work on site then perhaps the most effec-tive thing you can do is to keep it tidy. There are grey areas between each trade. The bricklayers will be working on the walls and take care to see that bricks are neatly pointed. In doing so any loose mortar they strike off will fall to ground. Outside, that is not a problem. But inside these 'snots' will accu-mulate at the base of the wall. Over time, if they are left they will harden so that it may take a full day to clear them up when the plumber wants to carcass or the carpenter wants to lay the floating floor. And all that was needed was for someone to go in at the end of the day and sweep them up and out.

Bricks and blocks get dropped everywhere. Broken half-bricks are left where they lie. Pick them up and place them beside the loaded-out bricks and, you never know, they might be used instead of a whole one being cracked in half! Both blocks and bricks are delivered bound with wire or plastic, which, when cut, gets everywhere and can be a lethal tripwire.

Make it your job to go in every night. Sweep up the oversites. Cover the sand heaps. Make sure the cement dust is properly stored in the dry. Turn back the scaffold boards nearest to the new brickwork to avoid any rain splashing mortar all over it. Check that all tools are stored away safely and that the mixer is turned down and covered. Clear walkways and make sure that all materials are neatly stacked and that, in particular, brick-and-block stacks are stable. If you do this, you will find that your site runs more smoothly; it will probably be the most effective and important work that you can physically do on site.

Some worthwhile DIY skills

While much of the above tries to get you to think twice about doing DIY, there are times when it is as well to know something about how the trades are done. There are indeed some jobs that the self-builder themselves might need to do, either after occupation or as part of general snagging. Listed below are some simple tasks and how to tackle them.

Setting out a building

Strip away any vegetation from the site, extending at least 1 metre beyond the proposed external walls. Study the plans for fixed points from which you can measure, such as the boundary. Measure the distance on the plan to these fixed points and put up a string line between two stakes set beyond the proposed building. Using the external dimensions of the proposed structure, put a stake in at the first corner of the building and tack a nail in the top, leaving it proud by about 25 mm. Hook a long tape on to that nail and measure out the length of the first wall along the string line to a second stake. Bang it in, checking it for position and upright as you go. Carefully measure and put a proud nail in the top.

Many builders use a 3:4:5 triangulation to set right angles. This is notoriously inaccurate over distance, and it is better to triangulate using Pythagoras' theorem. Multiply the length of each of the two outside walls by themselves and add together the two answers. The square root of the addition is the length of their diagonal.

Hook a tape on each of the two stakes and holding them both, one to measure the diagonal and one to measure the next outside-wall measurement, position the third stake. Bang this in and then carefully measure with each of the tapes to position the nail in the top. Repeat the process for the fourth stake to form the square or rectangle and then check that the resultant distance between the third and fourth stake is correct. Complex shapes should be broken down into handy rectangles or squares.

Stretch a string line around the nails to mark the shapes of the building. This needs to be transposed to profiles. Sight down each line and firmly bang in two stakes about 450 mm apart, about 5 metres beyond the building, so as to straddle any continuation of the line. Fix a 600 mm length of batten across the top of the pair. Repeat this at both ends of every line. Hook a string line on the first corner's nail and take it beyond the second corner to the profile. Pull tight and sight down it until it crosses the second nail. Mark the profile with a nail where the line crosses it. Repeat this for every profile. Internal foundation walls can be marked by measurement from the external string lines and profiles put up, if necessary. To find centre dig, measure half the thickness of the proposed wall along the profile (moving inwards) and mark with a nail. Put the lines to centre dig and using an upright spirit-level and a straight edge, mark the ground with lime for the digger to work to.

Putting up a close-boarded fence

A fence such as this can follow any gentle contours of the land rather than being stepped. Buy posts with the mortise slots already cut in, a recess for gravel boards and the top sloped, unless post caps are to be used. All timber should be pressure impregnated and treated with preservative. It is, however, a good idea to treat further the bottom ends of the posts. Mark out the line of the fence with the string line. Dig the post holes so that at least 600 mm of the post will be in the ground allowing for it to stand on a bed of ballast. Knock two 100 mm nails nearly all the way through a scaffold board. Stand the first post upright in both planes in the hole and rest the scaffold board on the top so that the nails will catch it and hold it steady, weighting the bottom with some heavy blocks. Fill the hole with rammed concrete and leave to set.

Shape the ends of the arris rails to fit into the slots. Leave the widest side alone and sharpen the rail rather like one half of a pencil to a blunt end, the same size as the slot, which will fit half-way into the post's thickness. Fit the arris rails into the first post. Sit the second post in its hole and slot the rails into its slots. Support the post in the same way as the first, checking for upright. Nail the rails to both posts by means of a nail angled downwards through the end of the rail into the post with an opposing nail coming upwards. Fill the hole with concrete and repeat the process down the line. Fit the gravel boards into the recess.

Nail the first feather-edge board, thicker end first, to the arris rails against the first post, resting on the top of the gravel board. Cut a timber spacer to allow a minimum 12 mm overlap. Nail the second board using this spacer at the top only and then check it for vertical before nailing to the lower rails. Nail all the other boards using the spacer. As you get close to the next post, calculate whether you need to increase the overlap in order to fill the gap with whole boards. Alternatively, carry on with the spacing and fill the final gap by reversing the last board and nailing it twice, thicker end first, against the post. Drill pilot holes through the capping strip, if required, and into the top of the thicker part of the boards and nail it home with the 25-mm nails.

Laying patio slabs

Most patios are laid with the slabs in neat rectangular grids. Staggering the joints can look most effective. Use a straight wall as the starting point or set up a string line. Consider whether you want the slabs right up to the wall of the house or with a 150-mm gravel margin. If you intend edging the patio with a low raised bed, consider whether you could build the wall off the last patio slabs, giving you scope to curve those walls and eliminate the need for cutting.

A good patio starts with the foundations. Remove the top vegetation and dig out to a depth of between 100 and 150 mm. Fill to within 25 mm plus the thickness of the slabs to the top, with a layer of broken bricks, hardcore or Type 1 roadstone. Compact with a heavy garden roller or a plate vibrator. Blind the hardcore with a layer of sharp sand and compact it again to make sure that the sand fills any crevices within it. Finally, lay a 20 mm layer of sharp sand, well smacked down with the back of a shovel and then smoothed off with a straight edge.

Allow for a fall of around 15 mm for every metre. Set pegs at the high side. Make a straight edge with a packing piece under one end and use this, plus a level, to determine the fall. Lay the slabs on large dollops of mortar, one to each corner of the slab and one in the middle. Tap them firmly into the mortar using a club hammer with a block of wood to protect them. Check for position and level, working away from one corner and checking for square. Square-edged slabs should be laid with a 10 mm gap using spacers. Bevel-edged slabs can be laid butted up to each other, but it is often best to allow a 6 mm gap so that the grouting mortar balloons out underneath the slab edge to give extra support.

Slabs can be cut by chiselling a line across the face of the slab with a hammer and bolster and then turning it over on a bed of sand and tapping along the back until it splits. It is difficult and can be wasteful. Alternatively, use an angle grinder to cut a deep score in the slab before tapping it until it splits. Be very careful with these machines. Follow the instructions and wear all the protective gear.

Grout with a dry mixture of 1:3 by volume, 1 part cement to 3 parts sand, brushed into the joints. Use a short length of garden hose to push the grout into the joints and smooth it off. Then sprinkle with a fine spray just to dampen. Leave to set and do not walk on it for two to three days.

Laying a concrete path

Mark out the pathway and remove the turf and topsoil down to a depth of around 200 mm. Allow for the width of the pegs and ply when calculating the width of the excavation. Knock pegs in the side of the excavation and tack the 100 mm strips of ply to them with the top of the ply as the top of the intended pathway. Use a level if you require the pathway to be level. Otherwise allow the top of the ply to follow the contours of the land. The ply should bend around most reasonable corners. If not, it may be necessary to make saw cuts or grooves part way through the ply on the outside edge. Lay the scalping, Type 1 roadstone or hardcore, in the bottom to within 100 mm of the intended surface and consolidate with either a roller or a whacker made from a square of ply fixed to the end of a stout piece of timber. If you use hardcore, it may be necessary to break up any lumps with a hammer so that there is no lump larger than a man's fist. Fill in and blind hardcore with sand or ballast.

Mix the concrete 1:3, cement to all-in ballast. Work out where you are going to start. It is often best to begin at the furthest point so that as you get tired, you have less distance to barrow things. Tip the concrete and rake it roughly level with the top, filling all corners and voids. Get a friend to work with you to tamp down the concrete using the straight edge. Gently saw the tamp along the path bringing with it any surplus. Then go back and, working

The kitchen begins to take shape.

in unison, tap the tamp on the top of the concrete to level it off with the top of the formers. This will bring the liquid (fat) to the surface. Install an expansion joint every 2 metres. Cut the expansion boarding and prop it upright by setting it in small mounds of concrete before infilling both sides.

If you are happy with the tamped finish, which is quite a good one for grip, you can make the path look better by running a plasterer's trowel around the edges, pushing the outside edge down a little to create a run off. When the concrete is nearly dry gently tap the formers to loosen them from the concrete. Leave full removal until the path is completely set. If a smooth finish is required, float the freshly tamped concrete with a plasterer's trowel, a float or the back of the shovel. Alternatively, you can make swirl patterns or brush the concrete with a stiff broom held at a low angle.

Laying block pavers
A driveway, pathway or patio is only as good as its base and its edging. Mark out the area to be covered and dig out to a depth of about 200 mm for pathways and patios; 275 mm for driveways. Dig out any soft spots and remove any roots or vegetation. Decide whether the paving is to follow the contours of the land or be laid to a level but, particularly with larger areas, try to engineer some crossfall or slope so that water can run off. Tanalised timber edging can be bent around corners and fixed to stakes driven in on the outside below the eventual ground level. Concrete edgings or blocks on edge in a soldier course must be bedded in concrete. Dig a spade-width trench another 100 mm deep around the perimeter. Fill this with dry-mixed concrete 1:4, cement to all-in ballast, and bring it up to a pyramid. Push the edgings into it and compact the concrete around their base with a gloved hand, taking care not to let it get higher than the base of the eventual sand course on the inside edge. Lay the hardcore to a depth of about 75 mm for paths and patios and 150 mm for driveways, consolidating it with the plate vibrator. If the driveway is going to have to take heavy-duty traffic, substitute the top 75 mm of hardcore with a dry concrete mix of 1:5, cement to all-in ballast.

Measure down from the top of the edgings to gauge the total thickness of sand. Spread sharp sand to about two-thirds of this depth and compact. Spread more sharp sand, levelling it out by means of pegs or marker boards, such that when the paviors are laid they stand 10–13 mm proud of the level required. For pathways, you can notch a straight board to fit over the edgings and drag this over the surface. Working from one end or corner, lay the blocks in your chosen pattern, taking care to butt them up close to each other. Herringbone is good for driveways as it resists the scuff of turning wheels. Stretcher bond can be effective in leading the eye for paths and patios. When you have laid all the whole blocks, fill in the remaining spaces with cuts. Run the plate vibrator over the blocks to work them down into the sand flush with the edgings. Spread kiln-dried sand over the blocks and brush it in to any crevices. Vibrate once more to work this sand between the blocks and lock them into position.

Pointing and repointing brickwork
Use an electric drill with a side-cutting bit or a cold chisel to rake out the old mortar. Soft mortars can often be taken out by knocking a 100 mm nail at an angle through a batten and dragging that, plough like, along the joint. Once the joints are open to a depth of about 12 mm, brush them out with a stiff brush.

If you are repointing part of a wall then you will want to match the existing. Track down the local sand-pits and make trial mixes to obtain the closest colour match. Lighten any cement-based mortar with lime. Do not discount the possibility that you can 'age' the mortar with dirt, soot or clay when it is dry. A mortar mix should never be stronger than the bricks. If it is, then the natural drying-out process of the wall will not be able to express itself through the bedding medium and will do so instead through the bricks with resultant spalling. A good mix for a cement-based pointing mortar would be 1:1:6, cement to lime to soft sand. Adding hydrated lime to water to a creamy consistency and then using sharp rather than soft sand can make a true lime mortar, suitable for softer and older brickwork.

Mix the mortar so it's quite stiff. Dampen the wall. Start from the top of the wall and work downwards. Pick up a quantity of mortar on the hawk and cut it into sausage shapes, pushing one strip to the edge. Pick up a short length with the pointing trowel and, holding the hawk beneath to catch any falling material, push the mortar into the vertical joints. Hold the hawk against the wall directly beneath horizontal joints and push the sausage of mortar into the bed with the pointing trowel. Do not smear the face of the brickwork. Wait until the mortar is beginning to set before shaping it. For a struck joint, simply sweep the edge of a trowel across and down the face of the brickwork and then brush off with a soft brush. More usual is a flush joint where a jointer or a short length of pipe is dragged along the mortar to create a slightly curved indent. Do the vertical joints first and, when you have ironed all the joints, remove any loose material with a soft brush. Recessed or raked joints, where the mortar is pushed back from the face of the brick, are not suitable for exposed conditions or for softer bricks. Weatherstruck pointing provides a sloping surface for water to run off. Recess the pointing about 5 mm at the top but bring it flush at the bottom. Make sure the vertical joints are all 'struck' in the same direction.

Cutting a doorway or opening in brickwork

If it is a load-bearing wall or if you are unsure, consult your local-authority Building Inspector or an engineer first. Mark the new opening on the wall and remove any skirting. Calculate the proposed door width including both legs of the lining, plus 25 mm. Calculate and mark out the height allowing for the lining plus 10 mm tolerance. Draw out the position of the lintel allowing about 15 mm for the bedding and packing under each end. Lay dust-sheets on each side. Cut away the plaster as neatly as possible. Cut a hole in the centre of the doorway, approximately 150 mm above where the lintel will be, using the drill, then the hammer and bolster. Thread a 150 ˘ 100 ˘ 1500 mm timber 'needle' through. Support it on each side, 500 mm from the wall with adjustable props set down on to scaffold boards.

Cut out the slot for the lintel and insert it, bedding it up with stiff mortar mixed 1:3, cement to sand, packing it tight with pieces of slate inserted into the mortar. Leave overnight. Chop out the rest of the opening. Drill holes at intervals down the sides. Starting at the top and cutting downwards with the bolster, cut out and remove the bricks and part bricks. Lightweight blocks can be sawn. Use a hand-held spray to keep down the dust and when the hole is cut clear up the debris before going on to the next stages. Remove the props and needle.

Make up the lining by attaching the two legs to the head allowing for 2 mm all around for door clearance. Alternatively, use ready-to-assemble linings with the head rebated to receive the legs. Fix the latch leg to the brickwork by drilling through the lining into the brickwork and using the frame fixings. Check for level in all planes, packing the leg out with slate or timber where necessary. Fix the hinge leg of the lining in the same way using timber packing pieces and adjusting for vertical in all planes plus level on the head. Fill in behind the lining with mortar and leave to set.

Refit the skirtings, stopping at the point where the architrave will start. If you need to make good the plaster, do this before fitting the architrave. Make good the needle hole with some of the old bricks and patch up the plasterwork. Mitre the angles of the architrave using the mitre block. Tack the architrave to the lining to mask the cut-away plaster and the join between that and the lining.

Building a brick garden wall
This assumes a 1-metre-high single-skin stretcher bond wall. Choose frost-proof bricks. Set foundations and wall with profiles. Foundations should be 300 ˘ 300 mm deep and wide with minimum 150 mm concrete; deeper in bad ground or heavy clay. With sloping ground, peg out to achieve the minimum concrete thickness at the highest ground or step the foundation by shuttering across the trench and making the steps equal to brick courses. Mix the concrete 1:5, cement to all-in ballast, and tamp to the tops of the pegs. Leave to cure.

Set lines to the outside brickwork and mark down to the foundation at each corner or at the ends of the wall. Mix the mortar to a cake-mix consistency, 1:6, cement to soft sand, adding plasticiser to the water. Load out the mortar-boards and stack bricks at convenient positions so you can reach them both while working.

To lay bricks, pick up a good measure of mortar on the trowel. Stand facing the way you will be laying and, with a backward swinging motion, bring a line of mortar towards you along the bed. Furrow the mortar with the point of the trowel. Holding a brick upright, butter the mortar on one end only, smoothing it down to each edge. Place the brick with the mortared end against the preceding brick and tap it into the bed with a slight pressure towards the joint. Keep the vertical joints (perps) thin. Strike off any protruding mortar with a clean upward sweep.

Build the corners or ends first. Lay three bricks in each direction and then build up to five courses, stepping back the bricks until you end up with just one brick. Use the gauge rod and keep checking for upright. Level each course along its line and across the diagonal. To infill the straight sections, insert line pins and stretch the line between the bricks at each end weighted to the front top (arris) edge by a brick laid across the line. Lay the bricks with the arris just back from the line to avoid pushing the line and bowing the wall. Lay towards the middle. Check the last few bricks to see if it is necessary to cut the last one or 'closure'. Introduce a pier or change of direction every 3 metres. Create the pier by turning around two bricks every other course with a header (half-brick) and two three-quarter closures on the other courses to maintain the bond. When the mortar is nearly dry, fill holes by pushing slightly dry mortar off the back of the trowel with a short length of 15 mm piping and then point by drawing this along each joint. Sweep with a soft brush.

Building a stone garden wall

While traditionally many dry-stone walls were laid without proper foundations it is, nevertheless, best to provide new walls with one. Keep below 1
metre in height for stone garden walls and batter (slope) the sides inwards
by about 40 mm on each side from a base width of around 400 mm.
Excavate a trench 500 ˘ 200 mm (width ˘ depth) or to firm ground. Tap level
pegs along the trench so as to provide a minimum of 100 mm concrete laid
in the bottom of the trench. Mix concrete 1:5, cement to all-in ballast, and
tamp to the top of the pegs. Choose your stone carefully. Flat or square
stones will be easier to lay in random courses, but in certain areas the tradi-
tion is for more rounded stones. Consider whether you are going to be
laying the stones in a sand-and-cement mortar or in soil. Cut two lengths
of batten 1 metre long and nail them together with a short piece at one
end to form a triangle that, when levelled upright, gives you the inward
slope for each side.

Search for a flat stone that will start off the wall as a bonding stone, the
full width of the base. Having laid the first bonding stone on a 25 mm bed
of soil or mortar, choose smaller stones of roughly the same height. Pull a
string line to keep the edges straight and lay these smaller stones with their
best face outwards to form the sides of the wall. Press them firmly into the
bedding mixture such that they slope inwards slightly and their face follows
the batter. Fill in the gap or core between these smaller stones with rubble
mixed with either soil or mortar. If you want to make the wall stronger,
substitute this for a concrete mix 1:5, cement to all-in ballast, making sure
that the mix fills in between the joints. Repeat this process along and up
the wall, from time to time employing a bonding stone at various levels
that spans the entire width of the wall at that point. Fill in any over-large
gaps between the main stones with smaller stones hammered into the
bedding medium.

At the top, which should be just over 300 mm wide, you have a choice
of capping. Either bed flat or square stones the entire top width of the wall
or bed flattish stones on edge as a soldier course. It is probably best that
these capping stones are bedded on mortar but there is no need for that
to show on the face edge. Walls built with soil can have plants introduced
or encouraged between the stones. If you decide to lay and point with
mortar, make sure that the pointing does not dominate the stone, which,
after all, is the most attractive feature.

Hanging a door

Cut off any 'horns' or stile extensions. Measure the height of the door
opening on both sides and then take off 10–12 mm at the bottom,
depending on the floor covering and 2 mm at the top, dividing the total
equally between the bottom and the top stiles.

Cut wedges or blocks to the thickness of the bottom clearance and
stand the over-wide door on these blocks with a friend holding it against
the opening on one side while you mark down both sides of the door,
sufficient to leave 2 mm clearance on each. Holding the door firmly,
using a workbench, plane down to the marked lines. Try the door in the
opening and if it will not fit comfortably, plane off a little at a time.
Remember you can always shave off more wood, but it is much more
difficult to put back.

For a new internal door, the top hinge should be set about 175 mm from the top of the door and the bottom hinge about 250 mm from the bottom. However, if you are replacing a door in an old frame, you will want to align the new hinges with those on the door jamb. Stand the door with its hinge stile up. Open the hinges and with the knuckle down and clear of the door, mark around them. Then draw a line on the side of the door as a guide for you to cut the hinge in by the thickness of its flap. Make a series of chisel cuts to the correct depth and then pare out the wood to the marked lines. Fit the hinge in the recess and screw in place.

Stand the door back up in the frame, in the open position on its wedges, and carefully mark the position of the hinge flaps on the door-frame, tracing their outline. Remember to make sure that the door is upright and that the hinges are parallel. Mark out the depth of the flaps and cut out the hinge recesses in the same way as you did on the door.

Hang the door with one screw in each hinge to start with in order to test whether you need to trim it or recess the hinges more. If the door appears to strain the hinges when closed you may need to insert a piece of cardboard behind the hinge in order to pack it out. When you have the door moving freely and shutting properly, screw in the remaining hinge screws.

Fixing a mortise lock
Remove the door and place it on edge with the lock side uppermost, securing it by use of a workmate or by clamping it firmly to a stable upright. At the place where the latch is to be fitted, mark a centre line down the edge of the door. Then, using the body of the latch itself as a guide, mark on this line the top and the bottom of the latch. Using a brace and a wood bit the same thickness of the latch body, use the marked centre line as your guide and carefully drill down into the door to about the same depth as the latch will need to go. When you have drilled out between the bottom and top lines, take a chisel and carefully pare out the wood, joining up the drilled holes to create a socket into which the latch will fit comfortably. When the hole is right, mark around the faceplate and then carefully pare out the wood until the faceplate is flush with its edge.

Before screwing it home, however, use the latch held against the side of the door to mark through to the door for the positions of the handle bar and the shape of the keyhole. Clamp a piece of wood on to the other side of the door to prevent splintering, and then drill right through into it using a bit that is only just bigger than the handle bar. For the keyhole you may have to use two different-size drill bits and then join up the holes with a padsaw. Fix the lock by screwing in the faceplate and cover plate, if it has one, and then fit the door furniture and handles, checking that the lock operates properly. Re-hang the door and carefully mark where the latch and bolt meet the opposing frame. If the door is slightly thinner than the reveal you will still want it to shut tightly so carefully measure to the front straight edge of the latch in order to position the striker plate. Draw around the striker plate and drill out the recesses for the latch and bolt. Pare out the wood with a chisel to recess the striker plate together with its protruding lip. Fix the striker plate in the recess. If you do need to adjust things a little, use cardboard behind the striker plate to tilt it or pack out the screw holes to move it forwards or backwards in the reveal.

Making up the door linings.

Laying/replacing floor-boards

Cut through the tongues of a board that runs to a joist. If there are no obvious nail holes this means that the boards are secret nailed though the tongues. If this is the case, mark the edge of the joist and cut though using either a floor-board saw or a circular saw set to precisely the same depth as the board. If you use a saw take care to cut at a shallow angle in order to avoid catching any wiring through the centre of the joists and watch out for pipework notched into the top of the joists. Ease the board up with a bolster and wrecking bar, slipping the bolster in to support the board as you lift it. Once you have one up the rest will follow relatively easily.

Squeaking flooring is often due to the joists flexing, caused by the absence of mid-span strutting or inadequately sized joists. Stiffen up the joists by using 50 ˜ 50 mm noggins, cut each end at 45 degrees, so as to form herringbone strutting cross-nailed in lines between the joists with solid blocking to the walls at each end.

Square-edged chipboard or ply boarding is laid in the same direction as the joists, with each edge cut on to and supported by a joist and supported by noggins nailed across and between the joists. Stagger the joints. Always leave an expansion gap of at least 9 mm to the walls and nail down using ring-shanked nails set about 9 mm from the board's edges and spaced no more than 300 mm apart. Tongue-and-groove chipboard boarding is laid across the run of the joists, with each end supported and cut to a joist or noggin, with staggered joints. Glue together the edges with PVA wood adhesive and fix the boards with ring-shanked nails at maximum 300 mm spacings. Leave a 9 mm expansion gap to the wall.

Cut new timber tongue-and-groove boards so that they will span the room, across the joists, with a 9 mm expansion gap at either end. If they are not long enough cut them to a joist and either randomly stagger the joints or arrange it so that the staggered joints are in line. Fix the first board, with the grooved edge 9 mm from the wall, using flooring brads or lost-head nails, two to a joist, 25 mm from each edge. You need to cramp the boards to counteract the inevitable shrinkage. Either hire a floor-board cramp or lay half a dozen boards and then fix a board just under a board's width away and use two triangular wedges of boarding that you can knock together to cramp the boards before nailing. Cut off the bottom section of the groove on the last board to facilitate fitting.

Fitting skirtings

Treat new boards with a suitable wood preservative before fixing. When fixing to timber, use either lost-head nails, driven home and filled, or counter-sunk brass screws. Fixing to masonry with cut or masonry nails is notor-iously difficult, as is drilling and plugging. Instead, use hammer screws. With these, the hole is drilled through the skirting and into the wall. The plugged screw is then pushed in and the screw hammered home. This expands the plug but allows for future removal. An alternative is simply to glue the boards to the wall, tacking them first to hold them in place.

Start with a wall with no outside angles, interruptions or openings. Measure the total length and fix the skirting from wall to wall. Inside angles are not mitred – they are scribed. This allows a snug fitting where the skirtings are not meeting in vertical planes or right angles. Tack or hold an over-length section for the next leg of skirting to the wall, butting up to the fixed section. Hold a ruler flat on the floor alongside the fixed skirting with a pencil held at the point where it touches the next board. Draw the ruler up the skirting, in and out of the profiles, marking them on to the other section. With a coping saw, carefully cut or fret out the shape you have marked. This should then fit snugly on to the fixed section.

If you need to join two sections along a wall, this is done by cutting each board at opposing angles of 45 degrees rather than just by butting them up to each other. External angles are mitred. Most mitre blocks only allow for cuts to be made at 45 degrees at a right angle. However, it is possible to mark the precise upright of the mitre for the corner using an adjustable angle. You can then clamp the skirting in the mitre box at this angle before cutting. If necessary, glue and pin the outside angles to each other and clamp across the corner by means of temporarily tacked blocks to hold the feet of a G-clamp.

Stopping a creaking staircase

If your staircase is open underneath or you can gain access via an under-stairs cupboard, then your chances of effecting a complete cure are greatly increased. If the underneath of the staircase is inaccessible or plaster-boarded then it is possible to effect some kind of a cure from above.

Working from below, get a friend to walk up and down the stairs as you crouch underneath ready to mark which treads creak. Staircases, viewed from below, are quite complicated affairs with the treads and risers fixed to each other and to the stringers with dowels and with a series of wedges, in both the vertical and the horizontal plane, that serve to hold each component rigid. Most times it is the natural shrinkage of the wood and the loosening of these wedges that causes the creaking. Tap out any loose wedges using a hammer and a flat chisel. Clean off any dry glue. If the wedge is damaged make up a new one using hardwood or hemlock. Apply wood glue to the wedge and tap it firmly back home. Triangular blocks are usually glued centrally in the angle between the tread and the riser. These too can come loose or even drop off. If they are loose, prise them off completely and clean off any dry glue. Using the chisel or a screwdriver prise the tread and riser apart a little and squeeze glue into the gap. Glue both edges of the block and refit it, tacking it in place with some small panel pins to hold it while it dries. Avoid walking on the stairs until you are sure that the glue has dried.

Working from above, if you cannot get access from below, it is possible to screw down through the tread and into the riser, so long as the riser is thick enough and not made of some flimsy ply. Countersink the screw into the tread and fill the hole with a dowel plug. It is also possible to introduce a triangular moulding to the angle between the tread and the riser, pinning and gluing this in place beneath any carpet. Technically, you must make sure that the tread maintains the minimum 220 mm required by the Building Regulations, but, in practice, this need not necessarily impede on the tread's width any more than carpet does as it turns the corner or stair rods would if they were employed.

Changing a tap washer

Turn off the water supply to the tap. If it is mains fed, turn off the water at the stopcock and drain down by opening the taps until water stops flowing. If it is fed from a tank, then either turn off the gate valve on the supply pipe or tie up the ball valve in the tank and drain the water by opening the taps.

When the water has stopped running put in the plug to prevent any screws going down and then put a towel in the basin to avoid scratches.

With a shrouded-head tap, prise off the colour-coded plastic cap at the top and undo the small screw that is exposed. Then release the handle by pulling gently up to expose the headgear. With a pillar-type tap, undo the small grub screw at the side and pull off the handle. Then unscrew the bell cover to expose the headgear. From this point onwards, both taps are very similar, although they do have slightly different washer types, so make sure that you have the correct one.

There are two nuts on the headgear. The top one is the gland nut. If the water is leaking from this then it is not the washer that is at fault and you might well clear up the problem by simply tightening this nut. The bottom nut is the headgear nut. Undo this nut, holding the tap firmly in place with your other hand as you do so to avoid putting pressure on the tap seating and cracking the basin. Lift out the headgear and you will see that there is a jumper or plunger arrangement at the bottom with the washer affixed to the end. This is either held on by friction or by a small nut that will need to be undone before prising off the old washer. Replace the washer and reassemble the tap in reverse order to the above.

Removing/replacing a radiator

There is no need to drain down the system so long as you are not altering or interfering with the pipework and upstands beyond the radiator valves and so long as, if you are replacing the radiator, you do so with one that is the same size (length). Nevertheless, in case of emergency, before you start any plumbing work make sure you know the location of the stopcocks or gate valves.

Lay towels or old sheets around the upstands, tucking them behind and around the pipes. The inlet valve is called the 'control' valve – if you have thermostatic radiator valves this is where they will be. Turn this to the 'off' position. The other valve is called the 'lockshield' valve. This valve is used to balance the system and make sure that each radiator in the run gets its appropriate share of the flow. Prise off the plastic cover and then, using a pair of pliers, close this valve, counting the number of turns needed to do so and making a note of the result.

The large horizontal nut between the valve and the radiator is called the 'union' nut. Put a bowl under the control valve (have another one handy) and undo this nut anticlockwise, looking from the radiator to the valve, while at the same time holding the nut joining the valve to the upstand firmly with a pipe wrench or molegrips. This prevents distortion of the pipework. Do not use excessive force. If necessary use a little penetrating oil.

As you undo the nut, water will start to escape. You can speed this up by undoing the air vent 'bleed' valve at the top with your radiator key. Repeat the process for the lockshield valve and then lift the radiator clear from its brackets. If you are using the old valve adaptors and blanking plugs for a new radiator, remove these and clean them with wire wool. Wind PTFE thread-sealing tape tightly around the male threads with a 50 per cent overlap on each turn and screw into place in the radiator. Hang or re-hang the radiator. Wind PTFE tape around the male threads of both valve tails and reconnect the union nuts, once again taking care not to distort the pipework. Open the control valve to let water back in while allowing the air to be expelled from the bleed valve. When it is full, close the bleed valve and open the lockshield valve by the noted number of turns.

Fitting an outside tap

The best tap position is outside the kitchen sink, taken off the rising main after the stopcock and the easiest way with 15 mm pipe is to use compression fittings. Check that you have sufficient space to work and that the tap will be in a usable position. From inside, drill through the wall with the long thin pilot. Then, from each side, drill through with the thicker bit. Mark from the hole to the rising main, after the stopcock. Measure or calculate the gap required to accommodate the tee fitting and make two marks on the pipe.

Turn off the stopcock and drain down by opening the taps. Cut the rising-main pipe at both marks. Cut square. Some water may come out so keep towels handy. File the ends smooth. Undo the caps of the tee connector and remove the olives (a soft copper material that compresses on to the pipe and seals as the cap is tightened), making a note of which way around they are. Put the caps and then the olives over each branch of the pipe using clothes-pegs to stop them slipping off or down. Smear some jointing compound around the pipe ends and spring into the fitting. Tighten up the caps with the branch pointing towards the hole in the wall. Connect an isolation or gate valve to a 150 mm length of pipe and then connect this pipe to the tee connector. Turn off the new gate valve. Turn the stopcock back on and check for leaks. If there are any, tighten up the fittings and check the valve.

Measure the length of pipe needed to connect the gate valve to the first elbow and another length, sufficient to go through the wall. Connect the elbow to both bits of pipe in the same way as you did the tee connector. Feed one pipe through the wall and connect the other to the gate valve. You may have to juggle this with both fittings loose. Cut the pipe on the outside to within 25 mm of the wall and fit the second elbow fitting, pointing downwards. Cut a 150 mm length of pipe and fit it to the wall plate elbow. Offer it to the other elbow and mark the position of the screw holes. Drill and plug. Fit the pipe to the upper elbow and then screw the wall plate elbow to the wall. Wind PTFE tape around the thread of the bib tap and screw to the wall plate elbow. If the bib tap does not incorporate a non-return valve, you will need to fit a double-check non-return valve between it and the stopcock. Turn on the gate valve and check for leaks. Mastic the gap around the pipe.

Fixing guttering
Be careful up ladders. If you are not comfortable or capable on a ladder, don't do it yourself. Wherever possible get a friend to hold the ladder. If you can tie the top, do so. Bang in a stake and tie the foot of the ladder to it. Don't lean out – move the ladder.

Using a plumb-line, mark the centre of the drain outlet at ground level, on the fascia board. The outlets are usually, but not always, near the end of the run of guttering. Fix a stop-end outlet, or a running outlet if it is in the middle of the run, with the centre of its downpipe at the mark and the top of the guttering section about 50 mm below the tile level. At the other end of the run, fit a gutter bracket so that the top of the gutter will be close to the tiles. Aim for a minimum fall of around 25 mm over 15 metres. If it is a hip-roof house, you will find that the original, and continuous, guttering allowed for it to run in different directions to various downpipes.

Using a string line between the higher and lower levels, mark and fix the guttering brackets, spaced no more than 1 metre apart with additional brackets at joints. Cut the guttering to length with a hacksaw and file the ends smooth. Tuck the back end into the brackets. Clip in the front end and dress the roofing felt into the gutter. Fit the wall brackets to a length of downpipe and fix it loosely against the wall directly beneath the outlet. Use

One room will inevitably become the storeroom.

offset bends plus a short straight length to create the 'swan neck' between the gutter outlet and the downpipe. When you have things right, tighten up the wall brackets. At the bottom, dress the downpipe into the hole provided in the gully grille. Alternatively, fix a shoe to send the water into the gully.

Changing a single-socket outlet to a double

Turn off the power at the consumer unit. On an old-fashioned fused board, remove the relevant fuse that protects the power circuit. On a modern consumer unit, switch off the appropriate miniature circuit breaker. Put the main power back on and then test to see that the circuit you will be working on is definitely not live by using an electronic circuit tester or by plugging in a lamp that you know is working. Unscrew the faceplate from the existing socket and disconnect the wires. There will be one set of wires into the back of the faceplate if it is a spur outlet, two if it is on a ring main and three if it is on a ring main and is also serving a spur outlet.

Gently remove the old box, easing the wires from it, and discard. Mark out the position of the larger box and cut out. With brickwork, mark the drill bit with tape to gauge the depth and drill all around the line before cutting out the hole with a hammer and chisel. Mark out the fixings for the mounting box, drill and plug. Knock out the appropriate blanked-off entry hole in the mounting box. Insert rubber grommets and feed the wires through the back of the box. Screw it to the wall. With plasterboard, cut out the board with a Stanley knife. The mounting box will have special lugs, which hold against the back of the plasterboard when the faceplate is tightened on to it. Knock out the appropriate blanked-off entrance hole, insert grommets and pull through the wires before easing the box into the hole.

To connect the new socket Check that the conductor ends of the wires are not frayed or blackened. If they are, cut back the sheathing and prepare them afresh. Sleeve any bare earth wires with green and yellow sheathing. Screw all the live red wires into the terminal on the back of the faceplate marked L. Screw all the neutral black wires into the terminal marked N. Screw all the earth wires into the terminal marked E.

Take care not to trap any of the wires when offering the faceplate back to the mounting box. Locate the faceplate fixing screws into the holes in the mounting box. Tighten them until the faceplate fits snugly. Do not over-tighten. Fill around and behind, if necessary with a decorative filler. Switch the power back on and test.

Patching plasterwork

For hard plaster, chip away any loose or crumbly material around the damaged area. Take care not to go too far. If there is some slight loss of adhesion in the otherwise sound plaster surrounding the hole, the repair work will probably serve to stabilise it. Brush away any dust and dampen the backing block or bricks. Mix the plaster and load an amount on to a hawk. Hold the hawk just below the lip of the hole and, with the trowel at an angle to the wall of about 45 degrees, push the mixture in and upwards. Do not let the trowel run flat over the mixture. Keep it at an angle, applying the pressure to the trailing edge so as not to drag the material back out. If necessary build up the plaster in layers, waiting until each layer is fairly stiff before applying the next. When the plaster in the filled hole has stiffened and nearly set, dampen it with the spray gun as you sweep the trowel over the surface, holding it at a slight angle and cleaning off the material that builds up on the trailing edge. Remove all blemishes but do not persist too long or beyond hard setting. If necessary, you can always sand off any remaining marks when it is fully dry.

To patch small holes in plasterboard you will need to provide a backing. Cut the hole square with a Stanley knife and a straight edge. Cut a piece of plasterboard 25 mm bigger, both ways, than the hole and then cut it in half. Squeeze filler or coving adhesive around three sides of one of the pieces of board. Insert it in the hole and pull it back against the plasterboard to stick it in place. Repeat this for the other side of the hole. Don't worry about the gap left down the middle by your fingers. Let things dry out and harden. Cut a piece of board about 3 mm smaller all around than the size of the hole and butter up the back. Press this gently into position, jiggling it slightly from side to side and taking care not to push too hard so as to dislodge the backing boards. When dry, fill gaps with filler and, when that is dry, sand smooth and decorate.

Two-coat rendering a wall

The most important elements of a good render are the preparation of the substrate and the mortar mix. Chip away any old render or loose mortar.

Brush off any organic growth or material. If the bricks have a smooth surface texture, chip away at the front of the bricks to create a key for the render. Finally apply a fungicide. If you are doing a whole wall rather than patching, it might be easier to set up vertical battens as a guide for the first (scratch) coat. Nail 10 mm battens vertically about 900 mm apart, packing them out where necessary to take up any undulations in the wall.

Render mortar should never be stronger than the walling material. The mixture for the undercoat on hard or non-porous materials such as dense clay bricks should be in the proportions, 1:0.5:4.5 by volume, 1 part cement to half a part lime to 4.5 parts sharp sand. For other bricks and for most blockwork this should be 1:1:6, cement to lime to sharp sand. Put half of all the materials into the mixer dry and run it until they are thoroughly combined. Add water slowly and then add the remainder of the materials, adding water as you go. Aim for quite a stiff mix for blockwork with a slightly wetter mix for bricks. Run the mixer until you have a thick, creamy sponge-mix consistency. Dampen the wall a little. Starting at the top, load the hawk and then pick up the mortar on the trowel. Pushing upwards in a slight arc and keeping a firm pressure, build up the render on the wall between the battens. Level off this undercoat by sawing the straight edge upwards along the battens. When each bay is filled, scratch the surface in a diamond pattern using the point of the trowel.

Allow to dry. Remove the battens and fill with the same mortar mix. Leave for up to a week to cure thoroughly. The topcoat mix for strong brickwork should be 1:1:6, cement to lime to sand. For blockwork it should be 1:2:9, cement to lime to sand, but in high-exposure areas this should change to 1:1:6, cement to lime to sand. Mix as before and apply to a depth of around 6 mm. For a smooth float finish, rub over with a wooden float. For pebbledash, increase the topcoat to 10 mm and then dash the stone aggregate into the still soft render and push home with a trowel. For a Tyrolean finish, hire a handheld machine that dashes a mixture of soft render and pebbles on to a dry unscratched undercoat.

Screeding a floor

Concrete floors are usually finished off with a sand-and-cement screed. In new houses the insulation can either be beneath the concrete oversite, above it and underneath the screed or a combination of the two. A screed laid directly on concrete can be a minimum of 50 mm thick. Sand-and-cement screed laid directly on insulation and a damp-proof membrane needs to be at least 65 mm thick. Modern proprietary screed mixtures can, however, be a lot thinner.

If laying the new screed on insulation, first make sure that the insulation is the correct flooring grade, that it is laid with the boards closely butted up to one another and that the membrane covers all parts of the floor and dresses up the walls at the edges. If laying the new screed on concrete, first prime the concrete by mixing up a slurry of cement dust, water and a PVA bonding agent, in equal parts. This should be applied in strips as the work of laying the screed commences.

Using a level, determine the lowest and highest points of the subfloor. Calculate your minimum screed thickness by reference to the highest point and mark this on the wall. Transfer this mark all the way around the room. If you cannot mark the walls, tack battens at various points to mark what will be the top surface of the screed.

Mix up the screed mortar in a mixer with 1:3, cement to sharp sand.

There is usually no need to add water as the sand will normally be damp enough, but your aim should be for a crumbly mix that, if squeezed in the hand, will hold together. It is best for one person to mix and deliver and the other to remain kneeling, working the screed and directing where the next loads are to be tipped. Work from the far wall out to a door and aim to work in 600 mm strips, the length of your straight edge. Put a small heap in one corner of the room and smooth it out to the finished level with a screed batten set into it, levelled to the marks on the wall and pointing in the direction in which you will be working. Repeat this at the other end of the first work area. Lay mortar between the battens and saw and tamp it level with the straight edge laid across the battens. Remove the battens and fill in the holes with mortar, smoothing it down with the trowel. Repeat this across the floor in 600 mm bands, smoothing out the surface with the trowel where necessary. Leave the floor for several days before walking on it. Trim any membrane before fitting skirtings.

Clean the house thoroughly before the decorator starts.

Ceramic tiling a wall

On a plain wall, measure up from the bottom with a tile set in the centre of the wall. Using a spirit-level, tack a batten along the wall at this height. Measure down from the batten to find the lowest point of the floor. Remove the batten and mark the top of a tile plus a spacer at this point. Replace the horizontal batten with its top edge on this mark. If there is more than one wall to tile, establish the lowest floor point and fix battens accordingly. Lay tiles and spacers along the floor so that you have an equal-size cut tile at each end.

Choosing from which end you wish to work, mark the position of the first full tile. With a plumb-line, transpose this mark up the wall and then fix a vertical batten between it and the corner. Where the battens meet is where the first tile will be fixed, supported by the lower batten.

If there is a window or feature in the wall it looks best if the tiles are centred on it. Mark out a gauge batten with the tiles and set it on the wall such that the tiles will meet in the centre with more or less the same cut tiles at either end. Use a plumb-line to transpose the tile spacings to the horizontal batten and then use the gauge batten to establish the first full tile and fix the vertical batten accordingly.

Apply adhesive to the wall with a combed spreader. Do not cover more than 1 sq. metre. Press the first tile on to the wall, bottom edge first and, using the spacers, continue until all the whole tiles are laid. After 12 hours, remove the battens in order to deal with the cut tiles. Most tiles can be cut by scoring and snapping with proprietary tools. You can also hire special tile cutters or a powered wet saw. Tiles can be reduced by small amounts with tile nibblers or pincers. Shapes can be cut from tiles by use of a small tile saw. To cut a hole in a tile, measure the centre of the pipe and cut the tile in half through this point. Then, using a template, score each half round and nibble away the excess. Put the cut edge of a tile to an inside corner. On outside corners, always start at least one angle with a full tile. Grout in accordance with the instructions on the packaging.

Hanging wallpaper

Calculate rolls required by dividing the average ceiling height into the average roll length (10 metres). Check that they are from the same batches. Buy the recommended paste. Sizing the walls with either special sizing paste or a weak paste solution will make it easier to move the paper on the wall. Mix the paste in the bucket as instructed on the packet. Tie string across the rim from each handle anchor to rest the brush and scrape off excess paste. Set up a plumb-line and mark the wall, one roll length from the first corner, less 12 mm. Start on the non-window walls, working away from the light, although if the paper has a strong pattern it can be best to centre this on the main focal point such as the fireplace.

Measure the height of the room plus 100 mm. Cut several lengths of paper, making sure that the over-sizing is sufficient to be able to match up the pattern. Lay pattern down, bottom end first, to one end of the table with the spare tucked behind string, tied loosely between the legs. Paste down the centre of the paper and then work out to the edges. Fold the pasted paper on to itself without creasing and complete the pasting. Hang the paper, leaving 50 mm at top and bottom and aligning it with the plumb-line. Release the folded section carefully so as not to tear it. Smooth out the paper with the paperhanging brush, working out to the edges to expel bubbles and remove creases. Run the closed scissors along the paper where it meets the ceiling and then cut along the crease. Do the same at the bottom. Smooth down the paper where it turns the corner.

Hang subsequent drops by butting them up to the preceding length. Cut the paper so as to turn an internal corner by 12 mm. Set the plumb-line to use the cut-off length as the first drop of the new run, overlapping its parent where it turns the corner. On external corners, cut the paper so that it turns the corner by 25 mm, then use the off-cut, butted to its parent, as the first drop of the next run. Use dart cuts around sockets and obstructions, then trim. Loosen faceplate screws, cut the paper and tuck under by about 3 mm before re-screwing. At reveals hang the paper and cut top and bottom where it overhangs, folding the paper into the reveal. To fill in at the reveal top cut a strip to match the width of the overhang above it. Paste it up and bring it forward to tuck under the main paper, matching the pattern. Then cut through the overlap with the Stanley knife, just above the reveal and seal the joint with the seam roller.

Laying quarry tiles

View the room from its main entrance and then find the centre of the wall directly in front of you and its opposite. Pull a string line between these two points down the middle of the room. Measure exactly half-way down the line. You now have the centre point of the room.

Lay tiles dry from this point along the line until you get to the last point where a full tile will fit. Don't forget to put in any spacers or allow 3 mm gaps for grouting. If the space left at one end is too small, move the tiles back along the line a little so that you have a reasonable-size cut at each end. Where the last tile ends, mark the centre line and then mark a second line at right angles to it. Find the right angle using a 3:4:5 triangle.

Lay tiles dry along this right-angle line until you get to the last spot where a whole tile can be laid. This is where the tiling will start. Mark the line and then create a third line from this point, parallel with the centre line. Fix straight-edge softwood battening along the second and third lines, nailing down into the concrete floor. The batten thickness should be at least twice the thickness of the tiles to allow for the mortar bed. Remember that while the battens should be secure, you will want to remove them later. If the floor is uneven, pack up the battens with cardboard so that you maintain a straight and preferably level top. Measure 600 mm or the nearest equivalent in tiles from the second line and fix a batten to the floor, parallel with it. Cut a batten or straight edge to span this last space plus the battens. Cut a notch out of each end the thickness of the tiles, less 3 mm, such that it will drop in between the battens.

Mix the mortar to a stiff cake-mix consistency, 1:3, cement to soft sand, and trowel it in between the battens to cover a 600 mm square. Use the notched board to level out the mortar. Dampen the tiles and sprinkle a little dry cement on the mortar before laying the tiles in approximately 600 mm squares or 16 at a time. Wiggle the tiles into the mortar level with the top of the battens. Wipe off any excess mortar using a damp cloth. When you have filled in this whole section move the third batten to start another one. Leave until set before removing the battens. Fill in the cuts at the edges. Cut tiles with a hired wet saw. Grout with a slightly wetter mortar mix, pushing it home with a short piece of hose or pipe. Wipe off excess mortar with a clean, damp cloth.

Replacing broken roof slates

Cracked or broken slates or tiles can let water into the roof and cause structural damage to the timbers. In windy conditions, they can also lead to wholesale stripping of the roof and pose a serious danger to passers-by. Always take care when working on a roof. Use a tower scaffold with appropriate boarding, guard rails and toe-boards to reach the eaves. Employ bracing and/or tie the tower through a window opening to a board across the reveal. Use a roof ladder, wheeled up the roof and then hooked over the ridge and, if necessary, employ sacks filled with straw under the resting points to protect the roof further.

Slates are usually nailed twice to the battens. Failure can be through the rusting of the nails or the cracking of the slate. Because slates are laid treble lapped, it is not possible to re-nail a replacement slate. A slater's rip is a long, thin implement with a fishtail hook at the end. Slide the rip up under the overlapping slates to pull out or cut off the old nails. Scour local reclamation yards to match the replacement slate for colour and thickness. Slates have the edges bevelled to the top/weathering surface. If you need to cut it to length or width, mark it by scoring a line with a nail, then place the slate, bevel-side down, on a bench or flat surface with the section to be cut off, overhanging. Using the edge of a bricklayer's trowel or a slater's axe (zax), chop off the excess. Cut a strip of lead or copper about 25 mm wide and 25 mm longer than the slate. Nail this strip to the batten through and between the slates immediately below the slate to be replaced. Slide the slate up and home so that the trailing edge is in line with the others. Fold the copper or lead strip up and over to secure the slate.

If you are replacing larger areas of slate you will need to drill or punch holes for the nails. If you punch them with the point of a zax, this will countersink the hole. Do not nail too tightly. Do not nail into lathes as they are not strong enough – in this case cut pegs of wood, insert them into the holes in the slate and hook the pegs over the lathe.

Replacing broken roof tiles

If your roof is clad with plain tiles or peg tiles then they are normally double or treble lapped. In severe-exposure areas every course will be nailed. In other areas only the verge, eaves and every third row could be nailed. Cut wedges from the 75 mm timber. Lift up the tiles on either side of the broken one and insert these wedges to hold them up. If the broken tile you have to replace is nailed, you will have to use a slater's rip to remove the nails and the tile. If not, then you will probably be able to wiggle it free, lifting the peg or nib over the batten. With interlocking tiles you will need to wedge up the tile immediately to the left of the broken tile as well as those directly above. Tiles with a particularly deep profile may require you to ease several of the surrounding tiles up or push them up on the battens. When the old tile is free, push the new tile into the vacated space and hook the nib or peg over the batten. Plain tiles may have been cut in order to gauge them across the roof. If you need to cut the new one always do this on the ground using an angle grinder and wearing the correct protective clothing and goggles.

To re-bed ridge tiles Knock off any loose or crumbling mortar and clean off the tiles for re-use. Make a mortar mix, 1:3, cement to soft sand, to a stiff cake-mix consistency. Lay two lines of mortar, one each side of the ridge, following the line of the old mortar. Dampen the ridge tile and press it into these lines of mortar, sweeping off any excess and filling into the profiles of the tiles below. If the profile is very deep you can bed dentil slips of tile pointing down the furrows. Pack the hollow ends with mortar and bits of broken slate or tile so that the mortar protrudes slightly from and above the end. Lay another two lines of mortar and press in the next ridge tile. Enough mortar should squeeze out to fill the narrow gap between the tiles but, if not, point up this gap. Verge tiles that become loose should be nailed back into position. In many cases there is a mortar pointing between the underside of the verge tiles and the undercloak. Remove any loose mortar. If the new mortar slumps too much, stiffen it by pushing pieces of slate or tile into it before smoothing off at the ends.

Ceramic floor tiling

Many of the techniques and principles described for the laying of quarry tiles and the fixing and setting out of ceramic wall tiles are applicable. However, if you are laying ceramic tiles, especially the thinner ones, on new screed laid over insulation with underfloor central heating, always use a flexible adhesive and grout. If you use a rigid fixer the inevitable settlement will produce fine hairline cracks in the tiles.

chapter nine

▋How to Stay On Time & On Budget

H ow is it that two self-builders, building similar houses to roughly the same specification, can have such varying experiences with costs and the time taken to complete their project? Luck does, of course, come into in it but, in the main, it is down to the management of the project and the ability to keep one step ahead of potential problems. Nobody can pretend that self-building is completely easy. It is not. It might not, in most cases, involve physical effort but it does demand constant thought and the only time to relax is when is it it is all over and you are sitting back in your new home.

To make sure that things go as right as possible and to sum up much of the information given in earlier chapters, here is a checklist of a few simple rules to follow at each of the stages.

What to do once you have found the plot

Make sure the finance is in place
Finding the plot might be the most difficult part of the whole project. But remember that you are not alone. There are thousands of others out there who would beat you to that plot if they could. So you need to have the right finance in place. Vendors won't wait for their money. They won't want to wait until you have sold your house. If you have no cash ready they will move on to somebody else. If you have freed up your equity by selling already or have the spare cash available, that is fine. Otherwise you will need to arrange a self-build mortgage in principle that will allow you to buy the land prior to selling your existing home.

Check out the planning
If a piece of land does not have planning permission or the certainty of it, then it is not a plot. If land is offered with planning permission check the dates. Check that it is still valid. As detailed in Chapter 5, The Planning Maze, there will be two types of planning permission in circulation until 2010; it is important to establish whether the consent is of the five- or three-year type. It is also vital to check that any subsequent application for Approval of Reserved Matters has been made in time to keep the consent valid.

Check out the access
Without access, the land is not a plot. Most plots need vehicular as well as pedestrian access. Make sure that the plot abuts a public Highway or, if a private road, that the necessary consents for you to use it are in place. Watch out for ransom strips – slivers of land that can deny access unless those owning them are paid off. Make sure that you can satisfy the requirements

of the Highways authorities in respect of visibility splays, turning circles, gradients and so on.

Check the boundaries

Make sure that what you are buying is the same size and shape on the ground as it is on the plans. Take some check measurements. Consider having a boundaries and levels survey carried out.

Pick the right solicitor

Not all solicitors or conveyancers are up to speed on land purchase and many might be baffled by simple problems that crop up during the legal process, many of which can be solved. If rights and documents are not clear, don't immediately abandon the project. Ask if a simple indemnity policy could solve the problem. Always remember that your solicitor is unlikely ever to see the land; if you can provide them with extra information that will short-circuit some of their enquiries, it will speed up the whole process.

Make sure you pick the right architect/designer

Choose somebody whose work you admire

Always goes on their track record. Look at their previous work. Talk to their previous clients. Investigate how their plans are received at the local authority. Check that they are *au fait* with the latest regulations and planning requirements.

Give them a 'starter for ten'

You can save time and a great deal of heartache on both sides if you give them a clear brief of what you want. If you have drawn plans, however bad, don't be bashful, show them to them.

Impress your budget upon them

Make sure they understand everything about building costs and the implications of design changes. The budget is paramount. They have to understand that if what they draw for you can't be built within it, it is not fit for your purpose.

Make sure their plans are clear

Unambiguous plans save time and money throughout the project. Cluttered or incomplete plans will drive you and your builders mad.

The planning process

Prior consultation saves time and money

Try to talk to the planners before you prepare your design brief. Take notes of their requirements. If that is not possible, read up as much as you can about their policies. If you need a Design and Access Statement, make sure it is comprehensive. If one exists already, make sure your proposals fit with its principles.

The first (scratch) coat of external render is now on.

Stay away from controversy
If you want your application to enjoy a smooth passage, make sure it is not contentious.

Check out local opposition
If you know who is going to be objecting and upon what basis, you can move to 'head them off at the pass'. Most objections are not valid in planning terms, but they can still delay a project. If you can mollify those who, after all, are going to be your new neighbours, then it pays to do so.

Check on the consultations and the timing of the application
If you have consulted the highways and environmental agencies beforehand, you will avoid wasting time with unacceptable applications. If you have primed the pumps locally and got people on your side, you will also speed up the process. Don't just wait for decisions. Keep abreast of to where the application has got and short-circuit problems as they arise.

Getting Building Regulations

Up-to-date knowledge is vital
The Building Regulations will continue to go through a dynamic period as governments come under increasing pressure in the face of climate change. This may not be in the form of a complete new set of regulations

as there are provisions within the Acts allowing for Statutory Orders to be made. It is important to make sure that at the time of your application all the professionals with whom you are working are fully conversant with the latest requirements.

Identify other professionals

It is a pound to a penny that other professionals are going to have to be brought on board to calculate the thermal and structural performances of your new home. Make sure that, if your architect/designer can't do these, you know to whom to go right at the outset.

Locating the right builder/subcontractors

Always go by recommendation

The best way of contacting labour is by recommendation and, indeed, you will find that if you mention a previous client, they will be much more amenable to quoting. However you get hold of labour, always make your own recommendation by tracking back and looking at their previous work as well as talking to their previous customers.

Check their schedule

It is no use getting a good price from a builder or subcontractor if they are going to be too busy to do your job. Check what work they have in the pipeline and only deal with them if they clearly identify a window of availability that fits in with your programme.

Keep them posted

Things inevitably slip in the run-up to commencement of work, and you will need to keep labour informed. It may mean that they are not able to do your job or, equally, that they have time to tidy up other jobs before they come to you.

Gearing up to start

Make sure all of the right consents are in place

You can't start work without planning permission. In England and Wales and in Northern Ireland, you can start without formal building-regulations approval, either on a Building Notice or by making an application and giving 24 hours' notice. If you have formal building-regulations approval, you will need to send in the commencement of work card and make sure that all of the other cards are sent in at the requisite time. In Scotland you must wait until the Warrant is issued before commencing work.

Get water on site

You will need water almost from day one, and it can take time to get the new supply organised. If there is any delay, arrange to take water from a friendly neighbour's outside tap or get a water bowser. Get butts or suitable water containers on site. Arrange a plumber for the stop-cock.

Sort out the access
The eventual access will have been dealt with at the planning stages. But you will need to make sure that there is suitable site access. This may be temporary and you may need to organise hardstanding and unloading points.

Get the fencing done
It is often easier to erect the main fencing before the main job starts. Security fencing needs to be arranged and erected.

Arrange storage
Think about where materials are going to be safe, out of the way of the contractors yet accessible. If access is limited, you may have to organise for off-site storage or hire fork-lifts or dumpers.

Think about spoil
If you can possibly make space or set aside an area for spoil then it will save you a considerable amount of time and money. It may even be useful at the later stages of the build. If it has to go, then organise to where and check the turnaround times of the lorries. It may require more than one vehicle if the site is to keep going.

Sort out site huts/toilets
These need to be positioned where they are accessible for storage, use and cleaning.

Arrange warranties well in advance
Most warranty companies will want notice of your intention to start work and may require three weeks' notice where there are trees. They may not take on responsibility for any works carried out prior to their approval and acceptance so it is important to think ahead on this one.

Arrange suitable self-build site insurance
Not having the right policy in place is a false economy that could jeopardise your entire project. You need Contractors' All Risk, Public and Employers' Liability.

Identify and order long-delivery materials
Some materials are on extremely long delivery and may need ordering well in advance of their requirement. Timber-frame companies may have lengthy lead-in periods, and you will need to co-ordinate their supply and erection with other site works if you are not to come to a complete stop.

Check out plant/tool hire
You may need plant or tools in pretty short order, and it is as well to open an account and gear things up well before you need them.

Check on the finance
You will want to know that all of the finance is in place before you start and to know when each tranche of the stage payments is going to be available.

Think about COD
Some materials, such as concrete, may be cash on delivery. The suppliers may take a cheque but that may be required in advance. Make sure you are not caught out at a stressful time.

Once work has commenced

Walk through the house in your mind
Keep on thinking about how things are going to be. You can't re-design on the hoof but you can minimise design conflicts by constantly keeping things under review.

Keep thinking ahead about materials
Think ahead for when materials will be needed and get them in on time and in the right quantities. Waste is expensive but running short can cost even more.

Keep thinking ahead about labour
Everybody working on your project is going to have other jobs on the go and they will require plenty of notice of when you are going to need them. It is a difficult balance for both parties to make. You are only concerned with your job and you won't want to be kept waiting. They can't leave their other clients in the lurch. That is why it is so important to keep in constant touch and to keep thinking ahead to when you will need them. Don't go looking for a trade in the immediacy of your need. It will cost you.

Make up your mind
Throughout the job there will be certain 'choice' items such as doors, sanitary-ware, kitchens and so on. Many of these are on long delivery and you will need to make up your mind early if you are not to introduce a delay.

Avoid changing your mind too often
Once or twice may be OK but if you make a habit of it you will delay the job and lose the windows of opportunity that tradesmen have set aside. Labour hates going back on a job and if you keep getting things done over and over again, relationships will break down.

Make sure key trades have plans and layouts
Recover all old and out-of-date plans and destroy them. Make sure that the electricians have the right layout plans with your requirements clearly marked by coloured symbols. Check that the plumbers know where radiators are to go or, with underfloor central heating, a detailed plan of the proposed layout. Check on the hanging of all doors and double-check that this accords with the position of electrical switches. Get a kitchen layout as soon as possible so that appliances and sockets are all in the right place and at the right level.

Gear up the inspections
You will need to make sure that the right inspection cards or building notice is given for the Building Inspector to attend. The same applies for the Warranty Inspectors and for any architectural progress certification.

Top coat of external render complete.

Gear up the stage payments

If stage payments are reliant on a surveyor visiting the site they may need notice. That may mean taking a flyer and asking them in advance of the stage being reached. But don't, on any account, let them come before you have actually got to the stage.

Check on-site security

Insurance will pay for stolen or damaged materials to be replaced or put right. But it won't pay for the time lost and a bad break-in could set you back weeks. Get a lock-up. Make sure that all movable items are safely put away. Keep the security fences up. Install PIR (passive infra-red) automatic security lights as soon as possible. Take home valuables if possible. Unwrap and de-crate saleable items.

Arrange approved contractors

Work within the Highway or to public sewers needs to be carried out by an approved contractor. Most authorities have lists of approved contractors,

Bringing in the services to the meter positions.

but there are often fewer than ten to each area and it can prove difficult to get on to their schedule. They are also expensive. Make the arrangements well in advance.

Site services
You will have arranged for quotations for a supply of electricity, gas and water at the earlier stages of the build. Water will be on site from the outset. Electricity and gas might not come in until the later stages. But you will need to gear them up for the supply and make sure that you have all of the necessary meter boxes and ducting in place. If you are using oil, you will need to get the tank installed and filled before you can fire the boiler and test the system.

Keeping abreast of the cashflow

Most self-build projects show a healthy margin at the end. But that does not always translate to a positive cashflow, and if you don't get the right finance or your stage payments are not set up right, you could run out of cash part-way through the job. Plan the cashflow and identify where you will be running short. Plan purchases to take the maximum credit. Try your hardest never get to the end of the week without having the money available for labour; if it looks likely warn them well in advance so that it does not come as shock. Make it clear that it will be forthcoming.

Keep the accounts and record recoverable VAT

Always keep receipts and enter them up each evening. That way you will not be at a loss to remember what they were for a few months down the line. Clearly list the recoverable VAT. It will save you loads of time later on and make it quicker to get your VAT reclaim in at a time when you might need the money.

Top five hold-ups

- **Things going wrong in the legal stages that could be put right** If there is a defective title, access can't be proved or beneficiaries of restrictive covenants or ransom strips can't be traced, ask if a simple single-premium indemnity policy could solve the situation.
- **Finance/cashflow problems** If you haven't got the right finance in place you could lose the plot. If you don't have a self-build stage-payment mortgage, it might be impossible to maintain a positive cashflow. Accelerator mortgages where the stage payments are given in advance rather than in arrears can be really useful. Try and avoid the stop–start syndrome of a self-build project that financially has been badly planned.
- **Delays on services** No matter how urgent your requirement the suppliers work to their own time-scale. Respond to their quotation and send in the payment as soon as possible. As soon as you have a reference number, arrange a date for the supply. Stick to that date if it is at all possible, but it is easier to put it back than bring it forward.
- **The wrong choice of builders/subcontractors/ professionals** Everyone is only as good as their last job. But you can weed out the wrong people by making the correct enquiries from previous clients or from those who have dealt with them in a work capacity. Never take on anybody on their own say-so. Always check them out.
- **Failure to think ahead** Self-building is all about forward thinking. You need to keep abreast of all requirements and second-guess eventualities or unforeseen problems. Never relax on this. For six months or so you have to be really on top of the game if you are to bring in your project on time and on budget.

chapter ten

How to Deal With Suppliers & Manufacturers

M anufacturers and suppliers, including builders' merchants, are all falling over themselves to deal with you as a representative of the huge self-build diaspora that they now recognise. But there are still some urgent considerations.

Buying on the Internet

Much of Internet shopping is largely parasitic upon existing retail and merchant outlets, relying on the ability of the would-be purchaser to hear of, touch, feel and see the product through some other forum. Within the self-build market, however, BuildStore have created a symbiotic relationship between itself and their merchant partners, Jewson, Builder Centre, William Wilson and others. The BuildStore trade account allows the self-builder to take advantage of the greater buying power of the group and set up individual trade accounts that enjoy discounts as good if not better than many major house builders. In addition, the possession of the BuildStore Trade Card enables the individual self-builder to gain the respect and attention of the members of staff within each branch of the builders' merchants, with access to a dedicated account manager.

Most builders' merchants will only allow a relatively small credit limit on private accounts. Those who have signed up to the BuildStore trade account have immediate access to a credit-account limit of £15,000, which is increased to £25,000 for those who are also taking a mortgage through BuildStore.

Guarantees and warranties

In UK law you cannot pass on the burden of a contract. If your purpose-made windows are supplied through your builder and they go out of business, you may not have recourse to the suppliers. Check the worth of any guarantee and if necessary insist on some form of collateral contract. Follow the instructions given with any purchase. Incorrect usage or installation could invalidate any guarantee. Structural warranties do not always cover items that are fundamentally important to the enjoyment of a home; warranty companies do require, though, that materials supplied have the necessary agreement certificate, and if they do not notice a failing during the inspection period, they might deny liability.

Suppliers' design and advice services

Many suppliers are prepared to put their facilities at the prospective buyer's disposal but be aware that this may be the sprat to catch the mackerel. It does, however, make complete sense to make use of kitchen and sanitary-ware suppliers prepared to undertake the design service. Specialist suppliers of plumbing and heating equipment will often provide a full take-off of not only their own but also ancillary supply. Ask all suppliers about after-sales back-up. Check on lead-in and delivery times. Read the suppliers' literature carefully and study the performance figures given in their published literature, comparing them wherever possible with their competitors.

Buying from abroad

There is no doubt about it that there are many bargains to be had abroad; savings can often be made by going directly to the foreign manufacturer or supplier instead of dealing with their UK agents. There are, however, pitfalls. Language barriers at the point of sale can be difficult. Cost of getting there and of delivery of materials can negate any supposed savings. Check on your guarantee position. Although in-store guarantees may be offered, what good will they do you if you have to add on the additional cost of travel. Many foreign companies set up business in this country, but these British subsidiaries might well refuse to recognise their sister company's manufacturer's guarantee. Always check compatibility with UK materials and compliance with local or statutory regulations.

Suppliers going bust

If a supplier goes bust before the goods are delivered then you effectively become an unsecured creditor for any monies you have paid. Given the length of time that it can take to sort out the financial affairs of a bankrupt company you will probably have no alternative but to write off the cost and look elsewhere for the materials. If a supplier goes bust after the goods have been delivered then you need to move quickly to make sure that they are secure from the attentions of creditors, who might feel they have the right to enter your site and re-possess the goods. Technically, if they are fixed then they are yours, but this is a grey area. If you have paid for them in full then title will have passed to you. If not, then you are probably better off making your own arrangements with the official receiver.

Purpose-made items

The words 'purpose made' have many connotations, the principal ones being special, costly and not easy to replace. If you are having purpose-made items then the lead-in times are likely to be greater and you will need to make allowances for this. Be careful to make sure that what is being made for you complies with all the necessary regulations and requirements of your warranty undertaker and Building Control. If you are likely to want additional matching items then it is a good idea to make the manufacturers aware of this when ordering so that they can keep any necessary templates. It should go without saying that wherever possible you should buy from established companies who are likely to be around to honour any guarantees.

Dodgy/cheap materials

Cheap doesn't always mean good – and can mean expensive. Check the quality of any goods being offered on the cheap. Remember that even if the materials are legal and of seemingly good quality, there might not be any come-back. Avoid the offers of the door-to-door tarmac salesman with no letter heading and no fixed address as it's a pound to a penny that it will all come up in short order. Resist the offers of cheap concrete or follow-on loads from drivers, as their bosses will be on to that one. If you are ever offered materials from unorthodox sources check the legality. If you unwittingly buy stolen goods then the title in those goods does not pass to you and you could find yourself considerably out of pocket. If you know about it or suspect it then you could find yourself on the wrong side of the law.

Discounts
Nearly all suppliers can be persuaded to give discounts, but few will offer them unless asked. As a private individual you should be aware that you are probably not initially being offered items as cheaply as, say, a builder would be. Even if you do negotiate a discount on the list price, be aware that some companies have different lists for different classes of customer and that you might still be at a disadvantage. If you are on good terms with your builders, ask them to obtain prices for the same item and then compare them. Sometimes, as when dealing with package-deal suppliers, it is not always appropriate to ask for an additional discount and many of those that do offer one, for say prompt or pro-forma payment, will have added the discount back into the costs in any event.

Changes in specification
In the small print of many agreements there is a right for the manufacturer to change the specification without notice. This might happen where, for example, the manufacturers find that there is a fault in the original design. They won't want to admit to the fault because that could leave them open to action by those who have already bought the goods. What you want is the goods you have ordered, and perhaps paid for, but what you don't want is faulty goods. You might have to be pragmatic here and either accept the rated design or, if it isn't suitable or doesn't fit, ask for your money back. Of course if you change the specification following order you will effectively be sending your delivery to the bottom of the list, so make sure that you specify exactly what you want in the first place.

What to do when things go wrong
Once delivery is made and items are paid for, your priority with the suppliers is considerably lessened as by then they are on to their next customer. Check all deliveries. Even when faced with an impatient lorry driver, check all items for scratches or damage and make a note on the delivery ticket. If you are not able to check then write 'goods unchecked' on the ticket. It isn't as good but it will give you some come-back. If the goods are incorrect or damaged then put them back on the lorry if at all possible. Resorting to legal action is the last option and should be considered only when all other avenues have been exhausted. Try to sort out the matter face to face with the suppliers and deal with people as near to the top as you can.

Deliveries
Most reputable suppliers will try to give at least 24 hours' notice of delivery, if only to ensure that there is someone there to assist in or direct off-loading. If you fail to turn up then the driver may make their own decision about where to put goods unless you give them specific instructions. Make suppliers aware of the immediate road conditions. If you are on a narrow lane or a site with restricted access it might not be possible to get large or articulated lorries in. Sometimes it is necessary to organise dumper or fork-lift trucks to bring in goods. At other times you might

need to arrange additional labour. Be aware that there might be waiting time added if you delay a delivery. If a lorry damages your property or the property of a third party then it is important to make a note of the driver's name and the vehicle number.

Supply and fix

Although specialist suppliers working within the self-build market have increased the choice and ability of the individual to purchase their own materials, many trades remain as principally supply and fix. Roof tiling is one where a supply-and-fix contract can often work out cheaper; electrical is another. This is principally because large discounts are available for bulk purchase of both primary and ancillary items. Plastering is a trade that is often best dealt with as supply and fix, simply because plaster has a shelf-life and if you supply the material then bad results could be blamed upon you. Plumbing is largely supply and fix for the more mundane of the materials and equipment. However, the self-builder is often able to supply specific items for fixing within the main contract.

With the scaffolding done, the house seems to break free of its cocoon.

Lead-in times

Many materials have long lead-in times that need to be addressed within your build programme. It is a failure to anticipate these that often results in the building falling behind schedule. Timber-frame companies will often require eight to ten weeks from order to delivery. If you are starting soon after receipt of planning permission then unless you are prepared to take a flyer on the order and, in many cases, the payment you might reach over-site and have to wait. Some of the more expensive and hand-made bricks and tiles are always on long delivery. Specially shaped bricks and tiles from mainstream manufacturers are only made to order. With second-fix and specialist items it might be as well to have alternatives in mind in case the delivery times become extended.

Wastage and returns

While there is often a charge for returns, any cost will be greatly outweighed by those involved in making up shortfalls; most self-builders would rather have something left over than have the site held up for the sake of, say, a few bricks. Reclaimed materials have a higher wastage factor than new ones and you might need to over order by up to 20 per cent on some second-hand bricks and tiles against the normal 5 per cent for new ones. Remember that materials such as second-hand bricks and tiles will be sourced by the suppliers from a particular demolition site; any subsequent deliveries might be significantly different. Quality is often and of necessity almost on a 'buyer beware' basis, so check that the items being supplied are fit for your purpose and comply with the necessary regulations.

Builders' merchants

Most builders' merchants entertain credit accounts from the individual self-builder. However, the credit limits imposed might be unrealistic and get swallowed up by the principal delivery items, reducing the account to a virtual cash-on-delivery basis. It is for this reason that it might be advisable for the self-builder to consider obtaining a BuildStore trade account, as referred to under 'Buying on the Internet' (p. 180). Some specialist merchants such as those dealing with plumbing and electrical materials are still prone to discriminate against accounts by non-trade people. In these cases it might be advisable to ask for the account in the name of 'Joe Bloggs Electrics/Plumbing or House Builder'. Builders' merchants are still unfriendly places for private individuals. BuildStore, through its trade account, is trying hard to make things better and succeeding slowly.

Service suppliers

Although there is a wider choice of supplier for the main services you will usually find yourself dealing with the principal undertaker or board for the connections. There is a considerable amount of paperwork involved; you will probably have to pay up front and allow a lead-in time of up to and sometimes beyond six weeks. Usually no work can start on site until water is available, so make sure that you have arranged a building supply. Electricity is not as critical, and many tradesmen use a generator. Be aware that service and drainage connections that entail work to the Highway can only be carried out by Approved Contractors. You can obtain a list of these from the local authority. They are expensive and in great demand.

Deposits and stage payments

Most specialist suppliers will require some sort of deposit, particularly before commencing manufacture of purpose-made items. Wherever possible keep the amounts to the minimum and insist that the deposit is returnable in the event of the supply being delayed through no fault of your own. Package-deal and timber-frame suppliers will more often than not require large stage payments in advance of deliveries. Make sure that these monies are paid only into a properly dedicated client's account and that the trustees of that account are authorised to pay the monies across to the main company account only when the staged contract has been fulfilled. Wherever possible, try to ensure that the stage payments accord with the value of the materials supplied.

Prime cost (PC) and provisional sums

These two costs are often confused. PC sums are prime-cost figures that relate to the supply of materials. Provisional sums usually relate to specific trades and are used when the actual specification is yet to be established. If there are PC sums for items to be supplied then you will need to establish whether they are the list price or take into account any available discounts. If the former, then you might consider that you should deduct the sum from the contract and purchase these items yourself. But beware the contracts that specify that the builder is still entitled to the profit element. Try to establish that provisional sums truly reflect the supply-and-fix cost of the relevant trade to its board and the NHBC requirements.

Theft, vandalism and damage

It is an unfortunate fact that many items go missing just after they are delivered. Whether this is because thieves keep a look out for high-value and easily disposable deliveries or whether there is a tip-off arrangement is debatable. Loss of certain goods at critical times can severely disrupt your programme, so when receiving goods make certain that they are secure or unpack and fit them as soon as possible to make it difficult for a thief to sell them on. Site insurance is a must for all self-builders, but this can never compensate for the loss of momentum to your project. If goods are damaged on delivery take this up with the suppliers. If they are subsequently damaged on site then, unless the value is greater than the excess, you might have to take it on the chin.

Problems with suppliers

From time to time even the best of suppliers are going to let you down. With many of them you will find that they have a *force-majeure* clause in their terms and conditions of sale that absolves them from any responsibility for knock-on problems. If what you have ordered does not arrive then you have two alternatives: continue to wait or buy elsewhere, the latter not as easy as it sounds especially if you have paid a deposit. And even if you can source an alternative, maybe the lead-in delivery time will be longer than the time in which the original suppliers now say they can get the goods to you!

There are a few simple rules to follow when dealing with suppliers. Firstly, don't pay for goods in advance unless you are sure of the source. If there is an element of bespoke manufacture then try to pay into a dedicated client's account or to a stakeholder who will release the money when the goods arrive. Sometimes it is better to walk away from a deposit. There are always alternatives. They may mean some compromise on your part but, in the end, if a company is unreliable at the beginning what on earth is it going to be like on after-sales service?

Whenever goods arrive they should be checked immediately. Even if the driver is impatient to be away, you need to check that the delivery is undamaged. If they won't wait, mark the delivery ticket 'Goods received unchecked'. If damage is subsequently found, you will have a stronger case for replacement. If goods prove to be unsatisfactory then you have the same rights as anybody buying from a shop, in that the goods should be 'of merchantable quality and fit for the purpose'.

A detached garage can often be left until last and even left off if money is tight.

Getting replacements from some firms is like getting blood out of a stone. On the other hand, most of the major builders' merchants and better-known suppliers working within the self-build industry know that their reputation is important and almost all will change faulty goods without demur. And you should have found that out in your initial enquiries with their previous clients.

chapter eleven

Costs, Cashflow & Who Does What

B efore any cost analysis, it is useful to know exactly who does what among the various building trades. The following list itemises tasks by trade for the groundworkers, bricklayers, carpenters, roofers, plumbers & heating engineers, electricians, plasterers, dry liners and tackers, decorators and ceramic tilers likely to be involved in your building project.

Tasks by trade on a typical job

The groundworkers
- Create entry into and clear site
- Lay hard base for access, deliveries and site storage
- Strip topsoil and store for re-use
- Set out house to suitably positioned profiles (this may be carried out by a surveyor/architect)
- Mark out centre line of dig with lime or similar
- Excavate foundation trenches to indicated or required depth
- Load spoil into dumpers for on-site storage/load spoil into tipper lorries for disposal off site
- Clean and bottom out trenches
- Position level pegs to indicate top of concrete
- Pour and lay footings concrete
- Lay foundation blockwork to DPC level, putting in cranked ventilators, all necessary drainage-exit lintels and/or sleeving for services (this may be undertaken by bricklayers)
- Level out subsoil in oversite
- Backfill trenches outside the building
- Fill cavities with lean-mix concrete
- Position floor beams on DPC
- Lay infill blocks in place
- Brush grout floor or fill and consolidate hardcore to oversite
- Sand blind hardcore
- Lay damp-proof membrane
- Position below-slab insulation
- Lay further damp-proof membrane
- Lay oversite concrete
- Excavate trenches for foul and surface-water drainage
- Lay drainage runs on pea shingle, bringing upstands to positions though oversite
- Haunch over all below-ground drainage in pea shingle
- Build all manholes

- Connect foul drainage to foul sewer/the boundary for road connection by others/install septic tank/cesspool/mini sewage-treatment plant. Install and lay any weeper drainage or outlets
- Construct soakaways and connect surface-water drains
- Backfill all drainage trenches
- Excavate all service trenches and backfill when supplies are laid
- Carry out specified and agreed hard and soft landscaping and fencing
- Lay driveways, pathways and patios to agreed specification

The bricklayers

- Lay blockwork foundations to DPC level
- Build honeycomb sleeper walls (timber-suspended floors only)
- Build in below-ground drainage exit lintels
- Build in cranked ventilators for beam and block floors, or airbricks and cavity sleeves
- Bed DPC
- Bed plates (timber-suspended floors only)
- Position floor beams and lay infill blocks (if the groundworkers do not do this)
- Brush grout flooring
- Build superstructure brickwork and blockwork
- Install cavity insulation as work progresses
- Create opening for windows and doors
- Install cavity closers
- Fit windows and door-frames (if appropriate)
- Build in meter boxes
- Bed lintels
- Lay padstones (where appropriate)
- Position steel joists and beams
- Lay first-floor beams and infill with blocks (if agreed)
- Brush grout flooring
- Install cavity trays (where necessary)
- Bed wallplate
- Build up gable ends
- Build chimney through roof
- Build internal brick features and fireplaces
- Point up flashings and trays
- Fill putlock holes
- Build feature walling to garden

The carpenters

First fix
- Cut, lay and level suspended ground-floor joists (mainly in Scotland)
- Fix decking (flooring) to suspended ground-floor joists (if appropriate)
- Cut, lay and level first-floor (chamber) joists and trimmers
- Fix door linings (casings) to openings in ground-floor blockwork
- Lay first-floor decking
- Make up and install first-floor studwork partitioning

- Install insulation to floor zones and studwork (unless done by a general labourer)
- Fix window boards
- Fix staircase flight
- Make up and fix garage door-frames
- Nogging out for plasterboard
- Hang temporary external doors (where appropriate for security)
- Make up tank stands in the loft (if using a vented plumbing system)
- Box out pipework (usually done at second-fix stage)
- Board out the loft (if appropriate) (done before tacking)

Roof
- Erect and complete roof using prefabricated trusses or cut and pitch a roof made on site from sawn lumber (to include gable ladders, valleys, hips, dormers or roof lights as well as any porch or bay-window roofs)
- Lay sarking boarding (Scotland only)
- Fix fascias and soffits, including, where required, any soffit or eaves ventilation
- Fix bargeboards where required

Second fix
- Lay insulation and decking to floating ground or first floors
- Assemble and fit staircase newels, balustrading, aprons and handrailing
- Hang all internal doors
- Fix all skirting, architrave and decorative timber mouldings
- Assemble and fit timber French doors
- Hang timber external doors
- Fit garage doors including personnel doors
- Hang doors to fitted wardrobes and cupboards and fit out, including slatted shelving to airing cupboard
- Fitting or fixing of loft traps
- Fixing loft ladders (if required)
- Installing insulation to ceilings (unless undertaken by a general labourer)

The roofers
- Cover in roof with underlay and rough batten
- Fix GRP valleys or attend plumber fixing lead valleys
- Bed or fix undercloak to verges
- Fix counter battens if necessary
- Gauge and fix tiling battens to suit tiles or slates
- Load out tiles/slates
- Lay roof tiles/slates, nailing as appropriate
- Lay valley tiles if appropriate
- Fix verge tiles/slates
- Interleave upstand and cover flashings to chimney
- Interleave lead soakers
- Attend to and interleave vent pipe skirts

Building the front garden walls.

- Fix or bed ridge and hip tiles
- Point up space between underside of tiles/slates and undercloak
- Clean off excess or spilled mortar

The plumbers and heating engineers
- Install standpipe for building supply
- Lay first-fix carcassing pipework
- Place tanks in the roof (where applicable)
- Run any gas pipework to boiler and outlets
- Make up any lead flashings or soakers to the roof
- Fix guttering & downpipes
- Fix vent pipes to drainage upstands and take them through the roof
- Fix skirts to vent pipes
- Fit hot-water cylinder
- Fix radiators to the wall and connect
- Lay underfloor central heating pipework
- Connect underfloor heating loops to the manifold
- Fit boiler and connect to system
- Attend to flues and chimney liners
- Connect boiler to oil or LPG tank (if applicable)
- Fit sanitary-ware
- Connect sanitary-ware to domestic plumbing and wastes
- Plumb in kitchen and utility sink units, washing machines, dishwashers, etc.

- Lag all exposed pipework
- Fire up boiler and test system
- Balance and commission system

The electricians
- Fit temporary consumer unit to building supply
- Install and connect earth rod
- Lay and fix all carcassing wiring
- Drill joists where necessary
- Fix backplates to outlets and controls
- Fix proprietary sheathing over wires in walls
- Fix and wire up faceplates to outlets
- Fix and wire up light pendants
- Fit and wire up ceiling and wall lights
- Fit and wire up all external and security lighting
- Fit and wire up extractor fans and cooker hoods
- Cross bond and earth all pipework and sanitary-ware
- Fit and wire up consumer unit
- Wire up thermostats and programmers
- Attend with plumber for testing of boiler and central heating
- Test the system

Compare this picture with the first photograph in the book. This really has improved the whole street scene.

The plasterers, dry liners and tackers
- Tack ceilings with plasterboard or gypsum fibreboard
- Fix all beading and lathing
- Float & set all masonry walls
- Dry line walls with plasterboard or gypsum fibreboard
- Tape and joint plasterboard walls or skimcoat all dry-lined walls
- Tape and joint ceiling boards
- Skimcoat ceilings or Artex ceilings
- Fix mouldings and coving
- Render external walls
- Screed floors

The decorators
- Snag and rub down all walls
- Fill all holes
- Rub down and fill all joinery
- Knot all timber to be painted
- Prime or undercoat all internal and external joinery and second-fix timber
- Gloss coat or stain all internal and external joinery
- Paint all walls with one mist coat and, usually, one topcoat
- Paint all ceilings with two coats of emulsion
- Paint all external render with two coats of proprietary finish

The ceramic tilers
- Lay all floor tiles with the correct adhesive
- Grout all tiles
- Fix all wall tiles using spacers
- Grout all wall tiles

Trade-by-trade cost analysis

Many self-builders will send off their plans to estimating companies, which, for a relatively small fee, will produce an eight to ten page print-out detailing the quantities and costs of both labour and materials. These are excellent. They are usually quite accurate and give the self-builder targets for which to aim and, hopefully, to beat. But they are not totally comprehensive. They will exclude many of the preliminary costs, such as architects/designers, service supply and site set-up, and the prime costs (PC) for items such as bathrooms and kitchens might be quite low. They would almost certainly also exclude costs for items such as fitted bedroom furniture and carpets and external works such as fencing, landscaping and turfing.

In any evaluation of building costs it is as well to go back to basic principles. Most self-builders will use the Average Build Costs tables in *Homebuilding & Renovating* magazine, at least in the first instance when starting the project. But £s per square metre is only ever going to be approximate and at some stage, before work commences, a proper costing is necessary, based on the actual drawings and the site circumstances.

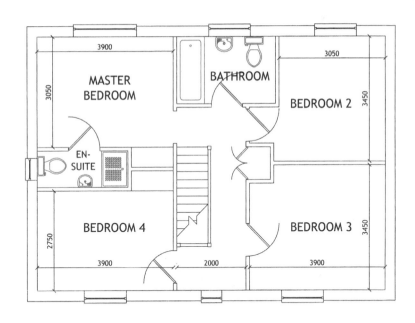

FIRST FLOOR LAYOUT

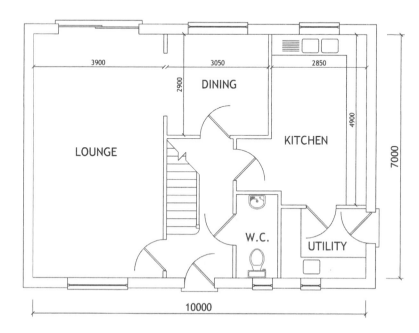

GROUND FLOOR LAYOUT

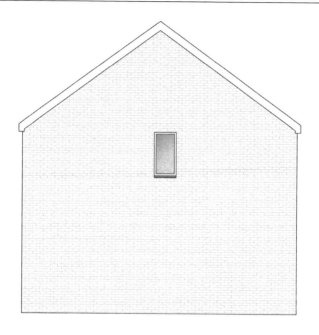

SIDE ELEVATION

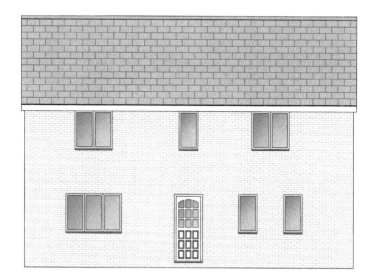

FRONT ELEVATION

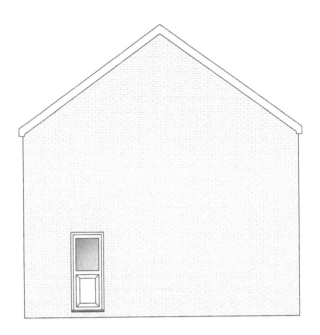

SIDE ELEVATION

REAR ELEVATION

What follows is a trade-by-trade analysis and build-up of costs for the basic four-bedroom house illustrated in the plans on pp. 194–6, plus a note of the factors that could serve to increase them. Finance costs are not included as these will certainly be unique to each individual. Some other costs, such as those for carpets and landscaping, are included in order to give a proper comparison with a fully finished home and bring the self-build project into line with the specification that most developers now follow. VAT is not generally included, except where it is non-recoverable and is, therefore, a direct cost.

Preliminaries and enabling works

Designer's fees, say, £2500 + VAT	£ 2937.50
SAP calculations £120 + VAT	£ 141.00
Engineer's fees £120.00 + VAT	£ 141.00
Planning fees	£ 265.00
Building Regulations fees	£ 535.00
Electricity supply	£ 900.00
Gas supply	£ 678.00
Water & sewage supply	£ 1170.00
Warranty	£ 1500.00
Site insurance	£ 513.00
	£ 8780.50

If an architect is used rather than a local designer then the costs for the drawings may rise to around £6000 or even more if site supervision is required. However, this is mitigated by the fact that engineer's fees and SAP calculations would be included. Service charges can vary considerably, depending on the distance the supply has to travel and the terrain it has to cross.

Groundworks

Enabling works

Site hut/storage 17 weeks @ £39.99 + VAT	£ 798.80
Toilets 17 weeks @ £27.99 + VAT	£ 559.10
5 tons Type 1 roadstone @ £20 p. ton	£ 100.00
Labour 1 day ganger + 1 @ £180 p. day	£ 180.00

Site strip

1 day digger (hire only) @ £189.04 + VAT	£ 222.12
1 day ganger + 1 @ £180 p. day	£ 180.00
Pegs	£ 15.00

Excavate

3 days digger @ £189.04 + VAT	£ 666.36
3.5 days labour ganger + 2 @ £260	£ 910.00
Soil away 6 loads @ £180.00 + VAT	£ 1269.00
Level pins	£ 30.00

Concrete foundations

1 day labour, ganger + 1, @ £180	£ 180.00
4 loads concrete @ £402.36 p. load	£ 1609.44
Pump hire £285 + VAT	£ 334.88

Foundation blockwork

45 m sq. blocks @ £7.50 p. metre	£	337.50
Blocklayers 45 m sq. @ £12 p. metre	£	540.00
Mortar	£	18.00
2 rolls DPC	£	6.66
1 bundle wall ties	£	43.60
Drainage exit lintels	£	64.00
Mixer hire 1 week @ £15 + VAT	£	17.63

Ground floor

70 m sq. floor beams @ £11.55	£	808.50
Infill blocks 65 m sq. @ £7.50 p. sq. metre	£	487.50
Cranked vents 18 @ £3.45	£	62.10
Labour – 2 days ganger + 2 @ £260	£	520.00

Drains

Digger hire 2 days	£	444.24
Labour – 6 days ganger + 2 @ £260	£	1560.00
8 ˜ 6m pipe @ £12.24	£	97.92
3 bags pea shingle @ £45 ea.	£	135.00
8 ˜ gullies @ £16.97 ea.	£	135.76
Fittings	£	390.21
6 No. inspection chambers	£	305.76
	£13,029.08	

It is in the ground that most cost overruns will occur. This costing is based on a trenchfill foundation. If a deep-strip foundation were utilised then the concrete costs would shrink but the foundation blockwork costs would increase. Trenchfill gets you out of the ground in one day and avoids problems with weather or unstable trenches.

Deeper foundations will cost correspondingly more depending on the amount of spoil and concrete. Unstable ground might mean changing to a piled or raft foundation with add-on costs of between £4000 and £8000. Some groundworkers will lay the foundation blocks. Others will prefer to leave it to the bricklayers. A solid concrete oversite could save between £500 and £800 but the beam-and-block floor provides a finite cost and is more acceptable to warranty providers.

Brick and blockwork/superstructure

Walling

12,283 bricks @ £260 p. 1000	£	3193.58
Labour – 11,184 bricks @ £450 p. 1000 including frame fixing, lintel bedding and insulation	£	5032.80
190 m sq. insulating blocks @ £8.80	£	1672.00
120 m sq. concrete blocks @ £7.50	£	900.00
Blockwork labour @ £12 per metre	£	3624.00
Mortar	£	324.00
External lintels	£	428.00
Internal lintels	£	236.00
Cavity insulation 160 m sq. @ £3.83	£	612.80
2 bundles wall ties	£	87.20

Retaining discs	£	27.57
2 rolls DPC	£	6.66
10 weeks' mixer hire	£	176.30
Skip	£	141.00

First floor

70 m sq. beams @ £11.55	£	808.50
65 m sq. infill blocks @ £7.50	£	487.50
Batten clips	£	52.50
Labour ganger + 2 @ £260	£	520.00
Crane hire	£	341.25

External windows and doors

uPVC supply	£	4000.00
Fitting	£	500.00

Scaffolding

12 weeks' hire @ £245.58 per week	£	2946.96
	£26,118.62	

Change to a more expensive brick will affect the material costs but is unlikely to affect the labour or ancillary costs. Change to a natural stone façade is likely to add considerably to the price with the requirement for a backing block plus the extra cost of the stone. The labour is also likely to shoot through the roof as this is an expensive and increasingly rare skill and, together with the extra materials, you could be looking at £7000–£10,000 extra. Change to rendered blockwork might seem a cheaper option but in fact because it involves two more trades, the plasterer and the decorator, and means that the scaffolding has to stay up longer, it could add £5 per sq. metre or close on £1000.

A timber first floor can save around £1100. The decking and insulation is also some £600 cheaper than the insulated screed floor. Some bricklayers will undertake the beam-and-block first floor; others prefer the groundworkers to come back to do it.

Any uPVC windows are usually supplied and retro-fitted by others. Timber joinery is fitted by the bricklayers as they go.

Carpentry

Roof

19 roof trusses @ £40 ea.	£	760.00
Wallplate 22 m @ £2.38	£	52.36
Plate straps	£	87.41
Fascia 22 m @ £5.10	£	112.20
Soffits 20 m @ £6.93	£	138.60
Nails & fixings	£	48.69
Binders and bracings 150 m @ 70p	£	105.00
Labour – 5 days carpenter + 2 @ £300	£	1500.00

First fix

Internal door linings 14 @ £14.32 ea.	£	200.48
Staircase flight	£	429.42
Newel post and base	£	215.48
Window boards 12 m	£	43.00

Pipe boxing & odds, say,	£	100.00
Loft hatch	£	48.05
Labour – 5 days carpenter @ £160	£	800.00

Second fix

14 doors @ £28.34 ea.	£	395.36
Furniture and fixings	£	145.41
Skirting 162 m @ £1.80	£	291.60
Architrave 140 m @£1.56	£	218.40
Balustrading & handrails, etc.	£	420.35
Second-fix labour – 8 days carpenter @ £160	£	1280.00
Kitchen units PC, say,	£	3500.00
Kitchen fitting, say 5 days @ £160	£	800.00
	£11,691.81	

For £1500–£2000 the trusses could be changed to attic trusses, which would then allow occupation of the roof at a later date. Of all the elective extras, this is perhaps the most cost-effective. Internal doors, kitchen units and joinery can cost considerably more but may not actually add value to the home.

Roofing

Undercloak	£	36.00
Breathable underlay 3 rolls @ £135.37	£	406.11
Battens 484 m @ 25p	£	121.00
Nails and clouts	£	280.78
Roof tiles		
1012 tiles)		
74 eaves tiles)		
80 top tiles)		
30 l/h verge)		
30 r/h verge) @ £2.08 ea	£	2550.08
25 ridge tiles @ £2.41 ea.	£	60.25
Mortar & colouring	£	25.00
Mechanical conveyor	£	88.13
Labour – 7 days roofer + 1 @ £220	£	1540.00
	£ 5107.35	

Hand-made plain clay tiles in lieu of concrete interlocking, as costed, might add around £10,000. Even machine-made clay tiles would add about £4000; natural slates would add around the same.

Breathable underlays might seem much more expensive than normal roofing felt but do not need additional ventilation to the roof void.

Plumbing and central heating

First fix

Pipe, fittings and wastes	£	852.78
Labour 6 days @ £200	£	1200.00

Second fix

13 radiators + TRVs	£	796.25
Boiler (gas-condensing)	£	892.53
Mains pressure cylinder	£	627.00
Controls	£	200.00
Sanitary-ware PC sum	£	1000.00
Labour 9 days @ £200	£	1800.00

Rain-water system

Guttering 4 ˉ 6 m @ £18.06 ea.	£	72.24
Brackets 14 @ 87p	£	12.18
Outlets 2 @ £4.12	£	8.24
Stop ends 4 @ £1.65	£	6.60
Downpipe 2 ˉ 6 m @ £16.08	£	32.16
Downpipe brackets 12 @ £1.86	£	22.32
Swan necks 4 @ £2.35	£	9.40
Rawl plugs and screws	£	14.81
Labour 2 days @ £200	£	400.00
	£	**7946.51**

Underfloor central heating could add around £1600 to the initial outlay but running costs might be much better as condensing boilers work more efficiently at the lower temperatures that are required.

Most modern houses now have a mains-pressure hot-water system, either using a standard boiler or a combi system.

You can spend considerably more on sanitary-ware but it might not be cost-effective: the 'wow' factor in bathrooms is often achieved with the accoutrements and accessories.

Rain-water goods are usually fixed by the plumber but can be carried out by another competent tradesperson. PVC sections are undoubtedly the cheapest. The soakaways and their connecting drains are carried out by the groundworkers.

Electrical

First fix

Cable, channel, sheathing, back boxes, etc.	£	242.00
Labour 5 days @ £165	£	825.00

Second fix

Faceplates, fans, consumer unit, pendants etc.	£	612.70
TV aerials (s&f)	£	200.00
Light fittings	£	300.00
Labour 5 days @ £165	£	825.00
	£	**3004.70**

It is all too easy to go over the top with this trade, doubling or even trebling the price. Think carefully about your needs. Mark up the plan and then mark the walls before the tradesperson starts. It is usual for the self-builder's light fittings to be fitted by the electrician.

Plastering and insulation

Ceilings
55 sheets ceiling plasterboard @ £5.29 ea.	£	290.95
Ceiling battens 150 m @ 25p	£	37.50
Tack ceilings – 2.5 days @ £220	£	550.00
Skimcoat ceilings – 2.5 days @ £220	£	550.00
Ceiling ancillary materials	£	138.01

Above ceiling insulation
14 packs insulation	£	341.88
Labour – 2 days @ £90	£	180.00

Walls
Dry lining 135 sheets plbd @ £5.29 ea.	£	714.15
Walling adhesive	£	228.92
Dry lining 3 days @ £220	£	660.00
Skimcoat walling materials	£	278.97
Skimcoat labour 6 days @ £220	£	1320.00
Skip	£	141.00

Floors
Flooring insulation 140 m. sq @ £5.36	£	750.40
Membrane	£	78.00
Readymix screed – 20 tons @ £49.95	£	999.00
Hoist	£	88.13
Labour 5 days @ £220	£	1100.00
	£	**8446.91**

Plasterers can be supply and fix or labour only. Hard plastering costs roughly the same as dry lining but will take considerably longer to dry out sufficient for it to be decorated. With dry lining one is also less likely to experience cracking. Coving can add £500–£900 but is rapidly going out of style in favour of cleaner lines. A plasterer might want a conveyor or hoist brought in for the first-floor screed, adding around £88.

The insulation to a cold roof void can only be put up once the ceiling is tacked. It can be done by the plasterers but is usually left to less skilled labour. The plasterers might not always want to lay the membrane and underfloor insulation; this can also be done by less skilled labour.

Decoration
72 litres trade emulsion	£	190.08
10 litres undercoat	£	47.10
10 litres satinwood	£	61.30
Fillers, solvents & cleaners	£	50.91
Brushes, sandpaper, etc.	£	25.55
14 days labour @ £110	£	1540.00
	£	**1914.94**

This trade is often undertaken by the self-builder. However, the decorator is also responsible for 'snagging' many of the problems left by other trades and the maxim 'prior preparation prevents poor performance' are certainly the watchwords. It is one of the cheapest in terms of labour costs and day rates.

Ceramic tiler

Floors

30 sq. m tiles @ £16	£	480.00
Adhesive, grout and additives	£	372.72
Labour @ £20 per sq. m	£	600.00

Walls

23 sq. m tiles @ £11	£	253.00
Adhesive, grout & spacers	£	127.49
Labour @ £15 per sq. m	£	345.00
	£ 2178.21	

Once again this trade is often taken on by the self-builder. Professionals do, however, do it much more quickly and neatly.

Carpets

110 sq. m @ £10.50 (s&f)	£ 1155.00	
	£ 1155.00	

It has become the norm for developers to put in carpets and, therefore, to be properly finished, a self-build home should also include these costs. Carpet can vary from £7.50 per sq. m up to £40 and even beyond.

External works

Driveway

Tarmac driveway 40 m sq. @ £20 (s&f)	£	800.00

Fencing

30 panels @ £15 p. post (s&f)	£	465.00

Paths and patios

Slabs 130 No. @ £2.50	£	325.00
All-in ballast – 2 tons	£	40.00
Cement 10 bags @ £2.83	£	28.30
Labour 4 days @ £180	£	720.00
Mixer hire 1 week	£	17.63

Turf

300 sq. m @	£	507.00
Labour 2 days @ £180	£	360.00
	£ 3262.93	

Savings can be made by swapping to a pea-shingle driveway at around half the cost.

Retaining walls can be very expensive. Keep all topsoil on site and as much subsoil as you need to make up levels. Remember stacked soil shrinks to under half its volume. Sending soil away is expensive – buying it back is even more so!

GRAND TOTAL	**£ 92,495.56**
+ 10% contingency	**£ 9,250.00**
	£101,745.56

= £726.75 per sq. metre

The rear garden view of the new self-built home that has been featured from beginning to end in this book.

Further Information

Books
Brinkley, Mark, *The Housebuilder's Bible*, Ovolo Publishing.
Dijksman, Ken, *The Planning Game*, Ovolo Publishing.
Holmes, Michael, *Renovating for Profit*, Ebury Press.
Snell, David, *Building Your Own Home,* Ebury Press.
Snell, David and Armor, Murray, *The New Home Plans Book*, Ebury Press.

Magazines
Build It www.self-build.co.uk Tel: 020 7837 8727
Homebuilding & Renovating www.homebuilding.co.uk Tel: 01527 834400
Self-build & Design www.selfbuildanddesign.com Tel: 01283 742950

Planning inspectorates and Appeal boards
England The Planning Inspectorate www.planning-inspectorate.gov.uk
    Tel: 0117 372 8754
Wales The Planning Inspectorate www.planning-inspectorate.gov.uk/cymru
    Tel: 02920 825007
Scotland The Scottish Executive Inquiry Reporters Unit www.scotland.gov.uk
    Tel: 0131 244 5649
Northern Ireland The Planning Appeals Commission www.pacni.gov.uk
    Tel: 02890 244710

Architectural, design and engineering associations and societies
Royal Institute of British Architects (RIBA) www.architecture.com
    Tel: 020 7580 5533
Royal Incorporation of Architects in Scotland (RIAS) www.rias.org.uk
    Tel: 0131 229 7205
Royal Society of Architects in Wales (RSAW) www.architecture-wales.com
    Tel: 02920 874753
Royal Society of Ulster Architects (RSUA) www.rsua.org.uk Tel: 028 9032
    3760
Royal Institute of Architects in Ireland (RIAI) www.riai.ie Tel: 00 353 1676
    1703
Associated Self-Build Architects (ASBA) www.asba-architects.org
    Tel: 0800 387310
Architects Registration Board (ARB) www.arb.org.uk Tel: 020 7278 2206
Royal Town Planning Institute www.rtpi.org.uk Tel: 020 7636 9107
The British Institute of Architectural Technologists www.biat.org.uk
    Tel: 020 7278 2206
The Institute of Civil Engineers www.ice.org.uk Tel: 020 7222 7722

Building trades associations
Federation of Master Builders www.fmb.org.uk Tel: 020 7242 7583
Guild of Master Craftsmen www.guildofmastercraftsmen.com Tel: 01273
    478449
HomePro/Fair Trades Ltd www.HomePro.com Tel: 0870 738 4858
Yellow Pages www.yell.com Tel: 0118 959 2111
Construction Federation www.constructionfederation.co.uk Tel: 020 7608
    5080
Joint Contracts Tribunal (JCT) www.jctcontracts.com Tel: 0121 722 8200
Association of Plumbing and Heating Contractors www.aphc.co.uk
    Tel: 02476 470626

Institute of Plumbing and Heating Engineering www.iphe.org.uk
Tel: 01708 472791
Council for Registered Gas Installers (CORGI) www.corgi-gas.com
Tel: 01256 372200
Oil Firing Technical Association Limited (OFTEC) www.oftec.co.uk
Tel: 0845 6585080
National Inspection Council for Electrical Installation Contractors
www.niceic.org.uk Tel: 020 7582 7746
National Federation of Roofing Contractors www.nfrc.co.uk Tel: 020
7436 0387
Thatching Advisory Services www.thatchingadvisoryservices.com
Tel: 01256 880828
The Painting & Decorating Association www.paintingdecoratingassociation.
co.uk Tel: 02476 353 776
British Interior Design Association www.bida.org Tel: 020 7349 0800

Government agencies and establishments
Ministry of Communities and Local Government www.communities.gov.uk
The Scottish Building Standards Agency www.sbsa.gov.uk
Scottish Parliament www.scotland.gov.uk
Northern Ireland Planning Service www.doeni.gov.uk
Department of Finance and Personnel (NI) www.dfpni.gov.uk
The Building Research Establishment (and BRECSU) www.bre.co.uk
Tel: 01923 664000
Health Protection Agency www.hpa.org.uk Tel: 01235 831600
HM Land Registry www.landreg.gov.uk Tel: 020 7917 8888
Registers of Scotland www.ros.gov.uk Tel: 0131 659 6111
Floodline www.floodline.com Tel: 0845 988 1188
The National Housing Federation www.housing.org.uk Tel: 020 7067 1010
The Housing Corporation www.housingcorp.gov.uk Tel: 020 7393 2000
HM Revenue and Customs www.hmrc.gov.uk Tel: 08450 109000
VAT self-build claims www.hmrc.gov.uk Tel: 0121 697 4000 and VAT
Helpline 0845 010 9000
SEDBUK boiler ratings www.boilers.org.uk

Self-certification schemes or bodies
BRE Certification Ltd www.brecertification.co.uk Tel: 01923 664100
British Standards Institution www.kitemartoday.com Tel: 01442 278607
ELECSA www.elecsa.org.uk Tel: 020 7864 9913
NAPIT www.napit.org.u Tel: 0870 444 1392
NICEIC Certification Services Ltd www.niceic.org.uk Tel: 08000 130900
Scottish Building Standards Registration Scheme (SELECT)
www.select.org.uk
Structural Engineering Registration Scheme (SER) www.ser-ltd.com Tel:
0207 201 9116

Special-interest groups or associations
Association of Selfbuilders www.self-builder.org.uk Tel: 0704 154 4126
Traditional Housing Bureau www.housebuilder.org.uk Tel: 01344 725757
Timber Research & Development Association (TRADA) www.trada.co.uk
Tel: 01494 569600 (England & Wales) 01259 272143 (Scotland)
British Woodworking Federation www.bwf.org.uk Tel: 0870 458 6951
Basement Development Group www.basements.org.uk Tel: 01344 725737
Glass and Glazing Federation www.ggf.co.uk Tel: 0870 042 4255
Disabled Living Foundation www.disabledliving.co.uk Tel: 020 7289 6111
Disability Alliance www.thedisabilityalliance.org.uk Tel: 020 7247 8776

Community Self-Build Association www.communityselfbuildagency.org.uk
 Tel: 020 7415 7092
Walter Segal Trust www.segalselfbuild.co.uk Tel: 020 7388 9582
Centre for Alternative Technology www.cat.org.uk Tel: 01654 705950
Society for the Protection of Ancient Buildings (SPAB) www.spab.org.uk
 Tel: 020 7377 1644
English Heritage www.english-heritage.org.uk Tel: 020 7973 3000
Council for the Protection of Rural England (CPRE) www.cpre.org.uk
 Tel: 020 7253 0300
Historic Scotland www.historic-scotland.gov.uk Tel: 0131 668 8600
Cadw www.cadw.wales.gov.uk Tel: 02920 500200
Environmental & Heritage Service (Ulster) www.ehsni.gov.uk
 Tel: 028 9023 5000
Council for British Archaeology www.britarch.ac.uk Tel: 01904 671417
Ancient Monuments Society www.theancientmonumentssociety.org.uk
 Tel: 020 7236 3934
Georgian Group www.thegeorgiangroup.org.uk Tel: 020 7387 1720
Victorian Society www.victorian-society.org.uk Tel: 020 8994 1019
Bat Conservation Trust www.bats.org.uk Tel: 0845 130 0228
Royal Society for the Protection of Birds www.rspb.org.uk Tel: 01767 680551

Government grants
England & Wales www.est.org.uk/housingbuildings/lowcarbonbuildings
Scotland www.est.org.uk/schri
Northern Ireland www.niesmart.co.uk

Renovation and reclamation specialists
The Lime Centre www.thelimecentre.co.uk Tel: 01962 713636
Strippers of Sudbury www.stripperspaintremovers.com Tel: 01787
 371524

Professional VAT reclaim assistance
Michael J. Flint www.mjfvat.btinternet.co.uk Tel: 01435 813360

Companies and agencies assisting in land finding
Plotfinder www.plotfinder.net Tel: 0906 557 5400
Plotsearch www.buildstore.co.uk/plotsearch Tel: 0870 870 9994
Rightmove www.rightmove.co.uk
English Partnerships www.englishpartnerships.co.uk Tel: 01908 692692

Exhibitions and shows
Homebuilding & Renovating Show (early spring at the NEC, Birmingham,
 late spring at Glasgow SECC, summer at East of England Showground,
 Peterborough, early autumn at Excel, London Docklands, late autumn
 in Harrogate Exhibition and Conference Centre and winter in
 Southwest Showground, Bath) www.homebuildingshow.co.uk
 Tel: 01527 834400
Ideal Homes Exhibition (every spring at Earl's Court, London)
Grand Designs Exhibition (held in the summer at Excel, London Docklands)
Selfbuild Ireland (shows in Belfast, Dublin, Cork & Galway)
 www.selfbuild.ie Tel: 0289 751 0570

Self-build and renovation centres
National Self-build and Renovation Centre – Swindon www.mykind-
 ofhome.co.uk Tel: 0870 870 9991
Scottish Self-Build and Renovation Centre – Livingston
 www.buildstore.co.uk Tel: 0870 870 9991

Self-build courses
Developing Skills (in association with *Homebuilding & Renovating*
    magazine – four- and two-day residential courses)
    www.selfbuildcourses.co.uk Tel: 01480 893833
BuildStore www.mykindofhome.co.uk Tel: 0870 870 9991
Constructive Individuals (weekend and three-week hands-on courses)
    www.constructiveindividuals.com Tel: 020 7515 9299
Centre for Alternative Technology (CAT) (various courses) www.cat.org.uk
    Tel: 01654 705981
Lime Centre (one-day courses, monthly in the summer)
    www.thelimecentre.co.uk Tel: 01962 713636
Society for the Protection of Ancient Buildings (SPAB) www.spab.org.uk
    Tel: 020 7377 1644

Self-build insurances
BuildStore Limited www.buildstore.co.uk Tel: 0870 870 9991
Project Builder www.project-builder-insurance.com Tel: 020 7716 5050
Self-Builder www.self-builder.com Tel: 0800 018 7660
Self-Build Zone www.selfbuildzone.com Tel: 0845 230 9874
Autoline Insurance Group (Eire & Ulster) www.autoline.co.uk
    Tel: 028 3026 6333
Renovation Zone www.renovationzone.com Tel: 0845 230 9874

Warranties
NHBC – Buildmark and Solo www.nhbc.com Tel: 01494 434477
LABC www.labcnewhomewarranty.co.uk Tel: 0845 054 0505
Zurich Self-Build Building Guarantee www.zurich.co.uk/buildingguarantees
    Tel: 0870 241 8050
Premier Guarantee www.thepremierguarantee.co.uk Tel: 0151 650 4343
Project Builder www.project-builder-insurance.com Tel: 020 7716 5050
BuildStore – BuildCare Warranty www.buildstore.co.uk Tel: 0870 870 9991

Specialist self-build companies, package-deal companies and timber-frame manufacturers
Border Oak Design and Construction Ltd www.borderoak.com
    Tel: 01568 708752
BuildStore Ltd www.buildstore.co.uk Tel: 0870 870 9991
T. J. Crump Oakwrights www.oakwrights.co.uk Tel: 01432 353353
Custom Homes Ltd www.customhomes.co.uk Tel: 01293 822898
Design & Materials Ltd www.designandmaterials.uk.com Tel: 01909 540123
Fleming Homes Ltd www.fleminghomes.co.uk Tel: 01361 883785
Frame Homes (South West) Ltd www.framehomes.co.uk
    Tel: 01872 572882
Maple Timber Frame www.mapletimberframe.com Tel: 01772 683370
Potton Ltd www.potton.co.uk Tel: 01480 401401
Scandia-Hus www.scandia-hus.co.uk Tel: 01342 327977
Scotframe Timber Engineering Ltd www.scotframe.co.uk
    Tel: 01467 624440
Taylor Lane Timber Frame Ltd www.taylor-lane.co.uk Tel: 01432 271912

Glossary of Building Terms

The words that follow may be unfamiliar outside the building industry or have specific meanings and uses peculiar to it.

Air tightness the stopping-up of all draughts
Apex the triangular section above the window in a dormer
Apron the decorative timber around a staircase opening
Architrave the timber moulding that masks the joint between the door-frame and the plaster
Arris a piece of timber with a triangular section
Balustrade and balustrading the bars and handrails around a staircase
Bat a half-brick
Batt slabs of fibre insulation
Batter to slope something, or something with a slope
Bed (noun) the horizontal joint in masonry; (verb) to lay something on mortar
Bellmouth the splayed junction of where a driveway enters the Highway
Bellstop an angled-out section of render above a window or opening
Binder a timber fixed longitudinally to provide stability
Blind/blinding the technique of using of a sand layer to prevent membranes being punctured
Box sash a window where the top and bottom casements slide independently up and down
Bracing a timber fixed diagonally to provide stability
Bressumer the visible beam over a fireplace
Butt (noun) a water barrel; a hinge; (verb) to join
Cantilever an over-sailing upper section
Carcassing to install the basic infrastructure
Casing a door-frame
Cavity tray a damp-proof membrane or course that interrupts moisture in the cavity and channels it harmlessly to the outside
Cesspit a tank for holding untreated effluent
Chamfer (verb) to slope or round off; (noun) a sloping section or edge
Chase to cut out a channel or groove
Collar (1) a tie, usually horizontal, between rafters at ceiling or floor level
(2) the fitting that joins two lengths of pipe
Compo (slang) mortar
Coping covering or weathering to the top of a wall
Corbel/corbelled stepped-out masonry or stone
Coving the rounded-off section at the junction of a wall and ceiling
Cruck a curved rafter or roof member
Curtilage the boundary of land or the limit of buildings
Dado at waist high of the wall with possible decorative moulding
Dashing the technique of applying one material to another by throwing it
Daywork price given by the day or the hour
Dead man a T-shape prop used to hold up plasterboard
Deep strip foundation trenches with concrete in the bottom
Dragon beam timber support and tie across the corners of a roof

Dressing the technique of flattening one material over another

Dog leg a right-angle bend

Dog plate toothed metal plate placed between timbers to strengthen the joint

Dormer a window protruding above the roof plane with its own roof section

DPC damp-proof course

DPM damp-proof membrane

Drip a groove or overhang that prevents water running back into the wall

Dubbing the technique of filling in and smoothing out depressions

Dust (slang) cement

Dwang (Scottish) interim support between structural members

Eaves the lower end of a roof, where it meets the walling

Espagnolette multi-point locking device or bolt

Fascia board that masks the bottom end of the rafters and carries the guttering

Filigree intricately carved and shaped timber

Fill the technique of packing to fill a gap; the make-up of land with available or suitable materials

Firrings tapered timber fixed to joists to provide a roof slope; sections of timber fixed to the side of other timber to provide extra strength

Fishplate a toothed metal plate used to join timber

Flashing a lead, plastic or roofing material strip let into a mortar line or cut into brickwork and sealed to allow the rain-water to run off the roof

Flaunch to smooth over with mortar

Floating (verb) to smooth over; (noun) bricks or stone remaining loose when mortar doesn't go off

Floating floor timber flooring laid on insulation

Flue chimney pipe

Frog indentation in a brick

Furniture ironmongery for a door or window

Gable the end of a building beneath a pitched roof

Gauge to measure by either volume or distance

Glulam beam a structural beam made from laminated timber sections

Going the horizontal distance of a tread or staircase

Green mortar, brickwork or stonework that has not yet set or 'gone off'

Hanger a metal device to support the ends of beams

Harling a technique for applying a coat of rough-cast render

Haunch to cover over

Hawk an implement to carry mortar or plaster

Head the top, horizontal section of a door-frame or window

Header a brick showing its shorter face

Hip the sloping junction between the outside angles of two roof planes

Hipped roof a roof that slopes back on to another roof plane

Infill the material, usually consolidated hardcore, used to fill in beneath a load-bearing floor

In situ describing something made or cast on site

Intumescent describing a material used around the perimeter of a fire door designed to expand and seal during fire

Jet a ladle with a long handle

Kingpost a single, vertical roof member

Lean mix weak concrete

Lining a door-frame

Measured rates pricing work by reference to the itemised or measured amount

Muck waste or unwanted soil; (slang) mortar

Mullion the vertical section or division strip in a window

Newel the upright support posts on a staircase

Nogging interim support between structural members

Nosing a projecting timber or part of a stair tread projecting beyond the riser

Ogee a moulding shape

Oversite the levelled-out subsoil beneath a floor or the concrete floor itself

Ovolo a moulding shape

Padstone a reinforced-concrete block used to prevent point loading and provide support beneath a beam, steel joist or purlin

Pargetting moulded decorative plasterwork or render

Pendant a hanging light

Perp/perpends the vertical joint in brickwork

Pig an uneven section in brickwork

Piled/piling concrete or steel sections driven or bored to lower foundation levels for support

Plate a timber on top of, within or fixed to a wall, used to support or fix other elements

Plinth a brick or stone section at the base of a wall

Plumb to carry out the plumbing; to make upright

Pricework work quoted as a lump sum

Point/pointing the face of the mortar joint in masonry

Proud to stand or lie above or beyond the surrounding material

Purlin timber support built into the walling and beneath joists or rafters

Putlock the short scaffold pole built into the walling to support the boards

Queen three-quarter-length brick

Queen post a paired, vertical roof member

Quoin corner stones or bricks

Raft a reinforced concrete slab

Rafter the top or sloping roof member supporting the roof covering

Rebate a stepped recess in timber or masonry

Reveal the visible part of the walling inside an opening

Ridge the apex of a roof

Rise the height of a tread or staircase

Rooflight a window lying within the roof plane

RSJ rolled steel joist

Saddle a sewer connection made on top of the pipe run

Sarking boarding timber boards laid over the roof members to provide structural stability

Sarking felt roofing underlay, laid beneath the tiles

Sash the glazed section of a window

Scarf/scarfing the technique of joining timber using a halved joint

Screed a smooth layer of sand-and-cement flooring

Scrim/scrim tape fabric or paper tape used to reinforce the joints in plasterboard

Septic tank a tank for storing and partially purifying effluent

Sill the external bottom lip of a window or opening

Skim/skimcoat a thin coat of plaster

Slinkies underground/underwater heat-collecting tubes for a heat pump

Slipper two open-channel sections of pipe joining at a gentle angle

Soakers lead sheets interleaved between tiles or slates and then dressed up the wall

Soffit the area beneath the rafters at the eaves

Soldier an upright-laid brick

Soleplate the timber upon which a timber frame is erected; the bottom rail of a timber frame

Solum the ground or concrete beneath the floor

Space heating the warming-up of the air within the home

Spar a rafter or top member of a roof

Sparking to carry out electrical works

Sparks an electrician

Spoil waste or unwanted material or subsoil

Spread a plasterer

Spreader beam a length of steel or reinforced concrete built into a wall to distribute any loading from above

Spreading the act of plastering

Square all angles and planes at 90°

Stile the vertical section of a door-frame

Strap metal used to fix two items together

Stretcher the long face of a brick as with *header*

Stringer the timber section covering up the run of staircase flights

Studding/studwork walling made from vertical sections of timber

Tabled verge where the gable wall is taken above the roof level and capped

Tack/tacking the technique of fixing plasterboard

Tamp the technique of smoothing-off concrete using a length of timber

Tanking the act of making waterproof

Template a pattern or guide, used as a gauge in cutting metal, stone, wood, etc.

Thermal bridging the transfer of heat from a warm element to a cold one

Transom the horizontal section or division within a window

Trenchfill the act of filling the foundation trenches almost to the top with concrete

Torching lime-mortar pointing or bedding to tiles or slates

Torus a moulding shape

Tosh to nail at an angle

Trimmer a joist that receives and supports other joists

Truss a sectional roof component

U value the measurement in watts of the heat flow though a sq. metre of any building material for every 1°C of temperature difference between inside and outside

Underpin the technique of reinforcing foundations by digging out beneath them and filling the void with concrete

Universal beam an I-shape steel joist

Valley the sloping junction between the internal angles of two roof planes

Verge the edge of the roof at the gable

Wallplate a longitudinal timber fixed to the top of a wall to take joists or trusses

Weepers perforated land drains

Weepholes the holes formed in walling to allow the egress of moisture

Index